The Chez Piggy Cookbook

Recipes From the Celebrated Restaurant and Bakery

Compiled by Victoria Newbury

FIREFLY BOOKS

ZALMAN YANOVSKY
(December 19, 1944–December 14, 2002)

ROSE RICHARDSON YANOVSKY
(January 15, 1938–March 18, 2005)

The Chez Piggy Cookbook is just one of the many legacies of the enduring partnership between Zalman Yanovsky and Rose Richardson, two extraordinary people who created an oasis of lively comfort — and so much more — in the heart of the small university town they called home.

Famously different in temperament and personal style, Zal and Rose effortlessly shared the qualities they regarded as essential to living a good life: joie de vivre, creativity, generosity, kindness, loyalty, a sense of social justice and a work ethic that wouldn't quit. For more than a quarter of a century, in big ways and small, they helped make Kingston, Ontario, a better place to live.

They are greatly missed by all who were lucky enough to know them, but that was just another of their gifts: You felt lucky to have known them. Zal's exuberant spirit and Rose's gentle wisdom live on in their friends and customers, in the social programs they sponsored and in the thriving businesses they left in the capable hands of their daughter, Zoe Yanovsky.

Backed by a staff that has always been more like family, Zoe carries on the traditions of one of Kingston's most-loved eateries. As Zal would have put it, "Viva Chez Piggy!"

— *The Editors*

A FIREFLY BOOK

Fourth Printing 2006

**Publisher Cataloging-in-Publication
Data (U.S.)**

Newbury, Victoria.
    The Chez Piggy cookbook : recipes
from the celebrated restaurant and
bakery / compiled by Victoria Newbury.
[240] p. : col. photos. ;   cm.
Includes index.
Summary: Cookbook with recipes from
the Chez Piggy Restaurant and bakery.
ISBN-13: 978-1-55209-296-5 (pbk.)
ISBN-10: 1-55209-296-8 (pbk.)
1. Chez Piggy Restaurant – Ontario.
2. Cookery – Ontario. I. Title.
641.5'09713'72 dc22   TX715.6C545
1998

**Library and Archives Canada
Cataloguing in Publication**

Main entry under title:

The Chez Piggy cookbook : recipes from
the celebrated restaurant and bakery
Includes index.
ISBN-13: 978-1-55209-296-5
ISBN-10: 1-55209-296-8
1. Cookery – Ontario – Kingston.
2. Chez Piggy Restaurant.
I. Newbury, Victoria, 1955 –   .
II. Chez Piggy Restaurant.
TX715.6.C545 1998   641.5'09713'73
C98-930986-X

Published in Canada by
Firefly Books Ltd.
66 Leek Crescent
Richmond Hill, Ontario L4B 1H1

Published in the United States by
Firefly Books (U.S.) Inc.
P.O. Box 1338, Ellicott Station
Buffalo, New York 14205

We acknowledge the financial support of
the Government of Canada through the
Book Publishing Industry Development
Program for our publishing activities.

Produced by
Bookmakers Press Inc.
12 Pine Street
Kingston, Ontario K7K 1W1
(613) 549-4347
tcread@sympatico.ca

Design by
Janice McLean

Edited by
Laurel Aziz

Food photography by
Garfield Peters

Food styling by
Laurel Aziz and Janice McLean

Front cover photograph by
Garfield Peters

Back cover photographs by
Garfield Peters (left) and
Stephen Homer (center and right)

Color separations by
Friesens, Altona, Manitoba

Printed in China

Chez Piggy
68-R Princess Street
Kingston, Ontario K7L 1A5
(613) 549-7673

Pan Chancho Bakery
44 Princess Street
Kingston, Ontario K7L 1A4
(613) 544-7790

Acknowledgments

Unless people come to it, a restaurant is not a restaurant for long. At Chez Piggy, we've been lucky to have a group of regular patrons who've been faithfully arriving at our door for almost a quarter of a century, and we'd like to express our appreciation for their ongoing loyalty. As important to a restaurant as its clientele is its staff, and we've been likewise fortunate to have had a wonderful and dedicated group of employees at both the restaurant and Pan Chancho. Our thanks to all of them, past and present. A special tribute to Vicki Newbury for her tireless contribution to the creation of this cookbook and to the restaurant, where she's been from the very beginning. Finally, thanks to the people at Bookmakers Press, who risked mixing business with pleasure to produce a book about their favorite watering hole and somehow lived to tell the tale.

— *Rose Richardson & Zal Yanovsky*

This book is dedicated to our friends George and Donna Montague, who came up with the cash, no questions asked.

Contents

Introduction

T he room is infused with light from windows that overlook a flagstone patio bordered by climbing vines and waist-high perennials. In the background, Etta James belts out the blues as the voices of patrons seated intimately at oak tables rise and fall in the cadence of good-natured cocktail-hour chat. Servers carrying savory appetizers and baskets of fresh crusty bread seamlessly crisscross paths. Passing the bar, they fire "May I order" drink requests at the bartender, who is in perpetual motion, mixing exotic cocktails and drawing amber-colored pints of beer. It's the dinner rush at Chez Piggy in Kingston, Ontario. Yet amid the relentless hum of a busy restaurant, the abiding sense is one of ease and comfort, generously served to all patrons with a healthy appetite for the good life.

Since the late '70s, people have come in droves to soak up the tastes, sights and sounds of Chez Piggy. In doing so, however, few may realize how closely the place imitates its owners, Rose Richardson and Zal Yanovsky. Everything about it—the food, the attitude, the atmosphere, the decor, the music, you name it—is a reflection of them. "You won't find anything else like it anywhere," says a longtime patron. "It's utterly unique in every way."

At first blush, Rose and Zal seem an unlikely pair, but the union is integral

PERFECT PARTNERS,
left to right: owners
Rose Richardson and
Zal Yanovsky turned
their love of food into
a way of life; a slice
of Peach Almond Pie
is a late-August favorite;
the Chez Piggy courtyard,
with its garden in full
bloom; chef Vicki Newbury
has been a part of Chez
Piggy's success since
the doors first opened
in February 1979.

Vegetarian Focaccette

to Chez Piggy's success. Calm and rational, Rose possesses a dignity and reserve that have earned her a natural authority and respect. In the balance of their partnership, these traits make her an invaluable filter and reality check for her husband's unrestrained energy. Zal, on the other hand, is a gregarious two-legged cyclone of enthusiasm, a man from whom ideas, plans and quips—both ingenious and wacky—endlessly flow. Tempering each other in marriage, they also share an understanding and a passion for food that has been cultivated by travel and by hours spent together in the kitchen. Like lightning in a bottle, that same passion for food has been harnessed and channeled into the restaurant. "We've always done things that we like and believe in," says Zal. "Somehow, we've been able to make that work."

The building that houses Chez Piggy is central to their success. In April 1978, Rose and Zal were looking for a location to open what Zal described as "a nice little bar." Hearing the local gossip, a landlord showed them a derelict limestone livery stable in downtown Kingston that was within two blocks of the Lake Ontario waterfront. The building's old tin roof was full of holes, its courtyard piled with garbage. The main floor, which had neither doors nor windows, had most recently been used as a cleaning-company warehouse and was filled with boxes of old coat hangers and barrels of dry-cleaning fluid. The second-floor loft, which had not been used since the 1920s, was accessible by way of a rickety barn ladder and was stocked with bales of musty, blackened hay. The 3,000-square-foot structure seemed too large for their cozy bar. "But," says Rose, "we knew that it was too nice to pass up."

The fearless risk-taking that followed echoes the tale of many small businesses struggling to launch during the late 1970s. Summarily turned down at every bank in town, the couple sank Rose's life savings and a loan from two trusting friends, George and Donna Montague, into the project ("I had blown all my savings in the '60s," says Zal, a former member of the band The Lovin' Spoonful).

Their commitment to the building heralded the renaissance of Kingston's

historic downtown. Overseeing every step and decision of the renovation, the couple worked as the project contractors alongside Lily Inglis ("world's shortest architect"), transforming the livery stable into a stylish restaurant that reflected their long-term plans. Solid limestone walls were stripped and exposed, and windows and doors were cut through them; plumbing, wiring and staircases were installed. Quarter-cut butternut was fashioned into a 20-foot bar. Tables and chairs were chosen to reflect the relaxed tone the owners were looking for. The kitchen, even after several remodelings over the past two decades, is still the same 350-square-foot area—an unbelievably compact working space for the number of cooks it accommodates on any one shift.

But if the painstaking restoration of one of Kingston's most unique architectural

structures tried the nerves of the partners—"Rose thought the place would never open," says Zal—it also piqued the curiosity of hundreds of people who passed by each day. When Chez Piggy opened in early February 1979, it was packed.

Dramatically understaffed, the 125-seat restaurant had only three people working in the kitchen serving up lunchtime nosh: omelettes, hash, latkes, salads, pâtés and extra-sharp grilled cheese on black bread. There was a bartender, whose stock-in-trade was a free-flowing tap of 99¢ premium draft beer served in frosty mugs, and a handful of food-loving waitresses, among them Victoria Newbury and Susan Newbury, who would eventually become Chez Piggy's chef and pastry chef, respectively. During those first few months, the restaurant ran out of food every day. "It was so successful and we were so busy,"

recalls Rose, "that I always had the feeling that things could spiral out of control." The pace was relentless, the 18-hour days deadly. "Zal would wake up in the morning and be so exhausted that he would burst into tears at the thought of going to work."

Today, the Chez Piggy staff numbers more than 100 employees and Rose and Zal have stepped back from the day-to-day operation of the restaurant. In the intervening years, a variety of cooks have left their mark on Chez Piggy, each eventually earning free rein in menu planning and recipe design. "Initially, we like them to make things our way," says Zal. "But each cook has an individual style, and we like to let them show that."

While this inherent diversity has earned Chez Piggy a reputation as a cook's restaurant, it has sometimes opened the door to criticism by food writers. "Our style comes from the cooks themselves," says Zal. "We have never jumped on any culinary bandwagon. There is no 'point of view.' We've had a Newfie chef, a Vietnamese chef, a couple of Jewish chefs, a Mexican cook and a Dutch cook. In that way, we've always been international."

The lack of pretense to *haute cuisine* on their menu makes Rose and Zal no less serious about serving good food. Quality ingredients—real lemon juice, freshly peeled garlic, premium olive oil, farm eggs, cream, fresh-baked bread and the best greens and vegetables available—are the backbone of their recipes. The combination of that care and the restaurant's incomparable ambience makes time spent at Chez Piggy one of life's sweeter experiences.

Maybe you can't take the atmosphere home with you, but much of Chez Piggy's magic can be found in this collection of recipes. "Don't follow them too strictly," says Zal. "Our recipes are guides that leave room for evolution. We like to make certain things differently each time. Each cook should feel free to put his or her own spin on a recipe. We didn't set out to rule the world. We wanted to do a nice thing to earn a living. Now we can share it around."

Who's on First?

A s a server passes the table carrying a sizzling order of Gambas al Ajillo, the restaurant fills with the mouth-watering aroma of garlic, chilies, olive oil and sautéed shrimp. While this Chez Piggy ritual is a routine event, the sight and scent of the small cast-iron frying pan never fail to whet the appetites of patrons.

Appetizers are a main attraction on the Chez Piggy menu. Over the past 20 years, nothing has changed and grown more dramatically. Like everything else, food goes in and out of fashion, and the selection found in this chapter can be attributed to that as much as to Rose and Zal's shared taste for variety. Rose lived in Madrid during the 1960s and became a great tapas grazer and a lifelong fan of that style of eating.

The "starters" at the restaurant provide customers with a chance to sample a range of foods from around the world—gambas from Spain, hummus from the Middle East, carpaccio from Italy, spring rolls from Vietnam—as well as more traditional fare like Stilton pâté.

For the cook at home, many of these recipes can stand on their own. But a special appeal also rests with the option of being able to mix and match a diverse collection of global tastes right in your own kitchen.

CHEZ PIGGY STARTERS, from left to right: Stilton Pâté with fresh Pan Chancho baguette and cured olives; eager wait staff get the spiel on lunchtime specials; hand-painted sign points the way to Chez Piggy; long-time staffer Brenda Spires-Holmes directs traffic on the summer patio.

GOAT CHEESE & RED-PEPPER SPREAD

Tastes great shmeered on a whole warm pita, cut into triangles,
or served as a cold vegetable dip.

3	red bell peppers	3
1 lb.	chèvre (goat cheese)	500 g
1 lb.	cream cheese	500 g
½ tsp.	balsamic vinegar	2 mL

Hold each red pepper on a long fork over the open flame of a gas stove or the coils of an electric stove until entire skin is blistered and blackened. Let peppers steam for 15 minutes in a paper bag or a bowl covered with plastic wrap. Then remove skins, stems and seeds.

In a food processor, blend roasted peppers, alternately adding chèvre and cream cheese in small batches. Continue to blend, and add vinegar.

Makes 2 cups (500 mL)

MARINATED GOAT CHEESE

Serve this delicious treat on a bed of ruby radicchio garnished with kalamata olives
and peperoncini—a pickled pepper available at Italian specialty stores.
Stored in a decorative glass jar, this marinated cheese makes a tasty holiday gift
that anyone would enjoy. Refrigerated, it keeps well for several weeks.
Chilled storage will cause the oil to cloud, but it will clear at room temperature.

1 lb.	chèvre (goat cheese)	500 g
1 Tbsp.	crushed dried chilies	15 mL
1 tsp.	whole black peppercorns	5 mL
1 tsp.	whole white peppercorns	5 mL
4	bay leaves	4
4	cloves garlic	4
2 Tbsp.	lemon zest	25 mL
2 cups	extra-virgin olive oil	500 mL
2 Tbsp.	lemon juice	25 mL
1	head radicchio, trimmed & washed	1
3	sun-dried tomato halves (dry or packed in oil), cut into strips, for garnish	3
	Peperoncini for garnish	
	Kalamata olives for garnish	

With a sharp knife, cut chèvre into ½-inch (1 cm) rounds, and place in a deep glass container or jar. Add chilies, peppercorns, bay leaves, garlic and lemon zest. Cover with oil and lemon juice. Refrigerate for 2 days. Remove cheese from oil, and serve at room temperature on a bed of radicchio. Garnish with sun-dried tomatoes, peperoncini and olives.

Serves 4 to 6

Guacamole
and Salsa

GUACAMOLE

*A delicious dip for corn chips and nachos, this guacamole
can also be served as a sandwich spread. To help minimize the natural darkening
of the avocado as it oxidizes, press plastic wrap tightly onto the surface.
Nonetheless, don't let any discoloration discourage you from using the guacamole
even after a few days in the refrigerator. Simply skim the top and serve.*

5	ripe avocados	5
1	tomato, diced	1
3 heaping Tbsp.	sour cream	45 mL
½	large red onion, diced	½
	Juice of 1 lime	
2	fresh jalapeños, minced	2
2	cloves garlic, minced	2
2 Tbsp.	chopped fresh coriander leaves	25 mL
	Coarse salt	

In a bowl, mash avocados into a chunky purée. Fold in tomato, sour cream
and onion. Stir in lime juice, jalapeños, garlic and coriander, and season with
salt to taste. Chill.

Makes approximately 5 cups (1.25 L)

Hummus With
Roasted Red Pepper
and Pita Bread

HUMMUS

Hummus has been on the Chez Piggy menu since the day the restaurant opened.
Because of the ongoing popularity of this dip, we make at least one large batch a day. Our
recipe is for garlic lovers only, but it can easily be toned down for timid palates by reducing
the amount of garlic. Hummus can be refrigerated for about three days but may need to be
freshened up with additional lemon juice or salt. Drizzle with sesame oil, and serve with
lemon wedges, kalamata olives and pita triangles (see page 202) on the side.
For an aromatic variation of this Mediterranean classic, add half a roasted red pepper
(see "Blistering Hot," page 19) and two tablespoons (25 mL) of feta cheese to the ingredients.

1	19 oz. (540 mL) can chickpeas, drained	1
	(reserve 4 Tbsp./50 mL juice)	
3	cloves garlic, chopped	3
3 Tbsp.	lemon juice	45 mL
2 Tbsp.	tahini (sesame paste)	25 mL
1 Tbsp.	sesame oil	15 mL
1 tsp.	coarse salt	5 mL
	Pinch freshly ground black pepper	

In a food processor, blend chickpeas, garlic, lemon juice, tahini, oil, salt
and pepper to a smooth paste, adding reserved chickpea juice as necessary
to desired consistency.
Serves 4

STILTON PÂTÉ

*A sharp-tasting spread for crusty bread, this pâté is equally at home on light rye
or on such hearty sandwiches as our salami and pepper sandwich on Pain Ordinaire.
Serve with French gherkins or pieces of roasted red peppers for garnish.*

1 lb.	Stilton cheese, room temperature	500 g
10 oz.	cream cheese, room temperature	300 g
½ cup	butter, room temperature	125 mL
2 Tbsp.	brandy	25 mL
½ tsp.	freshly ground black pepper	2 mL

Blend cheeses and butter in a food processor with a mixing blade, gradually
adding brandy and pepper. Spoon into a bowl, and serve immediately or chill.
Garnish with freshly ground pepper.

Makes a party-size appetizer

BLISTERING HOT

To roast a bell pepper, hold it on a long fork over the open flame of a gas stove or the coils of an electric stove until the entire skin is blistered and blackened. Let pepper steam for 15 minutes in a paper bag or a bowl covered with plastic wrap. Then remove skin, stem and seeds.

BLACK-OLIVE TAPENADE

Serve alone on crostini for a salty appetizer, or toss with warm pasta as a main course.

1 lb.	kalamata olives, pitted & coarsely chopped	500 g
4 Tbsp.	chopped rinsed capers	50 mL
2	anchovies, rinsed & chopped	2
4	cloves garlic, chopped	4
	Pinch dried thyme	
3 Tbsp.	olive oil	45 mL
1 Tbsp.	brandy	15 mL
1 Tbsp.	Dijon mustard	15 mL

Thoroughly mix all ingredients in a bowl with a wooden spoon and
refrigerate.

Makes 2 cups (500 mL)

SUN-DRIED TOMATO TAPENADE
ON CROSTINI

This savory tapenade is versatile—it's perfect as a spread for seasoned crostini or when used as a condiment for Potato-Crusted Goat Cheese (see page 22). Crostini are easy to make from a day-old baguette or other crusty loaf. Cut the bread into thin slices, brush it with olive oil, bake until crispy, and garnish with your favorite herbs. (Be careful, because they burn easily.) Store in an airtight container, and use with a variety of spreads and toppings.

4 oz.	sun-dried tomatoes	125 g
½ cup	olive oil	125 mL
2 Tbsp.	lemon juice	25 mL
3	cloves garlic, minced	3
¼ cup	capers	50 mL

Pour boiling water over tomatoes, and soak for 20 minutes or until soft. Drain, and blend with oil, lemon juice, garlic and capers in a food processor until thoroughly mixed. Serve on crostini.

Makes 2 cups (500 mL)

SPINACH, LEEK & TOMATO TERRINE

The three colorful layers in this unique vegetarian terrine maintain their integrity, yet their flavors combine for a light treat that can be served sliced on mixed greens and dressed with rémoulade or spread on garlic crostini or a fresh baguette.

SPINACH LAYER

1 lb.	fresh spinach, stems removed	500 g
2	eggs, lightly beaten	2
⅛ tsp.	ground nutmeg	0.5 mL
	Coarse salt & freshly ground black pepper	

Wilt spinach in a little boiling water (do not cook so much that it loses its fresh green color). Drain and cool spinach, then squeeze out excess moisture. Finely chop spinach, and mix with eggs and nutmeg, seasoning with salt and pepper to taste. Divide mixture in half, and set aside.

LEEK LAYER

1 lb.	leeks (white part only)	500 g
5 oz.	35% B.F. cream	150 g
¼ tsp.	dried thyme	1 mL
2	eggs, lightly beaten	2
	Coarse salt & freshly ground black pepper	

Trim leeks and wash well. Finely chop leeks, and place in a skillet with cream and thyme. Simmer over medium heat until cream is reduced and mixture is dry. Allow to cool. Beat in eggs, seasoning with salt and pepper to taste. Set aside.

Spinach, Leek
& Tomato Terrine

TOMATO LAYER

1	small onion, finely chopped	1
2	large cloves garlic, minced	2
2 tsp.	butter	10 mL
1	28 oz. (796 mL) can plum tomatoes, processed in a food mill, if possible	1
½ tsp.	dried basil	2 mL
2	eggs, lightly beaten	2
	Coarse salt & freshly ground black pepper	

Sauté onion and garlic in butter until onion is soft. Add tomatoes and basil, and simmer until no liquid remains. Add eggs, and season with salt and pepper to taste.

Preheat oven to 350°F (180°C).

To assemble the terrine, line the terrine mold with parchment paper. Spread half the spinach mixture on the bottom. Spread with all the leek mixture, then all the tomato mixture. Top with the remaining spinach mixture. Cover with parchment paper, and wrap the terrine in foil. Place in a roasting pan half filled with hot water.

Bake for 2 hours, checking the water level to be sure the pan does not boil dry. Remove the terrine from the oven, and place a weight on the top to press out liquid as it cools.

Serves 12

POTATO-CRUSTED GOAT CHEESE

*The crusty potato and the chalky texture of the goat cheese are
nicely balanced with the savory tastes of the tapenade.*

13 oz.	chèvre (goat cheese), 2-inch-diameter (5 cm) log	400 g
2	large potatoes, thinly sliced	2
2 oz.	sun-dried tomatoes	50 g
¼ cup	olive oil	50 mL
2	cloves garlic, minced	2
⅓ cup	capers	75 mL
1 Tbsp.	lemon juice	15 mL
	Olive oil for frying	
6 cups	mixed fresh baby greens	1.5 L
2 tsp.	Chez Piggy House Dressing (*see page 71*)	10 mL

Cut chèvre into ¾-inch-thick (2 cm) disks. Set aside.

Blanch potato slices in boiling salted water, being careful not to overcook.
Drain, and set aside.

Soak tomatoes in boiling water for 20 minutes or until soft. Drain and dry.
To make tapenade, thoroughly mix tomatoes, oil, garlic, capers and lemon juice
in a blender or a food processor.

Smear tapenade on one side of a slice of chèvre, and press between two
potato slices. Fry cheese-filled potato "sandwiches" in oil, browning both sides.
Serve hot on a bed of lightly dressed greens.

Serves 6

Potato-Crusted
Goat Cheese

ACARAJÉ

*Seasoned with a hint of shrimp, these wonderful Caribbean bean fritters
are mildly flavored and pair remarkably well with gingered shrimp sauce.*

2 cups	dried black-eyed peas	500 mL
½ cup	dried shrimp	125 mL
1	medium onion, coarsely chopped	1
	Coarse salt	
	Palm oil (dendé) or olive oil for frying	

Place peas in a bowl, cover with water, and soak overnight. Drain and rub
off skins. Set aside.

In a separate bowl, cover shrimp with water, and soak for 20 minutes. Drain.

In a food processor, grind peas, shrimp and onion together. Add salt to
taste. Heat oil in a heavy-bottomed pan over medium heat, and drop in
1 tablespoon (15 mL) bean purée for each fritter. Fry fritters until golden
brown. Drain and serve.

Makes 25 to 30 fritters

MOLHO DE ACARAJÉ

Use this shrimp sauce as a condiment for Acarajé (recipe above).

½ cup	dried shrimp	125 mL
1	medium onion, coarsely chopped	1
1 Tbsp.	chopped fresh chili	15 mL
1 Tbsp.	minced fresh ginger	15 mL
3 Tbsp.	palm oil (dendé) or olive oil	45 mL

Soak shrimp in water for 20 minutes, and drain. Place shrimp, onion, chili
and ginger in a food processor, and blend to a thick paste. In a skillet, sauté
the paste in oil for 5 minutes. Cool before serving.

Makes 1 cup (250 mL)

ROASTED GARLIC

Whether spread on a chunk of baguette or used as an ingredient in a recipe, roasted garlic is a treat not to be missed. Preheat oven to 400°F (200°C). Rub garlic cloves with olive oil, wrap in aluminum foil, and roast for 25 minutes. To make a larger quantity, arrange garlic buds or whole heads in a roasting pan, drizzle with olive oil and add a few splashes of wine or chicken stock or both. Cover with aluminum foil, and roast until tender.

BRANDADE DE MORUE

Provincial French cooking is featured in this sweet, rich salt cod purée, which, according to food writer Elizabeth David, originated in Nîmes. Serve it as a spread on crostini or with rustic bread. It is also an excellent thickener for fish soup.

1 lb.	salt cod	500 g
½ lb.	potatoes, peeled & cut into chunks	250 g
½ cup	olive oil	125 mL
6	large cloves garlic, roasted in olive oil	6
1 cup	35% B.F. cream	250 mL
	Croutons for garnish	
	Chopped fresh parsley for garnish	

Place cod in a deep roasting pan, and cover with cold water. Soak cod overnight until the extremely salty taste is gone, changing water twice, if possible. Check saltiness before cooking by tasting a bit from the center of the thickest portion. If sufficient salt has leached out, drain and flake. Set aside.

Cook potatoes in boiling unsalted water, then drain. In a large pot, heat oil, and add garlic, cod and potatoes. Stir with a wooden spoon while adding cream. Cook until half the liquid has evaporated and cod starts to break apart, indicating that it is done. Purée with a hand blender. Serve warm, garnished with croutons and parsley.

Serves 8 to 10

SMOKED SALMON PÂTÉ

You don't need to use prime slices of salmon for this pâté; scrappy end bits will work just as well. Serve on thin rye toasts or crackers, garnished with lemon zest and fresh dill.

7 oz.	smoked salmon	200 g
8 oz.	cream cheese	250 g
1 Tbsp.	coarsely chopped fresh dill	15 mL
¼ cup	lemon juice	50 mL
	Freshly ground black pepper	

Place salmon in a food processor, and blend until smooth. Add cream cheese, dill and lemon juice, and blend until mixed. Season with pepper to taste.

Makes a party-size appetizer

DUCK & GREEN PEPPERCORN PÂTÉ

The wild-duck flavor of this coarse terrine is enhanced with freshly ground
green peppercorns. To ensure the right texture, all the duck meat—including the liver
and heart, if you have them—should be cut into small pieces by hand.

5 lb.	duck, deboned (keep ¼ of fatty skin)	2.2 kg
1 cup	red wine	250 mL
¾ lb.	ground veal	375 g
1	duck liver	1
3 Tbsp.	brandy	45 mL
½ cup	chopped fresh parsley	125 mL
2 tsp.	dried thyme	10 mL
1 tsp.	coarse salt	5 mL
¼ cup	chopped shallots	50 mL
2	cloves garlic, chopped	2
	Pinch allspice	
2	eggs	2
2 Tbsp.	whole green peppercorns	25 mL
16	slices bacon	16
	Beet & Horseradish Relish (*see page 28*)	

Marinate duck meat and skin overnight in wine; drain in morning. Cut meat
into slices, then into thin strips. Julienne skin to yield ¼ cup (50 mL). Add to
duck, and mix with remaining ingredients, except bacon and relish. Line the
sides and bottom of a pâté pan with bacon, reserving enough slices to cover
top. Fill pan with pâté mixture, and top with reserved bacon. Set pâté pan in
a roasting pan half filled with water. Bake at 350°F (180°C) for 1¾ to 2 hours. Let
cool in pan, then turn out. Cut into ½-inch (1 cm) slices, and serve with relish.
Serves 10

The safest way to flame
alcohol for cooking is to
heat it in a pot until it
comes to a boil. Turn off
the heat. Light a long
fireplace match, and hold
it near the liquid—but not
touching—until it ignites.
Allow the flame to burn
itself out to ensure
that the alcohol has
completely evaporated.
Alternatively, put the
alcohol in a stainless steel
ladle and light it in
the same way.

LIVER & COGNAC PÂTÉ

A good basic pâté, this liver and cognac spread, dressed up with a dozen herbs and spices, is a rich, elegant treatment of an inexpensive meat. The spice mixture also complements other meat dishes, such as meat pies and beef stew.

SPICE MIXTURE

2 Tbsp.	whole white peppercorns, ground	25 mL
½ tsp.	crushed bay leaf	2 mL
½ tsp.	cloves	2 mL
½ tsp.	ground mace	2 mL
½ tsp.	ground nutmeg	2 mL
½ tsp.	paprika	2 mL
½ tsp.	dried thyme	2 mL
¼ tsp.	dried basil	1 mL
¼ tsp.	dried marjoram	1 mL
¼ tsp.	cinnamon	1 mL
¼ tsp.	dried sage	1 mL
¼ tsp.	dried savory	1 mL

Combine all spices in a food processor or a spice grinder. Store in a small jar for future use.

PÂTÉ

2 lb.	chicken livers	1 kg
3 Tbsp.	butter	45 mL
1	onion, sliced	1
1 tsp.	spice mixture	5 mL
1 tsp.	coarse salt	5 mL
½ cup	brandy	125 mL
12 oz.	cream cheese, room temperature	375 g

Trim chicken livers to remove fat and bile. Melt butter in a large skillet over low heat, and sauté onion until translucent but not brown. Increase heat to medium, and add livers, spice mixture and salt. Cook until livers are firm. Flame with brandy, and be sure to cook off alcohol, or pâté will taste bitter. Set aside and cool.

Blend cream cheese in a food processor until smooth. Add cooled liver mixture, and process again until smooth. Cover and chill before serving.

Makes a party-size appetizer

PÂTÉ MAISON

Layered with pork, veal, chicken and spinach,
this terrine is a treat for the eyes as well as the palate.

1 Tbsp.	dried sage	15 mL
1 tsp.	freshly ground black pepper	5 mL
1 tsp.	allspice	5 mL
1 tsp.	juniper berries	5 mL
1 tsp.	dried basil	5 mL
1 tsp.	dried marjoram	5 mL
1 tsp.	coarse salt	5 mL
½ tsp.	dried thyme	2 mL
4	cloves garlic, finely chopped	4
1 lb.	ground pork sausage	500 g
1 lb.	ground veal	500 g
½ cup	chopped fresh parsley	125 mL
1 lb.	chicken livers	500 g
2	10 oz. (300 g) pkgs. spinach	2

In a blender, food processor or mortar and pestle, finely grind together sage, pepper, allspice, juniper berries, basil, marjoram, salt and thyme.

Mix garlic, pork, veal, parsley and blended spices together in a bowl. Set aside.

Trim chicken livers to remove fat and bile, and chop. Set aside.

In a large pot, blanch spinach in 1 inch (2.5 cm) boiling water. Drain and squeeze out excess moisture. Chop, and set aside.

Preheat oven to 350°F (180°C). Line a pâté pan with wax paper. Divide the ground-meat mixture into three equal parts. Layer in pâté pan: one-third ground meat, chicken livers, one-third ground meat, spinach and remaining ground meat. Cover lightly with aluminum foil, and set in a roasting pan that has been half filled with hot water. Bake for 2½ hours, periodically checking the water level to make sure the pan does not boil dry.

When the pâté is cooked, remove from oven and cool. Set pan between two plates, and place a weight on top to squeeze out excess moisture. Chill overnight. The next day, turn out pâté, cut into ½-inch (1 cm) slices, and serve.

Makes 12 to 16 slices

BEET & HORSERADISH RELISH

*The natural sweetness of apple complements the taste of the beets in this relish.
It makes an excellent condiment for duck pâté, smoked duck or other game meat.*

5	medium beets	5
1	apple, unpeeled, finely diced	1
2 tsp.	prepared horseradish	10 mL
1 Tbsp.	apple-cider vinegar	15 mL
	Zest of 1 orange	
	Juice of 1 orange	
2 Tbsp.	olive oil	25 mL
	Coarse salt	

Place beets in a large pot, and cover with water. Bring to a boil, and cook
until still slightly firm. Cool, rinse in cold water, and peel. Finely dice the
beets, and mix with remaining ingredients, adding salt to taste. Cool and chill
for 30 minutes.

Makes 4 cups (1 L)

CAYENNE YAM CHIPS

We garnish our spicy jambalaya with these addictive chips. They also make a great snack.

3	large yams	3
	Peanut oil for deep-frying	
	Coarse salt	
	Cayenne pepper	

Peel the yams, and slice paper-thin. In a deep fryer or a heavy skillet, heat
oil over medium-high heat until it is hot but not smoking. To test oil, drop
in a single yam slice. The oil should bubble and crackle immediately.

Add yam slices in small batches, and cook until lightly browned. Remove
with a slotted spoon, and drain on paper towels. To get the crispest chips,
allow the oil to reheat between batches. Place drained chips in a paper bag,
sprinkle with salt and cayenne pepper to taste, and shake.

Serves 4 to 6

GRAVLAX WITH SWEET MUSTARD SAUCE

*This Scandinavian salt-cured salmon will melt in your mouth. The thickness
of the fillet you select will determine the curing time. A tail-end fillet needs a day to cure,
while a thicker midsection may take longer. The combination of different mustards
in the lightly blended sauce lends interest to its texture, consistency and flavor.*

SALMON

1 cup	loosely packed, coarsely chopped fresh dill	250 mL
1 Tbsp.	coarse salt	15 mL
1 Tbsp.	green peppercorns in brine	15 mL
2 Tbsp.	aquavit	25 mL
1 lb.	fresh tail-end salmon fillet, skin on	500 g

MUSTARD SAUCE

1 Tbsp.	grainy mustard	15 mL
1 Tbsp.	Dijon mustard	15 mL
1 tsp.	dry mustard	5 mL
4 tsp.	sugar	20 mL
2 Tbsp.	white wine	25 mL
2 Tbsp.	olive oil	25 mL

Mix together dill, salt, peppercorns and aquavit in a small bowl. Press onto
flesh side of salmon. Place salmon, skin side down, on a rack set in a tray.
Cover with plastic wrap, and place a weighted object on top. Refrigerate for at
least 1 day. After salmon has cured, scrape off the dill mixture. Angling your
knife on a sharp diagonal, thinly slice the flesh away from the skin.

To prepare mustard sauce, place all ingredients in a bowl, and whisk until
smooth and blended, or blend in a food processor.

Serve salmon with mustard sauce and sliced cucumbers or with boiled
potatoes.

Serves 6 to 8

SAVING THE MAYO

If the mayonnaise does not emulsify, it could be that the humidity of the air or the acidity of the mix is making it watery. You can save the batch by blending 1 egg yolk and 1 teaspoon (5 mL) hot water in a clean container. Slowly add the "broken" mixture to the fresh yolk. If the mayonnaise does not thicken, continue the process with another yolk and hot water in another clean container until you get an emulsified mixture that will incorporate the first broken batch of mayonnaise.

ASIAN CURED SALMON

Chez Piggy's recipe is a variation of the Scandinavian salt-cured classic infused with Asian spices, ginger, soy sauce and rice-wine vinegar. You'll have to anticipate your craving for this delicately flavored salmon, however, because it takes at least two days to cure.

WASABI MAYONNAISE

4 tsp.	wasabi powder	20 mL
1 Tbsp.	water	15 mL
1	egg	1
2 tsp.	lemon juice	10 mL
½ tsp.	red-wine vinegar	2 mL
1 Tbsp.	honey	15 mL
1⅓ cups	vegetable oil	325 mL
2 heaping Tbsp.	yogurt	25 mL

Prepare mayonnaise the day you plan to serve the salmon. Mix wasabi powder and water to form a paste. Using an electric or hand blender, blend wasabi paste with egg, lemon juice, vinegar and honey. Slowly add oil while continuing to blend, until mayonnaise is thick. Stir in yogurt. Refrigerate.

SALMON

1 lb.	fresh tail-end salmon fillet, skin on	500 g
2 Tbsp.	soy sauce	25 mL
1 Tbsp. + 2 tsp.	coarse salt	15 mL + 10 mL
⅓ cup	rice-wine vinegar	75 mL
⅓ cup	cider vinegar	75 mL
⅓ cup	white vinegar	75 mL
¼ cup	sugar	50 mL
2 Tbsp.	julienned fresh ginger	25 mL
1	fresh chili, sliced into rings	1
1 heaping tsp.	Szechuan peppercorns	5 mL
½	small onion,	½
	cut into half-moon slices, for garnish	

Coat the flesh side of salmon with soy sauce, and press 1 tablespoon (15 mL) salt on top. Wrap salmon tightly in plastic wrap, and cure for 2 days in the refrigerator.

After salmon has cured, mix vinegars with sugar, ginger, 2 teaspoons (10 mL) salt, chili and peppercorns to make a brine. In a saucepan, bring brine to a boil, then remove from heat. Unwrap salmon, and place in a container. Pour in warm brine. Cover with wax paper, and marinate for 24 hours in the refrigerator.

Remove salmon from brine, and pat dry. On a sharp diagonal, slice salmon thinly away from skin. Drizzle salmon with wasabi mayonnaise, and garnish with onion.

Serves 6 to 8

CARPACCIO

This dish originated in Harry's Bar in Venice. The freshness of the sirloin is important, since the meat is salt-cured rather than cooked. The cured beef is served in paper-thin slices with crusty bread, capers, slices of salty Romano cheese and mustard mayonnaise or a good fruity olive oil. Unsliced, carpaccio will keep for up to 10 days in the refrigerator.

MUSTARD MAYONNAISE

3	cold egg yolks	3
7 Tbsp.	Dijon mustard	90 mL
2 Tbsp.	lemon juice	25 mL
½ cup	vegetable oil	125 mL
1 cup	olive oil	250 mL
¼ cup	chilled white wine	50 mL

Prepare mayonnaise the day you plan to serve the carpaccio. With a hand blender, mix egg yolks, 3 tablespoons (45 mL) mustard and lemon juice. Gradually add vegetable oil. Add remaining 4 tablespoons (50 mL) mustard, and drizzle in olive oil to thicken mayonnaise. (Adding all the mustard at once may cause the mayonnaise to break.) Continue blending, and gradually add wine. If the batch is too thick, thin it with water or additional wine, adding only 1 teaspoon (5 mL) at a time. Refrigerate.

Makes 2 cups (500 mL)

CURED BEEF

10	cloves garlic, finely chopped	10
¼ cup	freshly ground black pepper	50 mL
¼ cup	coarse salt	50 mL
2 Tbsp.	coarsely chopped fresh thyme	25 mL
4 lb.	sirloin roast	1.8 kg
¼ cup	olive oil	50 mL
	Capers for garnish	
	Romano or Parmesan cheese, sliced, for garnish	

Mix garlic, pepper, salt and thyme in a large bowl. Rub roast with oil, and press spice mixture onto the meat. Set meat on a wire rack in a pan to keep it out of the drippings and to allow air to circulate on all sides. Loosely cover with wax paper. Refrigerate for 3 days.

When ready to serve, scrape spice mixture from all sides of roast. Slice thinly, discarding outer slice. Rub each slice with a few drops of olive oil. Add a dollop of mustard mayonnaise, and garnish with capers and cheese.

Makes a party-size appetizer

CHA GIO (Vietnamese Spring Rolls)

*These tightly wrapped cigar-shaped spring rolls are fried with an extra-crispy
paper-thin shell and served with a wonderfully light nuoc cham dipping sauce.
They are also delicious with fresh mixed salad greens or slices of cool English cucumber.
When cooked, cha gio will keep in the refrigerator and can be reheated in a deep-fat fryer
or by immersing in hot oil in a skillet. The key to rolling cha gio successfully
is to keep the rice-paper wrappers moist but work on a dry surface.*

NUOC CHAM

1 ¼ cups	water	300 mL
½ cup	lemon juice	125 mL
½ cup	sugar	125 mL
½ cup + 2 Tbsp.	Vietnamese fish sauce	125 mL + 25 mL
3	fresh chilies, chopped	3
3	cloves garlic, chopped	3
2	limes, juice & pulp	2

Place all ingredients in a jar, and shake to dissolve sugar. Set aside. (This
sauce will keep in an airtight container in the refrigerator for several days.)

SPRING ROLLS

1 oz.	Chinese black fungus	25 g
1 oz.	bean-curd vermicelli noodles	25 g
½ lb.	ground pork	250 g
½ lb.	shrimp, peeled & ground	250 g
½ lb.	ground chicken	250 g
¾ cup	grated carrots	175 mL
½	small onion, chopped	½
2	cloves garlic, minced	2
½ tsp.	freshly ground black pepper	2 mL
½ tsp.	coarse salt	2 mL
1	egg	1
1 cup	beer	250 mL
1 cup	water	250 mL
1 lb.	pkg. (6-in./15 cm sheets) rice paper	500 g
	Peanut oil for deep-frying	

In separate bowls, soak fungus and noodles in warm water until soft. Drain
and chop. In a large bowl, thoroughly mix fungus and vermicelli with pork,
shrimp, chicken, carrots, onion, garlic, pepper, salt and egg. Set aside.

In a pie plate, stir together beer and water. Separate sheets of rice paper, and
dip, one at a time, into beer mixture, then lay flat, allowing liquid to soften rice
paper. Wick excess moisture. Place damp wrapper on a dry surface for rolling.

Shape 2 tablespoons (25 mL) meat filling into a cylinder, and place in the
center of a sheet of rice paper. Fold the sides into the middle. Fold bottom up,
and tuck under filling to prevent air pockets. Roll tightly. Deep-fry in peanut
oil. Serve hot with room-temperature nuoc cham.

Makes 24 spring rolls

Cha Gio With Nuoc Cham

CHA LEM (Vegetarian Spring Rolls)

You will find egg-roll skins in the frozen-food case of your favorite Asian market.

3 cups	mashed potatoes, mashed with 1 minced clove garlic	750 mL
1 cup	shredded, blanched green cabbage	250 mL
½ cup	wilted spinach	125 mL
½ cup	softened bean-curd vermicelli noodles	125 mL
1	medium onion, chopped & sautéed	1
½ cup	grated carrots	125 mL
	Coarse salt & freshly ground black pepper	
1	1 lb. (500 g) pkg. 6-inch (15 cm) egg-roll skins	1
1	egg yolk, lightly beaten	1
	Peanut oil for frying	

Using your hands, combine potatoes, cabbage, spinach, noodles, onion and carrots, and season with salt and pepper to taste. Separate egg-roll skins, and spread flat in a diamond pattern in front of you (that is, one corner pointing toward you and the other pointing away). Place 2 tablespoons (25 mL) potato mixture on each skin. Brush top corner with egg yolk.

Fold bottom corner to center and over filling. Fold both sides into the center. Roll toward the top yolk-brushed corner. Set aside, and repeat until all rolls are filled. Heat oil in a skillet until it spits when a drop of water is added (roughly 350°-375°F/180°-190°C). Fry until golden brown. Drain on paper towels.

Makes 24 spring rolls

POH PLA
(Fresh Spring Rolls With Clear Dipping Sauce)

This recipe is the Thai variation of the fresh spring rolls that are common to Asian cooking. Nam pla, or fish sauce, is the flavor base for this sauce. It is an amber-colored liquid made from fish that has been fermented and strained.

DIPPING SAUCE

1 cup	cold water	250 mL
½ cup	sugar	125 mL
4 Tbsp.	fish sauce	50 mL
2	fresh chilies, finely sliced	2
2 Tbsp.	lime juice	25 mL

In a large bowl, mix water and sugar until sugar is dissolved. Add remaining ingredients, and stir.

Makes 1 cup (250 mL)

SPRING ROLLS

1 cup	dried shrimp	250 mL
2 cups	bean-curd vermicelli noodles, soaked & cut into 1-inch (2.5 cm) lengths	500 mL
4	fresh chilies, sliced	4
4 tsp.	fish sauce	20 mL
2 tsp.	lime juice	10 mL
2 Tbsp. + 1 cup	grated white radish	25 mL + 250 mL
2 tsp.	sugar	10 mL
1	12 oz. (341 mL) bottle of beer	1
16	sheets rice paper (each 6 in./15 cm)	16
32	small shrimp, deveined & lightly poached in salted water	32
16	fresh basil leaves	16
16	small pieces soft leaf lettuce	16
3	carrots, grated	3

Soak dried shrimp in hot water for 10 minutes. Drain and chop. In a large bowl, mix dried shrimp, noodles, chilies, fish sauce, lime juice, 2 tablespoons (25 mL) radish and sugar. Set aside.

Combine ½ of the beer and an equal amount of warm water in a pie plate. Dip a sheet of rice paper into beer mixture, and spread on a flat surface. Lay 2 fresh shrimp on rice paper, and top with 1 tablespoon (15 mL) noodle mixture. Add 1 basil leaf and 1 piece lettuce, but do not overfill. Fold the sides to the inside, and roll snugly. Repeat, using all the filling. Mix carrots with remaining 1 cup (250 mL) radish in a large bowl to serve as garnish. Serve dipping sauce in a side dish.

Makes 16 spring rolls

CHILLED MUSSELS WITH ROMESCO SAUCE

*A good garnish for steamed, chilled mussels, this nutty Spanish sauce
works well with pasta. The shells of fresh mussels should be tightly sealed
or pull closed when lightly tapped. Avoid broken or cracked shells, and
never serve mussels that do not open fully during cooking.*

SAUCE

½	tomato, peeled	½
¼ cup	olive oil	50 mL
1	red bell pepper	1
1	fresh chili or ½ dried ancho chili	1
3	cloves garlic	3
¾ cup	toasted whole almonds	175 mL
½ tsp.	red-wine vinegar	2 mL
	Pinch coarse salt	

MUSSELS

4 dozen	mussels	4 dozen
1 cup	white wine	250 mL
	Coarse salt & freshly ground black pepper	

To make sauce, pan-fry tomato in 1 teaspoon (5 mL) oil until browned.
Set aside.

Hold red pepper on a long fork over the open flame of a gas stove or the
coils of an electric stove until the entire skin is blistered and blackened. Let
pepper steam for 15 minutes in a paper bag or in a bowl covered with plastic
wrap. Then remove skin, stem and seeds.

If using dried ancho chili, soak in warm water until soft, then drain.

Place tomato, remaining oil, roasted pepper, chili, garlic, almonds, vinegar
and salt in a food processor, and blend to a paste. Set aside. (Sauce can be
refrigerated but should be brought to room temperature before serving.)

Immediately before cooking, wash mussels and remove beards. Heat a
heavy-bottomed saucepan over medium-high to high heat, and add mussels,
wine and salt and pepper to taste. Cover and cook until mussels open; discard
any that do not open fully during cooking. Chill mussels, and remove from
shells.

Serve mussels on the half-shell topped with 1 teaspoon (5 mL) sauce. Makes
a great party appetizer.

Serves 4

Mussels Piri Piri

MUSSELS PIRI PIRI (Mussels With Portuguese Oil)

Provide lots of bread for sopping up the juices of the spicy mussels in this delicious dish.

1/2 cup	olive oil	125 mL
4	bay leaves	4
1 Tbsp.	lemon zest	15 mL
1/4 cup	lemon juice	50 mL
3 Tbsp.	crushed dried chilies	45 mL
6	cloves garlic, julienned	6
5 dozen	mussels	5 dozen
1 cup	white wine	250 mL
1/4 cup	chopped fresh parsley	50 mL

In a small bowl, mix together oil, bay leaves, lemon zest, lemon juice, chilies and garlic. Immediately before cooking, wash mussels and remove beards. Gently heat seasoned oil in a heavy-bottomed saucepan. Increase heat to high, and add mussels and wine. Cover and cook until mussels open; discard any that do not open fully during cooking. Serve in bowls, and garnish with parsley.

Serves 4 to 6

SCALLOP SEVICHE IN AN AVOCADO HALF

A refreshing light lunch or dinner appetizer for a hot summer day, scallop seviche has an added advantage for the cook: no heat required. The scallops "cook" in the citric acid of the lime and orange juices. Sea scallops can be sliced for this recipe, while bay scallops can be left whole. Firm up scallops for slicing by tossing them into the freezer for a few minutes. Fresh cod cut into ¼-inch (6 mm) chunks makes an excellent substitute for the scallops.

1 lb.	scallops, patted dry & sliced paper-thin	500 g
½ cup	freshly squeezed lime juice	125 mL
¼ cup	freshly squeezed orange juice	50 mL
1	medium tomato, diced	1
½	red bell pepper, thinly sliced	½
1	small red onion, thinly sliced	1
1 dozen	small green olives, halved	1 dozen
1	clove garlic, finely chopped	1
1	fresh chili or jalapeño, seeded & finely chopped	1
½	dried ancho chili, seeded & chopped	½
2 Tbsp.	chopped fresh coriander leaves or mint	25 mL
	Coarse salt	
2-4	ripe avocados	2-4

In a large bowl, mix together all ingredients, except avocados, seasoning with salt to taste. Marinate in the refrigerator for at least 2 hours.

Peel, halve and core avocados. Using a slotted spoon, fill avocado halves with scallop seviche.

Serves 4 to 8

GAMBAS GAMUT

Gambas can easily be turned into a light salad. In the final minutes of cooking time, add ¼ cup (50 mL) dry sherry and the juice of ½ lime to the skillet. Set aside, and serve at room temperature.

SCALLOPS MADAGASCAR

Pan-browned scallops tossed in a light, creamy sauce with a hint of Pernod make this a mouth-watering seafood dish. If you like the buttery crunch of pastry, serve the scallops on phyllo triangles. The scallops taste equally satisfying over rice.

½ cup	35% B.F. cream	125 mL
⅓ cup	sour cream	75 mL
1	leek (white part only), cleaned & julienned	1
6	sheets phyllo pastry	6
½ cup	melted butter	125 mL
1 Tbsp.	butter	15 mL
1 lb.	bay scallops	500 g
¾ tsp.	green peppercorns, crushed	4 mL
	Coarse salt	
	Freshly ground black pepper	
1 Tbsp.	Pernod	15 mL

To make crème fraîche, mix cream and sour cream in a bowl with a spoon; cover and leave at room temperature overnight. Within 24 hours, pour mixture into a cloth-lined colander that has been set in a bowl and refrigerate, allowing the cream to drain for 2 to 3 hours, or until there is about ½ cup (125 mL) thickened cream. Discard the liquid, and refrigerate crème fraîche until needed.

Blanch leek in boiling water, drain, and set aside.

Preheat oven to 350°F (180°C). Spread sheets of phyllo pastry, and cut them in half. Layer the 12 sheets on a baking sheet, brushing melted butter between each sheet and on the top layer. Using a sharp knife, cut the squares into triangles. Bake for 10 minutes or until lightly browned.

Melt 1 tablespoon (15 mL) butter in a skillet, then increase heat to medium-high. Add scallops, and toss until browned, about 2 minutes. Add leek, peppercorns and crème fraîche, and cook, stirring, for about 2 minutes. Season with salt and pepper to taste. Flame the Pernod (*see "Light My Fire," page 26*), and pour it over the scallop mixture. Serve immediately.

Serves 4

GAMBAS AL AJILLO

A delicious starter for any meal, these Spanish-inspired garlic-fried shrimp should be served in the cooking pan, hot from the stove, with lots of crusty bread to soak up the mouth-watering spicy oil. For a variation of gambas, which we call Grilled Ginger Shrimp, mix two tablespoons (25 mL) ginger with the other spices.

½ cup	olive oil	125 mL
28	large shrimp, peeled & deveined	28
2 Tbsp.	coarsely chopped fresh chilies	25 mL
2 Tbsp.	coarsely chopped garlic	25 mL
	Coarse salt	

Heat a heavy-gauge pan, such as a cast-iron skillet, over high heat until hot, and add oil. Dip a shrimp tail in the oil to test that it is hot enough; the tail should turn pink immediately. Add shrimp, and briefly cook one side. Turn, then add chilies and garlic. Do not let the garlic brown, or the gambas will be too bitter to enjoy. Season with salt to taste.

Serves 4

Gambas al Ajillo

*There's only one sure test
for saltiness with salt cod,
and it's a simple one.
After soaking the cod,
break open the thickest
part and taste it.
If it's still too salty, the
fish needs another soaking.*

SALT COD FRITTERS WITH MANGO SALSA

The hearty fish flavors of these Jamaican fritters are beautifully tempered by the succulent sweetness of mango. In this recipe, it is important to eliminate as much salt from the flesh of the fish as possible, which may call for repeated soakings in fresh water.

MANGO SALSA

2 oz.	tamarind pulp	50 g
4 cups	water	1 L
4	medium unripe mangoes	4
2 cups	malt vinegar	500 mL
1 cup	sugar	250 mL
½ cup	golden raisins	125 mL
½ cup	finely chopped fresh ginger	125 mL
1 Tbsp.	coarse salt	15 mL
1 tsp.	finely chopped garlic	5 mL
1 tsp.	finely chopped fresh chilies	5 mL
½ tsp.	allspice	2 mL

In a saucepan over low to medium heat, soften tamarind pulp in 4 cups (1 L) water for about 20 minutes. When seeds and pulp are softened and volume of liquid is reduced by half, strain the mixture, pushing as much pulp as possible through the sieve. Reserve the liquid.

Peel and dice mangoes, and combine with vinegar and ½ cup (125 mL) reserved tamarind water in a pot. Bring to a boil, and cook, stirring, for 10 minutes. Add remaining ingredients, and simmer over low heat for 45 minutes. Allow salsa to cool.

Makes 4 cups (1 L)

FRITTERS

½ lb.	salt cod	250 g
1½ cups	flour	375 mL
½ tsp.	coarse salt	2 mL
2	medium eggs, lightly beaten	2
3 Tbsp.	unsalted butter, melted	45 mL
1¼ cups	milk	300 mL
1	fresh habañero chili, seeded & chopped	1
2	scallions, chopped	2
1	clove garlic, chopped	1
1 Tbsp.	chopped fresh parsley	15 mL
½ tsp.	dried thyme	2 mL
½ tsp.	allspice	2 mL
	Peanut or vegetable oil for deep-frying	

Soak cod in lots of cold water overnight. In the morning, drain and test for saltiness. If necessary, change water and soak for an additional few hours, then drain. Set aside.

Place flour and salt in a large bowl. Beat eggs with butter, and add to flour. Gradually stir in milk, and let batter stand for 30 minutes.

In a separate bowl, mash cod with chili, scallions, garlic, parsley, thyme and allspice. Stir into batter. The finished fritter mixture should be the consistency of cooked porridge.

Add oil to a heavy-bottomed skillet over medium heat, and drop in 1 tablespoon (15 mL) batter for each fritter. Deep-fry fritters until golden brown. Drain on paper towels, and serve with salsa.

Makes 24 fritters

BRAEWATS

These Moroccan chicken-filled pies are prepared in a light, crispy phyllo shell.

4 lb.	chicken, cut into portions	1.8 kg
2	cloves garlic	2
½	onion, grated	½
½ cup	mixed chopped fresh parsley & coriander leaves	125 mL
¼ tsp.	saffron	1 mL
½ tsp.	freshly ground black pepper	2 mL
½ tsp.	ground ginger	2 mL
1 cup	butter	250 mL
	Pinch coarse salt	
3 cups	water	750 mL
2 Tbsp.	vegetable oil	25 mL
½ lb.	slivered blanched almonds	250 g
⅓ cup	icing sugar	75 mL
1½ tsp.	cinnamon	7 mL
1	1 lb. (500 g) pkg. phyllo pastry	1

In a large pot, place chicken, garlic, onion, parsley and coriander, saffron, pepper, ginger, ½ cup (125 mL) butter, salt and water. Bring to a boil. Reduce heat, and simmer for 1 hour.

In the meantime, heat oil in a pan, and brown almonds. Drain, dry and grind them. Mix almonds with sugar and cinnamon. Set aside.

Remove chicken from the pot, and drain. Debone meat, and shred in a food processor. Mix chicken with almond mixture, and set aside.

Preheat oven to 425°F (220°C). Clarify remaining ½ cup (125 mL) butter.

Cut folded phyllo sheets into four pieces. Unwrap one roll, lay one sheet flat, and brush with butter. Lay a second strip on top of the first, and brush with butter. Place 1 tablespoon (15 mL) filling in the bottom corner of the length of pastry. Fold diagonally from the bottom corner to the opposite side. Continue this triangular folding pattern until pastry is enclosed. Repeat steps, using all pastry and filling. Bake for 10 to 15 minutes, or until pastry is browned. Serve hot or cold.

Makes 36 to 40 pastries

RISOTTO MILANO-STYLE

For a risotto variation, add a pinch of saffron (about 20 strands) to the Basic Risotto recipe when sautéing the onion, and serve with Osso Buco (see page 144). Arborio rice is available at Italian specialty stores.

BASIC RISOTTO

Risotto is a classic northern Italian rice dish that can be served as a first course or a side dish or can be dressed up to stand on its own. The methodical addition of small amounts of hot cooking liquid and the constant stirring are the keys to giving risotto its full flavor and creamy texture. Use a heavy-bottomed pot to prevent the rice from sticking.

8 cups	rich chicken stock (see Basic Stock, page 46)	2 L
4 Tbsp.	butter	50 mL
1 Tbsp.	olive oil	15 mL
1	medium onion, diced	1
2 cups	arborio rice	500 mL
¾ cup	dry white wine	175 mL
	Coarse salt & freshly ground black pepper	
	Butter for garnish	
½ cup	freshly grated Parmesan cheese	125 mL

Add stock to a medium-size saucepan, bring to a boil, then set aside.

In a heavy-bottomed pot, heat butter and oil. Stir in onion, and sauté over low heat until onion is soft and translucent but not browned. Add rice, and stir for about 3 minutes to coat with oil and butter. When rice is shiny and translucent, add wine.

Continue to stir until wine has been absorbed. Add enough hot stock just to cover rice, and cook over low heat, stirring frequently, until stock is absorbed. Adding only ¼ cup (50 mL) stock at a time, repeat process until all stock is used. Rice should have a creamy texture, but the grains will retain their integrity. Season with salt and pepper to taste, and garnish with a dollop of butter, and sprinkle with cheese. Serve immediately.

Serves 6

SUN-DRIED TOMATO & PINE NUT RISOTTO

Vicki Newbury created this recipe using leftover puttanesca ingredients.

3	sun-dried tomato halves	3
1	medium onion, diced	1
1	clove garlic, minced	1
3 Tbsp.	olive oil	45 mL
1¼ cups	arborio rice	300 mL
1½-2 cups	chicken stock (see Basic Stock, page 46)	375-500 mL
1	roasted red bell pepper, diced	1
	(see "Blistering Hot," page 19)	
¼ cup	pine nuts	50 mL
3 Tbsp.	chopped fresh herbs (basil, parsley, thyme)	45 mL
	Coarse salt & freshly ground black pepper	

Rehydrate tomatoes by soaking in water. Remove from water, reserving liquid, and dice. In a large skillet, sauté tomatoes, onion and garlic in oil until onion is translucent. Add rice, and stir until rice is fully coated with oil. Pour ½ cup (125 mL) reserved water into pan, and cook, uncovered, over low heat, stirring constantly with a wooden spoon until water is absorbed. Add stock, ½ cup (125 mL) at a time, stirring until all liquid is absorbed. Just before serving, stir in roasted pepper, pine nuts and herbs. Season with salt and pepper to taste, and serve immediately.

Serves 6 to 8

RISOTTO CAKES
WITH TOMATO HERB SAUCE

At the restaurant, we often have leftover risotto. Experimentation with frying risotto patties led to adding a few ingredients to lighten the cakes and help them retain their shape. The more ingredients added to the initial risotto recipe, the more interesting the finished cake.

SAUCE

1	onion, thinly sliced	1
2	cloves garlic, chopped	2
¼ cup	olive oil	50 mL
½ cup	white wine	125 mL
1	28 oz. (796 mL) can whole tomatoes, crushed	1
¼ cup	chopped fresh herbs (thyme, basil, parsley & chervil)	50 mL

Over medium heat, sauté onion and garlic in oil until onion is translucent. Pour in wine, and cook for 5 minutes. Add tomatoes, and simmer, uncovered, over low heat for 20 minutes. Stir in herbs immediately before serving, or use as a garnish.

Makes 4 cups (1 L)

CAKES

5 cups	cooked risotto	1.25 L
2	eggs	2
2 Tbsp.	flour	25 mL
¼ cup	half-and-half	50 mL
	Clarified butter or olive oil	

In a large bowl, mix together risotto, eggs, flour and cream. Form into hamburger-size patties. Heat butter or oil in a skillet, and cook patties until golden brown. Spoon tomato herb sauce over patties, and serve.

Makes 8 to 10 patties

THE
AL DENTE
'BITE'

There are various ways to prepare risotto, and the final texture comes down to individual taste. In our opinion, perfect risotto should have an al dente "bite" to it. In general, the rice grain should retain its integrity, but the finished consistency can range from creamy soft to a crunchy, nutty center.

Beautiful Soup

Z al has always been a fabulous soup maker. He also loves to eat soup, and as a result, soups are one of Chez Piggy's strengths, considered by many to be a signature element of the menu. In fact, everyone who works in the kitchen enjoys creating them too, perhaps because, from the cook's point of view, it's really a chance to be innovative and spontaneous.

Great soup begins with a good stock. Our kitchen is always filled with the aroma of a large stockpot simmering from early morning to make a flavorful base for the soup of the day.

Zal's favorite soups tend to be the kind you can stand a spoon up in. Rich and hearty, Chez Piggy soups likewise often rely on lavish amounts of olive oil, cream, if it's called for, and butter, for which there is no substitute, according to Zal. Not all of these recipes reflect that approach, however; many are subtle, the understated seasoning gathering momentum with each spoonful.

Beyond that, it's all adaptation, intuition and luck. We exploit these to the fullest by combining the tastes that work together in other preparations—lime with shrimp, tomato with pesto, leek with Stilton, squash with ginger—to create unforgettable soups.

EAT, DRINK AND BE
HARRIED, from left to
right: general manager
Nick Waterfield takes time
to raise a glass of cheer
with a Chez Piggy patron;
limestone walls hint of the
restaurant's architectural
history; hectic life in the
staff lane; relocated to
Kingston's lower Princess
Street in 2002, the new
and improved Pan
Chancho now boasts a
bakery, a courtyard café
and a private dining room.

STOCK TIPS

Stock should never be boiled, since fat and protein drawn out of meat and bones are readily dissolved and will leave a fatty residue in the finished stock. Simmering, on the other hand, gently draws out the flavor from the meat, keeping the fat separate from the stock so that it is easier to skim.

Once the stock is defatted, however, boiling it during the preparation of soup will not adversely affect the flavor.

BASIC STOCK

This recipe provides the base for a variety of homemade soups. Roasting the bones and vegetables isn't necessary but will produce a clearer, richer stock. Leaving the fat on the surface until you use the stock will seal in flavors for up to a week. When making fish stock, avoid using strong-tasting salmon bones.

4 lb.	chicken, duck, beef, lamb, veal or ham bones	1.8 kg
	or fish bones, heads & tails	
	or seafood shells	
1	medium onion, cut into chunks	1
1	clove garlic	1
1	carrot, cut into chunks	1
2	stalks celery, cut into chunks	2
4 qt.	water	4 L
½ cup	fresh parsley stems	125 mL
1	bay leaf	1
1 tsp.	whole black peppercorns	5 mL

Preheat oven to 375°F (190°C). Combine bones, onion, garlic, carrot and celery in a roasting pan, and roast for 35 minutes. In a stockpot, heat water to a simmer, and add roasted bones and vegetables, parsley, bay leaf and peppercorns. Simmer chicken bones for 2 to 3 hours; lamb, veal or ham bones for 3 to 8 hours; and beef bones for up to 10 hours. For fish or seafood stock, simmer for 30 minutes. Strain and chill overnight. Skim fat just before using.
Makes 12 to 16 cups (3-4 L)

VEGETABLE STOCK

If you don't have bones on hand, this flavorful vegetarian option can be used in any recipe that calls for meat stock. Use your imagination, and add whatever range of mild vegetables you like, but avoid strong-flavored members of the brassica and pepper families.

2	carrots, unpeeled	2
	Tops from 2 leeks	
1	onion, unpeeled	1
3	cloves garlic, unpeeled	3
1	bunch fresh parsley leaves or stems	1
1	bay leaf	1
1 cup	button mushroom stems	250 mL
1 Tbsp.	whole black peppercorns	15 mL
1 cup	white wine (optional)	250 mL
3 qt.	water	3 L

Combine all ingredients in a stockpot. Simmer for 30 to 60 minutes. Strain and chill.
Makes 12 cups (3 L)

BROWN STOCK

*Roasting the bones infuses this stock with a rich flavor, providing a tasty base
for gravies or sauces. Once clarified, it can also be used as the stock consommé
for strong meat soups, such as beef and barley.*

6 lb.	meat bones	2.7 kg
2 Tbsp.	vegetable oil	25 mL
1	carrot, chopped	1
1	stalk celery, chopped	1
2	onions, chopped	2
2	cloves garlic	2
1 Tbsp.	tomato paste	15 mL
2 cups + 4 qt.	water	500 mL + 4 L
2 cups	red wine	500 mL
1 tsp.	whole black peppercorns	5 mL
½ cup	fresh parsley stems	125 mL

Preheat oven to 375°F (190°C), and roast bones in a large roasting pan for
45 minutes.

Add oil to a large stockpot, and brown carrot, celery, onions, garlic and
tomato paste over medium heat. Add roasted bones. Drain fat from roasting
pan, and deglaze with 2 cups (500 mL) water, stirring in all meat bits from the
sides of the pan. Pour this liquid into stockpot, and add wine, 4 quarts (4 L)
water, peppercorns and parsley. Partly cover, and simmer for 6 hours. Let cool,
and refrigerate. Skim fat just before using.

Makes 12 to 16 cups (3-4 L)

FLAVORED BROWN SAUCE

*Made without flour, this thick, rich sauce provides a nice taste with no overpowering meat
flavors. Add any one or combination of brandy, Calvados, lemon zest, rosemary,
sage, porcini or wild mushrooms to flavor this brown sauce. Use on duck leg and roasted
or grilled lean meats or as a base to make stock. The sauce can be frozen for future use.*

12 cups	brown stock *(recipe above)*	3 L
	Flavoring of your choice:	
	1 cup (250 mL) brandy or Calvados	
	or zest of 1 lemon	
	or 3-inch (8 cm) piece fresh ginger, sliced,	
	or other flavoring	

Skim fat from chilled stock. Add your choice of flavoring, and boil stock
down until only 2 cups (500 mL) remain, approximately 5 to 6 hours. When
hot, the sauce will be thick like syrup; when chilled, it will be firm like fudge.

Makes 2 cups (500 mL)

ROASTED GARLIC SOUP

When roasted, garlic becomes sweet and aromatic and, combined with potatoes, forms the backbone of this creamy, flavorful soup.

1	whole head garlic, peeled	1
1	onion, diced	1
1 Tbsp.	olive oil	15 mL
4 cups	chicken stock (*see Basic Stock, page 46*)	1 L
1 cup	35% B.F. cream	250 mL
2 cups	diced peeled potatoes	500 mL
	Coarse salt & freshly ground black pepper	

Preheat oven to 400°F (200°C). Rub garlic and onion with oil, and wrap in aluminum foil. Roast for 45 minutes. Let cool.

Place roasted garlic and onion, stock, cream and potatoes in a large saucepan, and cook over medium heat until potatoes are tender. Let cool slightly, place in a food processor, and purée. Return soup to saucepan, and simmer. Season with salt and pepper to taste.

Serves 4 to 6

FIERY GALANGAL SOUP

The basic vegetable-and-rice-noodle broth of this soup features lime juice,
tamarind water and coconut milk in a hot-and-sour Thai combination.
Once the broth is created, you can generously add ingredients such as chicken
or shrimp to make a more robust dish. "Sambal" is an Indonesian term for sauce.
It is a chili purée that you can buy at Asian specialty stores.

2 qt.	chicken or shrimp stock (*see Basic Stock, page 46*)	2 L
2	kaffir lime leaves	2
1	1-inch (2.5 cm) piece fresh galangal, sliced	1
1	2-inch (5 cm) piece lemongrass, chopped	1
1	1-inch (2.5 cm) piece fresh ginger, sliced	1
4	fresh chilies, sliced	4
⅓ cup	coconut milk	75 mL
¼ cup	fish sauce	50 mL
3 Tbsp.	lime juice	45 mL
3 Tbsp.	tamarind water (*see Mango Salsa, page 40*)	45 mL
4 oz.	rice noodles	125 g
2 cups	fresh bean sprouts	500 mL
4	scallions, chopped	4
¼ cup	chopped fresh coriander leaves	50 mL
	Hot chili sambal for garnish	
2	limes, sliced	2

Bring stock to a boil. Reduce heat, add lime leaves, galangal, lemongrass,
ginger, chilies, coconut milk, fish sauce, lime juice and tamarind water, and
simmer for 1 hour. Strain soup and reserve broth.

Soften noodles in warm water, then drain. Divide noodles, bean sprouts,
scallions and coriander among serving bowls, and cover with hot broth. Serve
garnished with sambal, with a slice of lime on the side.

Serves 4 to 6

APPLE & CHEDDAR CHEESE SOUP

We consider this recipe a great Canadian combination of flavors: the sharpness of old Cheddar and the sweetness of apple juice.

8 cups	chicken stock (*see Basic Stock, page 46*)	2 L
3 cups	apple juice	750 mL
4	cloves garlic, chopped	4
2	carrots, peeled & cut into chunks	2
1	stalk celery, cut into chunks	1
1	medium onion, cut into chunks	1
3	tart apples, unpeeled, cut into chunks	3
½	red bell pepper, cut into chunks	½
1 tsp.	ground cardamom	5 mL
	Coarse salt & freshly ground black pepper	
3½ Tbsp.	butter	52 mL
¼ cup	flour	50 mL
5 cups	35% B.F. cream	1.25 L
5 cups	grated sharp Cheddar cheese	1.25 L
¼ cup	brandy	50 mL
	Chopped fresh parsley or croutons for garnish	

Place stock and apple juice in a large pot, and bring to a boil. Reduce heat, and add garlic, carrots, celery, onion, apples and red pepper. Simmer until vegetables are soft, then add cardamom. Season with salt and pepper to taste. Blend to a smooth purée with a hand blender or in a food processor. Set aside.

In a separate pan, melt butter over medium heat. Add flour, and cook for 5 minutes. Stir in cream, and whisk, cooking until mixture thickens. Add cheese, stirring until melted. Flame brandy in a ladle (*see "Light My Fire," page 26*), and pour into cheese sauce. Mix thoroughly.

Bring puréed soup base to a boil. Stir in cheese sauce. Immediately remove from heat. Garnish with parsley or croutons.

Serves 10 to 12

LEEK & STILTON SOUP

*This soup is a Chez Piggy favorite. Although Stilton is a strong cheese
on its own, its flavor is subtle in this recipe, in which it is combined with leeks.
You can derive more flavor from the leeks by holding one back, dicing it,
sweating it in butter and using it in the cheese sauce.*

8 cups	chicken stock (*see Basic Stock, page 46*)	2 L
2 cups	dry white wine	500 mL
1	medium onion, diced	1
1	stalk celery, diced	1
3	cloves garlic, minced	3
7-8	leeks, thinly sliced	7-8
2 tsp.	dried thyme	10 mL
2 tsp.	dried oregano	10 mL
2 tsp.	freshly ground black pepper	10 mL
3 Tbsp.	butter	45 mL
2 Tbsp.	flour	25 mL
4 cups	35% B.F. cream	1 L
¾ lb.	Stilton cheese, crumbled	375 g
	Coarse salt & freshly ground black pepper	
2	scallions, chopped, for garnish	2

Place stock and wine in a large pot, and boil for 20 minutes. Reduce heat,
add onion, celery, garlic, leeks, thyme, oregano and 2 teaspoons (10 mL)
pepper, and simmer until vegetables are tender, about 1 hour.

In a separate pot, melt butter. Stir in flour, and cook for 5 minutes. Stir in
cream, and heat until thickened. Add cheese, and cook, stirring, until melted.

Bring soup to a boil, and stir in cheese sauce. Immediately remove from heat.
Season with salt and pepper to taste. Garnish with scallions.

Serves 8 to 10

SHRIMP BISQUE WITH VANILLA
& CHIPOTLE CHILIES

To make the shrimp stock, you will need three to four pounds (1.5-1.8 kg) of shrimp shells simmered in nine cups (2.25 L) of water for 30 minutes. Since it is not likely that you will have this much shrimp on hand at one time, you will need to save the shells from gambas and other dishes and store them in the freezer. Chipotle is a smoked, dried jalapeño.

1	medium onion, finely diced	1
2	cloves garlic, minced	2
2 Tbsp.	butter	25 mL
2 Tbsp.	tomato paste	25 mL
4	fresh tomatoes, peeled & diced	4
1	chipotle, soaked & puréed	1
½ tsp.	cumin seed, toasted & ground	2 mL
2 cups	35% B.F. cream	500 mL
8 cups	shrimp stock (see *Basic Stock*, page 46)	2 L
2 Tbsp.	brandy, flamed	25 mL
	(see *"Light My Fire,"* page 26)	
5 Tbsp.	vanilla extract	65 mL
	Coarse salt	
	Olive oil	
24	shrimp	24
	Crostini for garnish	
	Chopped scallions for garnish	

Sauté onion and garlic in butter until soft and transparent. Add tomato paste, tomatoes, chipotle and cumin. Fry for a few minutes, then stir in cream and stock. Bring to a boil, then reduce heat, and simmer for 15 minutes. Stir in brandy and vanilla. Season with salt to taste, and keep warm.

Heat oil in a skillet, and sauté shrimp. Place shrimp in bowls, and spoon tomato mixture on top. Garnish with crostini and scallions.

Serves 6 to 8

COCONUT LIME SOUP WITH SHRIMP

*Sweet-and-sour Asian flavors are cut by the richness of coconut milk
in this fresh, light soup. For a stronger-tasting seafood base,
simmer the shrimp shells in the chicken stock, then strain them out.*

4 Tbsp.	vegetable oil	50 mL
1	red bell pepper, finely diced	1
1	green bell pepper, finely diced	1
2	fresh green chilies, minced	2
1	onion, finely diced	1
	Pinch turmeric	
3	cloves garlic, minced	3
6 cups	chicken stock or mixture of half chicken & half shrimp stock (*see Basic Stock, page 46*)	1.5 L
1½ cups	coconut milk	375 mL
	Juice & pulp of 6 limes	
2 cups	diced tomatoes	500 mL
2 Tbsp.	honey	25 mL
	Coarse salt & freshly ground black pepper	
18	large shrimp, peeled (reserve shells)	18
2 Tbsp.	chopped scallions	25 mL

Heat 2 tablespoons (25 mL) oil in a large skillet, and sauté red pepper, green pepper, chilies, onion, turmeric and two-thirds of garlic. Set aside.

Place stock in a large pot, and bring to a boil. Reduce heat to low, and stir in coconut milk, lime juice and pulp, tomatoes, honey and sautéed vegetables. Simmer for 10 minutes. Season with salt and pepper to taste, and keep warm.

Heat remaining 2 tablespoons (25 mL) oil in a skillet. Add shrimp and remaining one-third of garlic, and sauté until cooked, turning once. Remove shrimp, and cut in half lengthwise. Add to soup just before serving. Garnish with scallions.

Serves 6

STORING SEASHELLS

Seafood stock is probably going to be one of the hardest things to create at home, because you'll rarely have the required number of shells on hand. Reserve and freeze leftover shells as they are available, or make and freeze small quantities of stock when you can. Another option is to visit your friendly neighborhood fish store and ask for castoffs. To avoid an overly strong-tasting stock, try to match the stock ingredients to the finished soup.

FISHERMAN'S SOUP

This seafood soup is a fennel broth flavored with piri piri and thickened with brandade, which underscores the fish theme. As the final touch, we add haddock, shrimp and mussels and garnish the entire creation with rouille. Just be patient, and prepare all the elements before you assemble the dish—it's worth the effort.

BRANDADE

1 lb.	salt cod	500 g
½ lb.	potatoes, peeled	250 g
½ cup	olive oil	125 mL
6	large cloves garlic, roasted in olive oil (*see page 24*)	6
1 cup	35% B.F. cream	250 mL

Place cod in a deep roasting pan, and cover with cold water. Soak for 2 days, changing the water twice, if possible. Check saltiness before cooking by tasting a bit from the center of the thickest piece. If sufficient salt has leached out, drain.

Cook potatoes in boiling unsalted water. In a large pot, heat oil. Add garlic, cod and potatoes. Stir with a wooden spoon while adding cream. Cook until half the liquid has evaporated and cod starts to break apart, indicating that it is done. Purée with a hand blender. Set aside.

ROUILLE

½ tsp.	saffron	2 mL
3	cloves garlic	3
3	fresh chilies	3
2 Tbsp.	lemon juice	25 mL
4 tsp.	tomato paste	20 mL
½	pimiento or roasted red bell pepper	½
1	egg	1
2	egg yolks	2
1-1½ cups	olive oil	250-375 mL
½ cup	vegetable oil	125 mL

In a mortar and pestle, grind together saffron, garlic, chilies and lemon juice, and let stand for 20 minutes. Place mixture in a blender, add tomato paste, pimiento or roasted pepper, egg and egg yolks, and blend. Gradually drizzle in olive oil, then vegetable oil until rouille thickens. Set aside.

PIRI PIRI

½ cup	olive oil	125 mL
4	bay leaves	4
1 Tbsp.	lemon zest	15 mL
¼ cup	lemon juice	50 mL
3 Tbsp.	crushed dried chilies	45 mL
6	cloves garlic, julienned	6

In a small bowl, mix all ingredients together. Set aside.

BROTH

¹⁄₄ cup	olive oil	50 mL
¹⁄₄ cup	well-stirred piri piri	50 mL
2	onions, sliced	2
1	fennel bulb, finely sliced	1
2 Tbsp.	tomato paste	25 mL
2 tsp.	fennel seed	10 mL
2 tsp.	saffron	10 mL
2 cups	white wine	500 mL
8 cups	shrimp or fish stock (*see Basic Stock, page 46*)	2 L
36	large shrimp	36
1 lb.	fresh haddock or monkfish, cut into chunks	500 g
5 dozen	mussels, washed & debearded	5 dozen
1 cup	brandade	250 mL
	Chopped fresh fennel for garnish	
	Crostini	

In a large heavy-bottomed pot, heat oil and piri piri. Add onions, fennel bulb and tomato paste. Cook over medium heat until onions and fennel are soft and browned slightly. Add fennel seed, saffron, wine and stock. Simmer for 25 minutes. Just before serving, bring broth to a boil. Add shrimp, haddock and mussels, and poach for about 2 minutes. Discard any mussels that do not open fully during cooking. Stir in brandade.

Serve in individual bowls, distributing seafood equally. Garnish with rouille and fennel, and serve with crostini.

Serves 10 to 12

Fisherman's Soup

NAVY BEAN SOUP WITH HAM

*A tip to ensure success is to add the tomato paste
only after the beans are fully cooked. Otherwise, the acid content
of the tomatoes will prevent the beans from becoming tender.*

1¼ cups	dried navy beans, sorted & rinsed	300 mL
3 Tbsp. + 1 tsp.	butter or chicken fat	45 mL + 5 mL
1	onion, diced	1
1	stalk celery, diced	1
1	carrot, diced	1
2	cloves garlic, chopped	2
1	bay leaf	1
1 tsp.	dried thyme	5 mL
1 tsp.	coarse salt	5 mL
6 cups	chicken or ham stock or a combination of the two (*see Basic Stock, page 46*)	1.5 L
2 Tbsp.	tomato paste	25 mL
2 cups	diced cooked ham	500 mL

Coarse salt & freshly ground black pepper
Chopped fresh parsley for garnish

Cover beans with water, and soak overnight. The next day, drain beans.

In a large pot, heat 3 tablespoons (45 mL) butter or chicken fat, and sauté onion, celery, carrot and garlic until soft. Stir in beans, bay leaf, thyme and 1 teaspoon (5 mL) salt. Add stock, and bring to a boil. Reduce heat to low, and simmer for 1½ to 2 hours, until beans are soft. You may need to add small amounts of water to get the right consistency.

When beans are cooked, heat remaining 1 teaspoon (5 mL) butter or chicken fat in a separate heavy-bottomed pot. Add tomato paste, and cook, stirring, being careful not to burn it. Remove 2 cups (500 mL) beans with liquid from soup pot, add to tomato mixture, and mash. Return this thickener to the soup. Add ham. Season with salt and pepper to taste. Garnish with parsley.

Serves 6 to 8

BEAN, POTATO & RED-PEPPER SOUP

Here is a fancy rendition of bean and bacon soup
dressed up with potatoes, tomatoes and red peppers.

1¼ cups	dried navy beans, sorted & rinsed	300 mL
4 qt.	chicken or ham stock (*see Basic Stock, page 46*)	4 L
1	ham bone	1
4	large potatoes, peeled & diced	4
1	bay leaf	1
¼ lb.	ham, diced	125 g
¼ lb.	bacon, diced	125 g
2 Tbsp.	butter	25 mL
2 cups	diced onions	500 mL
2	carrots, diced	2
3	cloves garlic, chopped	3
1	stalk celery, chopped	1
2	red bell peppers, diced	2
1	28 oz. (796 mL) can whole tomatoes, crushed with liquid	1
	Coarse salt & freshly ground black pepper	

Cover beans with water, and soak overnight. The next day, drain beans.

In a large stockpot, bring stock, beans and ham bone to a boil. Reduce heat to a simmer, and cook for 45 to 60 minutes. Add potatoes and bay leaf, and continue to simmer until beans and potatoes are tender. Stir in ham.

In a cast-iron skillet, cook bacon until crisp. Melt butter in skillet with bacon. Add onions, carrots, garlic and celery. Cook until tender, then add to soup. Stir in red peppers and tomatoes, and simmer for 7 to 10 minutes to blend flavors. Remove ham bone. Season with salt and pepper to taste.

Serves 6 to 8

BLACK BEAN SOUP
WITH CHEDDAR & ONIONS

One leftover we all love to find in the restaurant refrigerator in the morning is black beans, simply because they make a fantastic soup base. When using leftover cooked beans, reduce the amount of stock to 12 cups (3 L) and add the beans directly to the soup along with the bacon. But don't wait until you have leftover turtle beans—this recipe is also worth making from scratch.

6 qt.	stock (*see Basic Stock, page 46*) or water	6 L
1½ lb.	dried black beans, sorted & rinsed	750 g
1	ham bone	1
1	12 oz. (341 mL) bottle of dark beer	1
3	bay leaves	3
¼ lb.	bacon, diced	125 g
4 cups	diced onions	1 L
3	finger-hot chilies, chopped	3
6	cloves garlic, minced	6
3 Tbsp.	cumin seed, toasted & ground	45 mL
1 tsp.	freshly ground black pepper	5 mL
1 tsp.	dried oregano	5 mL
1 tsp.	dried thyme	5 mL
2 Tbsp.	lime juice	25 mL
	Coarse salt & freshly ground black pepper	
½ cup	chopped fresh coriander leaves for garnish	125 mL
1	sweet onion, minced, for garnish	1
1 cup	grated sharp Cheddar cheese for garnish	250 mL
1 cup	chopped red & green bell peppers for garnish	250 mL

Cover beans with water, and soak overnight. The next day, drain beans.

Place stock or water in a large pot, and add beans, ham bone, beer and bay leaves. Simmer over medium heat until beans are soft, about 1½ hours, adding small amounts of water, if necessary, to keep beans covered. Reduce heat to low, and remove ham bone and bay leaves.

Heat a cast-iron skillet over medium heat, add bacon, and cook until crispy. Remove bacon with a slotted spoon, and set aside. Reduce heat to low, add onions, chilies and garlic to bacon drippings, and cook until soft. Add onion mixture and bacon to the soup pot. Stir in cumin, pepper, oregano, thyme and lime juice. Season with salt and pepper to taste. Heat through, and serve garnished with coriander, onion, cheese and red and green peppers.

Serves 8 to 10

CURRIED RED LENTIL SOUP

*The flavors of curry spices combined with red lentils and sweetened with coconut milk
are a natural marriage in this soup inspired by Indian cuisine. The result is
thinner than split-pea soup but hearty enough to make a light meal.*

2 Tbsp.	butter	25 mL
2	onions, diced	2
1	carrot, finely diced	1
4	cloves garlic, chopped	4
1	1-inch (2.5 cm) piece fresh ginger, peeled & chopped	1
2 tsp.	curry powder	10 mL
1 tsp.	ground cumin	5 mL
½ tsp.	turmeric	2 mL
2 cups	red lentils	500 mL
6 cups	vegetable stock (*see page 46*)	1.5 L
1½ cups	coconut milk	375 mL
	Fresh coriander sprigs or chopped scallions for garnish	

Melt butter in a large pot over medium heat, and sauté onions, carrot, garlic,
ginger, curry powder, cumin and turmeric until onions are translucent. Stir in
lentils until coated with butter. Add stock and coconut milk, and simmer over
medium heat until lentils are mushy, about 1 hour. Garnish with coriander
or scallions.

Serves 8 to 10

SPICED LENTIL SOUP
WITH PRESERVED LEMON

Inspired by Moroccan cuisine, this variation of curried lentil soup uses preserved lemon for a tart taste. If you happen to have half an overripe papaya, as we often do at the restaurant, mash it along with the honey and add to the soup to sweeten.

2	cloves garlic, chopped	2
	Pinch saffron	
7 cups	chicken stock (*see Basic Stock, page 46*)	1.75 L
	Vegetable oil for frying	
1	carrot, finely diced	1
1	red bell pepper, finely diced	1
1	onion, finely diced	1
1	fresh chili, chopped	1
2 Tbsp.	chopped fresh ginger	25 mL
1½ cups	red lentils	375 mL
4	cloves	4
½ tsp.	ground cardamom	2 mL
1 tsp.	coriander seed	5 mL
2 tsp.	cumin seed	10 mL
3 Tbsp.	honey	45 mL
	Juice of 2 limes	
1	preserved lemon, rinsed & finely diced (*see page 176*)	1
	Coarse salt & freshly ground black pepper	
2 Tbsp.	chopped fresh coriander leaves for garnish	25 mL

One hour before preparing soup, grind garlic and saffron together in a mortar and pestle. Set aside.

In a large pot, bring stock to a boil. Reduce heat, and simmer.

In a skillet, heat oil, and sauté garlic-saffron mixture, carrot, red pepper, onion, chili and ginger until onion is yellow and soft. Stir vegetable mixture into stock. Add lentils, stirring so that they don't stick together.

In a dry skillet, lightly toast cloves, cardamom, coriander and cumin. Grind and add to soup along with honey, lime juice and preserved lemon.

Continue simmering soup, stirring occasionally, until lentils have almost disintegrated, about 20 minutes. Season with salt and pepper to taste, and garnish with coriander.

Serves 6

Curried Carrot Soup
With Coconut Milk,
Cashews & Coriander

CURRIED CARROT SOUP WITH COCONUT MILK, CASHEWS & CORIANDER

Ginger, garlic, curry powder and coconut milk make flavorful seasonings for this mild grated-carrot soup. For a spicier version, add extra curry powder.

3 Tbsp.	butter or olive oil	45 mL
2	onions, diced	2
1	stalk celery, diced	1
3	cloves garlic, chopped	3
1	3-inch (8 cm) piece fresh ginger, chopped	1
2 Tbsp.	curry powder	25 mL
1½ lb.	carrots, peeled & grated	750 g
6 cups	chicken stock (*see Basic Stock, page 46*)	1.5 L
2	kaffir lime leaves	2
3¼ cups	coconut milk	800 mL
	Coarse salt & freshly ground black pepper	
1	bunch fresh coriander, chopped, for garnish	1
½ cup	chopped cashew pieces for garnish	125 mL

Heat butter or oil in a large pot, and sauté onions, celery, garlic and ginger over medium heat. Add curry powder, and continue cooking until onions are soft. Add carrots, and sauté. Add stock and lime leaves, and simmer until carrots are fully cooked. Using a hand blender or a food processor, purée soup. Stir in coconut milk, and heat through. Season with salt and pepper to taste. Garnish with coriander and cashews.

Serves 10 to 12

AFRICAN YAM & PEANUT SOUP

Flavored with peanut butter and the tart taste of lime juice,
this sweet-potato soup is a thick and hearty offering.

6 cups	chicken stock (*see Basic Stock, page 46*)	1.5 L
2 Tbsp.	butter	25 mL
2	medium onions, diced	2
3	cloves garlic, minced	3
2	fresh chilies, minced	2
1 cup	diced tomatoes	250 mL
2	yams, cooked & mashed	2
1 tsp.	cumin seed, toasted & ground	5 mL
1	2-inch (5 cm) stick cinnamon	1
3	cloves, ground	3
2	cardamom pods	2
1½ cups	crunchy peanut butter	375 mL
¼ cup	lime juice	50 mL
	Coarse salt & freshly ground black pepper	
4	scallions, sliced, for garnish	4

In a large pot, bring stock to a boil; reduce heat to medium-low.

In a skillet, melt butter over medium heat, and sauté onions, garlic and chilies until soft. Add tomatoes, and cook for 5 minutes. Add tomato mixture, yams, cumin, cinnamon, cloves and cardamom to stock. Stir in peanut butter and lime juice, and simmer for 20 minutes. Season with salt and pepper to taste. Garnish with scallions.

Serves 8

GINGERED SQUASH SOUP

Winter squash that has been seasoned with garlic and fragrant spices—ginger,
cardamom and coriander—makes a delicious and heavy-textured base for soups.
With that in mind, you can lighten the taste of the finished soup by omitting the butter
and stirring in yogurt in place of the cream. For the richest color, use pepper
and butternut squashes, and be sure to cut the carrot into small pieces,
since it will take the longest to cook.

8 cups	chicken stock (*see Basic Stock, page 46*)	2 L
6 cups	coarsely chopped peeled winter squash	1.5 L
1	onion, cut into chunks	1
1	carrot, cut into small chunks	1
½	red bell pepper	½
1	small sweet potato or parsnip, cut into chunks	1
3-4	cloves garlic	3-4
1	2-inch (5 cm) piece fresh ginger, peeled	1
2 tsp.	ground cardamom	10 mL
2 tsp.	ground coriander	10 mL
3 Tbsp.	honey	45 mL
¼ cup	brandy	50 mL
1 Tbsp.	butter	15 mL
½ cup	35% B.F. cream	125 mL
	Coarse salt & freshly ground black pepper	
	Sliced toasted almonds for garnish	

Place stock in a large pot, and bring to a boil. Reduce heat, add vegetables, garlic, ginger, cardamom and coriander, and simmer until vegetables are tender. Stir in honey. Flame brandy in a ladle (*see "Light My Fire," page 26*), and add to soup. Simmer for 10 minutes.

Using a hand blender or a food processor, purée soup, then return to pot over low heat. Stir in butter and cream. Season with salt and pepper to taste, and garnish with almonds.

Serves 8 to 10

CORN CHOWDER WITH HAM

This soup is best when it is made with freshly picked sweet corn.
Because Zal believes that "glistening fat greatly enhances the taste
and appearance of this soup," he recommends using the chicken fat skimmed
from the stock in place of butter for making the roux.

12 cups	stock, made from chicken & ham bones	3 L
	(see Basic Stock, page 46)	
12	ears corn, kernels removed (reserve cobs)	12
1	medium onion, diced	1
1	carrot, diced	1
1	stalk celery, diced	1
1 tsp.	dried savory	5 mL
2	cloves garlic, minced	2
2 tsp.	ground cumin	10 mL
½	red bell pepper, diced	½
1 cup	diced cooked ham	250 mL
1½ cups	mashed potatoes	375 mL
1 Tbsp.	chicken fat or butter	15 mL
1 Tbsp.	flour	15 mL
1½ cups	35% B.F. cream	375 mL
	Fresh chives for garnish	

Bring stock to a boil in a large pot, and add reserved cobs. Reduce heat, and simmer for 30 minutes. Remove cobs, and add onion, carrot, celery, savory, garlic and cumin. Cook until vegetables are tender. Add corn, red pepper and ham.

Remove 3 cups (750 mL) soup, and in a separate bowl, blend into potatoes. Return potato mixture to soup, and mix thoroughly. Continue to simmer.

In a separate pot, warm chicken fat or butter over medium heat. Add flour, and cook for 5 minutes. Stir in cream, and continue stirring until thickened.

Bring soup to a boil, and stir in cream sauce. Immediately remove from heat. Garnish with chives.

Serves 8 to 10

RUSSIAN GAZPACHO

For beet lovers who don't like borscht and want to enjoy a tasty cold soup in summer.

2 lb.	beets, cooked & peeled	1 kg
1	medium red onion	1
1	medium red bell pepper	1
1	large English cucumber, unpeeled	1
8	radishes	8
3	cloves garlic	3
1 cup	olive oil	250 mL
2 cups	chilled & defatted chicken stock	500 mL
	(see *Basic Stock, page 46*)	
1/3 cup	lemon juice	75 mL
2 Tbsp.	red-wine vinegar	25 mL
2 Tbsp.	sugar	25 mL
2 cups	crushed ice	500 mL
1 tsp.	coarse salt	5 mL
	Lemon slices for garnish	
	Fresh mint for garnish	

In a food processor, purée beets, onion, red pepper, cucumber, radishes and garlic with oil. Pour into a large bowl, and stir in stock, lemon juice, vinegar, sugar and ice. Add salt, and chill. Garnish with lemon slices and mint.

Serves 8 to 10

WHITE GAZPACHO

Rose and Zal first tasted this soup in Spain; Anne Linton developed it for the restaurant.

2 cups	finely ground almonds	500 mL
5	cloves garlic	5
1	loaf French bread, crust removed, cubed	1
6 cups	cold water	1.5 L
1/4 cup	olive oil	50 mL
1 tsp.	coarse salt	5 mL
2 Tbsp.	sugar	25 mL
1/4 cup	white-wine vinegar	50 mL
	Halved green grapes for garnish	

In a food processor, blend almonds and garlic. Place bread cubes in a large bowl, and cover with water. Soak until soft, then squeeze out excess water, and reserve. Blend bread with garlic mixture in a food processor. With food processor running, drizzle in oil, and mix until well blended. Transfer mixture to a large bowl, and whisk in reserved bread water. Add salt, sugar and vinegar. Chill. Serve in chilled bowls, and garnish with grapes.

Serves 6

CHILLED AVOCADO SOUP
WITH CORIANDER SALSA

This thick and simple soup pairs the creamy texture of avocado with citrus and Mexican spices. The soup's similarities to guacamole make coriander salsa a natural choice for a garnish.

SALSA

3	tomatoes, diced	3
½	red bell pepper, diced	½
1	fresh chili, minced	1
2	cloves garlic, minced	2
½ cup	chopped fresh coriander leaves	125 mL

Mix all ingredients together in a bowl. Refrigerate until needed.

SOUP

3	avocados	3
4 tsp.	lemon juice	20 mL
8 tsp.	lime juice	40 mL
2 tsp.	ground cumin	10 mL
1 tsp.	chili powder	5 mL
2 cups	35% B.F. cream	500 mL
3 cups	chilled & defatted chicken stock	750 mL

(see Basic Stock, page 46)
Coarse salt & freshly ground black pepper

Place avocados, lemon juice, lime juice, cumin and chili powder in a food processor, and purée. Transfer to a large bowl, and stir in cream and stock. Season with salt and pepper to taste. Chill. Serve in chilled bowls, garnished with a generous portion of salsa.
Serves 6

**Chilled Avocado Soup
With Coriander Salsa**

CHILLED CURRIED BLUEFISH SOUP

Curry spices are the strong seasoning for the distinctive taste of bluefish.

2 Tbsp.	vegetable oil	25 mL
1	large onion, finely diced	1
1 tsp.	chopped finger-hot chili	5 mL
1½ tsp.	chopped fresh ginger	7 mL
1 tsp.	chopped garlic	5 mL
1 Tbsp.	curry powder	15 mL
1 tsp.	ground fenugreek	5 mL
6 cups	chicken stock (*see Basic Stock, page 46*)	1.5 L
¼ cup	lime juice	50 mL
1 Tbsp.	brown sugar	15 mL
1 cup	puréed tomato	250 mL
¼ cup	finely diced red bell pepper	50 mL
¾ lb.	bluefish, cut into ½-inch (1 cm) cubes	375 g
1½ cups	35% B.F. cream	375 mL
1 cup	yogurt	250 mL
1 tsp.	coarse salt	5 mL
½ tsp.	freshly ground black pepper	2 mL
1 Tbsp.	chopped fresh dill for garnish	15 mL

In a large pot, heat oil over medium heat, and sauté onion, chili, ginger, garlic, curry powder and fenugreek until onion is soft. Add stock, lime juice, sugar, tomato, red pepper and bluefish. Simmer for 10 minutes, or until fish is cooked. Remove from heat. Stir in cream and yogurt, and add salt and pepper. Chill. Garnish with dill.

Serves 8

A New Leaf

Chez Piggy salads don't rely on lettuce. We make salads with tomatoes, beans, cabbage, root vegetables, fish and meat. These days, we're also fortunate to have year-round access to arugula, oak leaf lettuce, beet greens, watercress, radicchio and endive—baby greens that serve as a great background to more substantial ingredients.

Carrot Salad à la Jirik, a lemon-juice-dressed salad with a garlicky kick; Red Cabbage Salad with mustard seed and sultanas; Warm Spinach Salad With Pancetta Dressing & Asiago Cheese; Black Bean Salad; and, in season, a combo of juicy vine-ripened tomatoes, fresh basil and feta are just a few of the Chez Piggy spins on salads. Like many of our appetizers, these salads, lightly and simply dressed, can—and often do—serve as a main course.

HOG WILD, from left to right: Mila Macapugas works cold-prep line for the dinner rush; a piggy homage in the main-floor bar; Chef Cuong Ly and Eric Connell grill to perfection; staff members Amy Robinson and Louise Corsi mug alongside Chez Piggy's biggest ham, owner Zal Yanovsky.

SALADE NIÇOISE

This substantial salad makes a great appetizer or main-course dish.

1	head romaine lettuce, washed & separated	1
2	tomatoes, cut into wedges	2
1	red onion, sliced	1
1	green bell pepper, sliced	1
2 dozen	green beans, trimmed & blanched	2 dozen
2	potatoes, cubed & cooked	2
2	hard-cooked eggs, sliced	2
8	anchovies	8
1	7 oz. (200 g) can tuna, drained	1
1 dozen	kalamata olives	1 dozen
	Chez Piggy House Dressing (*see facing page*)	

Arrange lettuce, vegetables, eggs, anchovies, tuna and olives in a large bowl, and drizzle with a small amount of dressing.

Serves 4

CHEZ PIGGY HOUSE DRESSING

*Making a basic vinaigrette is easy, and it's hard to beat garden-fresh greens
tossed with fruity olive oil and lemon juice or a mild vinegar. When making
salad dressing, taste it until the flavor is right for you, and don't be afraid
to experiment with different kinds of oils, vinegars and mustards. Leftover dressing
can be refrigerated for one day, but after that, it will lose its tartness.*

½ cup + 2 Tbsp.	olive oil	150 mL
4 tsp.	lemon juice	20 mL
1 Tbsp.	red-wine vinegar	15 mL
1 tsp.	Dijon mustard	5 mL
	Coarse salt & freshly ground black pepper	

Whisk ingredients together in a bowl, or shake in a jar.
Makes ¾ cup (175 mL)

WARM SPINACH SALAD WITH PANCETTA DRESSING & ASIAGO CHEESE

*Vicki Newbury devised this recipe as a way of making the most of mature spinach,
which can be a bit tough and is too intense for lightly dressed preparations. The result
is a hearty salad seasoned with the taste of pancetta and asiago cheese.*

½ cup	diced pancetta	125 mL
1	small tomato, seeded & diced	1
2 Tbsp.	diced red onion	25 mL
½ tsp.	grainy mustard	2 mL
2 Tbsp.	olive oil	25 mL
1½ tsp.	red-wine vinegar	7 mL
	Freshly ground black pepper	
1 lb.	spinach, washed, dried & torn into bite-size pieces	500 g
½ cup	grated asiago cheese	125 mL

Lightly fry pancetta, and drain off fat. In a bowl, combine pancetta with
tomato, onion, mustard, oil and vinegar. Season with pepper to taste. Transfer
dressing to a heavy-bottomed pan, and warm over low heat.

Place spinach in a large salad bowl. Cover with warmed dressing, and toss.
Garnish with cheese, and serve immediately.

Serves 4

ASPARAGUS & HARD-COOKED EGG SALAD

*This is the ultimate salad for asparagus lovers. Asparagus season is short,
so you'll want to eat this every day while you can.*

	Juice of 1 lemon	
1 Tbsp.	balsamic vinegar	15 mL
½ tsp.	Dijon mustard	2 mL
⅔ cup	olive oil	150 mL
2	shallots, chopped, or 2 Tbsp. (25 mL)	2
	very finely chopped red onion	
1	egg, hard-cooked, white separated from yolk	1
1 Tbsp.	capers, coarsely chopped	15 mL
2 Tbsp.	chopped fresh chervil or chives	25 mL
	Coarse salt & freshly ground black pepper	
2 lb.	asparagus, trimmed & rinsed	1 kg

In a bowl, mix together lemon juice, vinegar, mustard, oil and shallots or
onion. Finely chop egg white, and add to vinaigrette. Set aside.

Finely chop egg yolk, and mix with capers and chervil or chives. Add salt
and pepper to taste. Set aside.

Tie asparagus in bundles, and cook upright in boiling salted water until stem
ends are tender. Refresh under cold water, and drain.

Arrange asparagus on individual plates. Drizzle with vinaigrette. Garnish
with egg-yolk mixture.

Serves 4 to 6

Asparagus &
Hard-Cooked Egg Salad

MARINATED SEAFOOD SALAD

This is a fresh-tasting salad of squid, shrimp and scallops mixed
with tomato, olives, sweet red pepper and onion and dressed with a citrus juice.
It is crucial to cook the seafood in separate batches, using fresh water and wine for each.
The squid should be poached in boiling water for only 30 to 45 seconds.

2 cups	water for each batch of seafood	500 mL
½ cup	white wine for each batch of seafood	125 mL
½ lb.	squid, cleaned & sliced	250 g
½ lb.	medium shrimp, peeled & deveined	250 g
½ lb.	bay scallops	250 g
¼ cup	lime juice	50 mL
¼ cup	orange juice	50 mL
1	medium tomato, diced	1
1	red bell pepper, diced	1
1	red onion, diced	1
1 dozen	green colossal olives, minced	1 dozen
1	clove garlic, minced	1
1	finger-hot chili, minced	1
2 Tbsp.	chopped fresh coriander leaves	25 mL
	Coarse salt & freshly ground black pepper	

Place water and wine in a pot over low heat, and bring to a simmer. Poach squid, shrimp and scallops separately, changing the water and wine for each. Remove with a slotted spoon. Drain and cool. Toss seafood with remaining ingredients, seasoning with salt and pepper to taste. Refrigerate for at least 1 hour.
Serves 4 to 6

RED CABBAGE SALAD

When the restaurant opened, this recipe was our original sandwich salad,
and we still love it today. Sultana raisins add a sweetness to the lightly
marinated red cabbage. The salad improves if it is left overnight.

½ cup	sultana raisins	125 mL
½ cup	cider vinegar	125 mL
½ cup	vegetable oil	125 mL
¼ cup	lemon juice	50 mL
	Coarse salt & freshly ground black pepper	
1	small red cabbage, trimmed & coarsely grated	1

Soak raisins in hot water for about 10 minutes to plump, then drain. Whisk together vinegar, oil and lemon juice, and season with salt and pepper to taste. Combine cabbage and raisins, and toss with dressing.
Serves 6 to 8

GREEN CABBAGE SALAD

A little lighter than the red cabbage salad that preceded it at the restaurant, this salad features colorful sweet peppers.

½	green cabbage, thinly sliced	½
1 cup	grated carrot	250 mL
½	red bell pepper, diced	½
½	green bell pepper, diced	½
½	yellow bell pepper, diced	½
½	red onion, diced	½
2 tsp.	poppy seed	10 mL
1 cup	white-wine vinegar	250 mL
1 cup	vegetable oil	250 mL
¾ cup	brown sugar	175 mL
½ cup	water	125 mL
2 Tbsp.	lemon juice	25 mL
1 Tbsp.	coarse salt	15 mL

Coarse salt & freshly ground black pepper

In a large bowl, combine vegetables and poppy seed. Set aside.

Heat vinegar, oil, sugar, water, lemon juice and 1 tablespoon (15 mL) salt in a saucepan until sugar dissolves. Pour hot dressing over vegetables. Season with salt and pepper to taste. Marinate for 2 hours. Chill before serving.

Serves 10 to 12

SMOKED DUCK BREAST SALAD WITH ONION CONFIT

*Onion confit is so delicious that it can stand as an ingredient in salad
or pasta, as a condiment or even on its own on crostini. But here,
we have combined it with smoked duck and fresh greens.*

ONION CONFIT

4	onions, thinly sliced	4
⅓ cup	brown sugar	75 mL
	Pinch ground mace	
¼ cup	currants	50 mL
2 cups	red wine	500 mL
1 cup	olive oil	250 mL
2 Tbsp.	balsamic vinegar	25 mL

SALAD

3 Tbsp.	olive oil	45 mL
3 Tbsp.	vegetable oil	45 mL
3 Tbsp.	lemon juice	45 mL
6 cups	assorted fresh baby greens	1.5 L
2	smoked duck breasts, very thinly sliced	2

Preheat oven to 350°F (180°C). To make onion confit, mix onions, sugar,
mace, currants, wine, oil and vinegar together in a bowl. Place in a shallow
pan, and bake for 1½ hours, or until liquid has been absorbed. Let cool,
then refrigerate.

To make salad, mix together oils and lemon juice in a bowl or a jar. Toss
greens with just enough dressing to moisten. Ring individual plates with onion
confit. Mound greens in center, and lay slices of duck on top.

Serves 4

WARM DUCK SALAD

*In this luscious salad, rich-tasting duck, which has been simmered in red wine
and stock until the meat is falling off the bone, is combined with green beans,
tomatoes and carrot and served on a bed of fresh greens.*

4	duck legs	4
1 cup	red wine	250 mL
1½ cups	duck stock (*see Basic Stock, page 46*) or water	375 mL
1	head romaine or leaf lettuce	1
1 cup	mixed fresh herb sprigs	250 mL
10 cups	mixed baby greens, endive or watercress, washed	2.5 L
2 Tbsp.	balsamic vinegar	25 mL
1 Tbsp.	lemon juice	15 mL
½ cup	olive oil	125 mL
1 tsp.	Dijon mustard	5 mL
	Coarse salt & freshly ground black pepper	
3 dozen	green beans, trimmed & blanched	3 dozen
3	tomatoes, cut into wedges	3
1	carrot, finely julienned & blanched	1

Heat a skillet over medium-high heat until it is very hot. Fry duck legs, skin
side down, to render fat. Brown on both sides, and drain fat. Add wine and
stock or water, and cook, uncovered, over medium heat for 2 hours. Remove
duck legs, cool slightly, strip meat from legs, slice, and set aside.

In a large bowl, mix lettuce, herbs and greens. Divide greens among six
individual plates.

Heat vinegar, lemon juice, oil and mustard in a skillet. Season with salt and
pepper to taste. Add beans, tomatoes, carrot and duck meat. Warm through.
Serve over greens.

Serves 6

MEDITERRANEAN SALAD

*This variation of a Greek salad is served on a seasoned slice
of grilled eggplant and dressed with a light, lemony vinaigrette.*

DRESSING

Scant ¼ cup	lemon juice	50 mL
⅓ cup	olive oil	75 mL
2 Tbsp.	vegetable oil	25 mL
2	large cloves garlic, minced	2
1 tsp.	chopped fresh thyme	5 mL
	or ½ tsp. (2 mL) dried	
1 tsp.	chopped fresh oregano	5 mL
	or ½ tsp. (2 mL) dried	
	Coarse salt & freshly ground black pepper	

Combine lemon juice, oils, garlic, thyme, oregano and salt and pepper to
taste in a jar or a shaker, and mix. Set aside.

SALAD

1	medium eggplant, cut lengthwise into 4 to 8 slices	1
	Olive oil	
½	English cucumber, cut into chunks	½
1	red bell pepper, cut into chunks	1
1	green bell pepper, cut into chunks	1
1	yellow bell pepper, cut into chunks	1
2	medium tomatoes, cut into chunks	2
2	large red onions, cut into chunks	2
½ cup	chickpeas	125 mL
½ cup	pitted & sliced kalamata olives	125 mL
4 oz.	feta cheese, cubed	125 g
	Salad greens	

Brush eggplant slices with oil, and grill on both sides until lightly browned.
Brush with dressing, and set aside.

Place cucumber, peppers, tomatoes, onions, chickpeas, olives and cheese in
a large bowl, and toss with enough dressing to moisten. Set aside.

Arrange greens on individual plates. Place 1 or 2 slices of eggplant on top.
Spoon on salad ingredients.

Serves 4

TOMATO, BASIL & FETA CHEESE SALAD

*In most northern regions, tomatoes are local, fresh and delicious for only a few months
of the year. During those months, this salad is a daily feature on our menu.
It is a simple yet satisfying combination of sweet summer tomatoes and basil
along with feta cheese and olive oil. Do not drown the salad in dressing.*

6	large tomatoes, sliced	6
1	red onion, thinly sliced	1
1 cup	crumbled feta cheese	250 mL
½ cup	chopped fresh basil	125 mL
	Chez Piggy House Dressing (*see page 71*)	

Layer tomato and red-onion slices on a platter. Top with cheese and basil.
Drizzle with dressing to taste.
Serves 4

BEET & YOGURT SALAD WITH MINT

*Mint and yogurt make a creamy summer-tasting dressing for fresh beets.
The beets should be cooked carefully so that they are tender without being too soft.*

3 lb.	beets, cooked, peeled & cooled	1.5 kg
	Juice of 1 lemon	
2 Tbsp.	olive oil	25 mL
1 cup	yogurt	250 mL
2 Tbsp.	chopped fresh mint	25 mL
⅛ tsp.	coarse salt	0.5 mL

Cut beets into bite-size wedges, and place in a large bowl. Combine remaining ingredients, and toss with beets.
Serves 6

MOROCCAN BEET SALAD

Naturally sweet, fresh beets work well with the pungent Moroccan seasonings.

1 lb.	beets, cooked, peeled & cooled	500 g
1 Tbsp.	sugar	15 mL
	Juice of 1 lemon	
	Juice of 1 orange	
1 tsp.	orange zest	5 mL
1 Tbsp.	olive oil	15 mL
¼ tsp.	ground cumin	1 mL
	Pinch paprika	
	Pinch cinnamon	
2 Tbsp.	chopped fresh coriander leaves	25 mL
	Coarse salt	

Cut beets into bite-size wedges, and place in a large bowl. Combine remaining ingredients, seasoning with salt to taste. Toss with beets. Marinate in refrigerator for at least 1 hour before serving.

Serves 4

MOROCCAN CHICKEN SALAD
WITH COUSCOUS

*Using a variation of the seasonings typically found in Moroccan
cuisine, Vicki Newbury created a colorful main-course summer salad
featuring chicken and couscous sweetened with honey and ginger.*

4	boneless, skinless chicken breasts	4
3 Tbsp.	lemon juice	45 mL
3 Tbsp.	olive oil	45 mL
3	cloves garlic, chopped	3
1½ tsp.	ground ginger	7 mL
1 tsp.	ground cumin	5 mL
	Pinch saffron	
2 cups	couscous	500 mL
2 cups	hot water	500 mL
12	green beans, blanched & sliced diagonally	12
1	sweet potato, peeled, diced & blanched	1
1	carrot, peeled, diced & blanched	1
½	red bell pepper, diced	½
12	green queen olives, pitted & chopped	12
½ cup	chopped golden raisins	125 mL
½	red onion, chopped	½

DRESSING

2 Tbsp.	lemon juice	25 mL
4 Tbsp.	olive oil	50 mL
2 Tbsp.	honey	25 mL
1 tsp.	ground ginger	5 mL
2 tsp.	ground cumin	10 mL
2 shakes	Tabasco sauce	2 shakes
½ cup	chopped fresh mint and/or fresh coriander leaves	125 mL
	Coarse salt & freshly ground black pepper	

Preheat oven to 350°F (180°C). Place chicken in a baking dish. Mix together lemon juice, oil, garlic, ginger, cumin and saffron. Pour mixture over chicken, turning chicken to coat evenly, then bake, uncovered, for 15 to 20 minutes. Chill, and chop chicken into bite-size pieces.

Soak couscous in hot water until water is absorbed, about 15 minutes. Toss couscous with chicken, beans, sweet potato, carrot, red pepper, olives, raisins and onion.

Whisk dressing ingredients together in a bowl, seasoning with salt and pepper to taste. Dress and toss salad.

Serves 8

Braewats With
Preserved Lemon
& Olive Salad

PRESERVED LEMON & OLIVE SALAD

In combination, the strong tangy-flavored lemons and salty olives balance each other. This salad works best as a relish or condiment for a variety of Moroccan dishes, such as Braewats (see page 41). You'll need to have preserved lemons on hand to make this recipe.

3	preserved lemons (*see page 176*)	3
1 cup	chopped kalamata or green colossal olives	250 mL
2 Tbsp.	olive oil	25 mL
2	cloves garlic, chopped	2
¼ cup	chopped fresh parsley	50 mL
½ tsp.	sugar	2 mL
¼ tsp.	ground cumin	1 mL
¼ tsp.	paprika	1 mL
	Pinch cayenne pepper	

Rinse and dice rinds of preserved lemons. Mix together in a bowl with olives. Toss with remaining ingredients.

Serves 4 to 6

COUSCOUS SALAD
WITH PRESERVED LEMON

We recommend serving this salad with any sliced cold meat along with vegetables to add extra color and flavor.

2 cups	couscous	500 mL
2 cups	warm water	500 mL
¾ cup	olive oil	175 mL
1	onion, diced	1
2 Tbsp.	peeled & chopped fresh ginger	25 mL
2	cloves garlic, chopped	2
1	carrot, peeled & diced	1
1	zucchini, diced	1
1	red bell pepper, diced	1
¾ cup	chopped fresh coriander leaves	175 mL
½ cup	chickpeas	125 mL
½	preserved lemon, finely diced (*see page 176*)	½
1½ tsp.	ground ginger	7 mL
1 tsp.	cinnamon	5 mL
½ tsp.	cayenne pepper	2 mL
⅓ cup	lemon juice	75 mL
¾ tsp.	coarse salt	4 mL
½ tsp.	freshly ground black pepper	2 mL

Place couscous in a shallow tray, and cover with warm water. Let stand for 25 minutes, or until water is absorbed. Break up any clumps with your fingers. Cover with a dampened towel, and set aside while you prepare the other ingredients.

Heat ¼ cup (50 mL) oil in a skillet, and add onion, fresh ginger, garlic and carrot. Sauté until carrot is tender but not fully cooked. Add zucchini and red pepper, and continue to cook for about 3 minutes, or until zucchini is just soft. Let vegetables cool.

To make dressing, combine remaining ½ cup (125 mL) oil, coriander, chickpeas, preserved lemon, ground ginger, cinnamon, cayenne, lemon juice, salt and pepper. In a large bowl, toss together vegetables, couscous and dressing.

Serves 8 to 10

Rare Roast Beef on
Whole Wheat Bread With
Carrot Salad à la Jirik

CARROT SALAD À LA JIRIK

*This salad—named after its creator Tomas Jirik—has been in the
Chez Piggy repertoire since day one. Grated carrots, lemon juice and parsley
are the dominant flavors in this fresh-tasting salad.*

1 lb.	carrots, peeled & grated	500 g
¾ cup	chopped fresh parsley	175 mL
½	medium red onion, diced	½

DRESSING

Scant ¼ cup	lemon juice	50 mL
½ cup	olive oil	125 mL
2	large cloves garlic, minced	2
	Coarse salt & freshly ground black pepper	

Combine carrots, parsley and onion, and set aside.

Mix lemon juice, oil and garlic together in a large bowl. Season with salt
and pepper to taste. Add dressing to carrot salad, and toss.

Serves 4 to 6

ETHIOPIAN RED LENTIL SALAD

We always get rave reviews whenever this lentil salad is on the menu.
The secret is not to overcook the lentils, so check them frequently as they boil.
Brown lentils can be used in place of red, but you will need to cook them longer
and to add more red-wine vinegar to enliven their heavier flavor. This salad
can be served in place of rice with almost any main course.

1 lb.	red lentils	500 g
3	scallions, julienned	3
1	red bell pepper, julienned	1
2	jalapeños, seeded & slivered	2
⅓ cup	red-wine vinegar	75 mL
¼ cup	olive oil	50 mL
	Coarse salt & freshly ground black pepper	

Cook lentils in boiling salted water for about 6 minutes, until just tender.
Drain and cool immediately, rinsing under cold running water. Combine
scallions, red pepper, jalapeños, vinegar and oil. Toss lentils with dressing,
seasoning with salt and pepper to taste.

Serves 4 to 6

SPICED CHERRY TOMATOES

These are wonderful on their own but are absolutely fantastic when combined with Ethiopian Red Lentil Salad (see facing page). If you do serve them with the lentil salad, however, substitute a green bell pepper for the jalapeños in the lentil mixture, because you'll get plenty of spicy kick from the cherry tomatoes alone. Serve the lentil salad surrounded by cherry tomatoes, and drizzle with a bit of the tomato marinade for extra flavor.

1 Tbsp.	brown sugar	15 mL
½ tsp.	coarse salt	2 mL
2 Tbsp.	white vinegar	25 mL
6 Tbsp.	olive oil	75 mL
1 Tbsp.	chopped fresh ginger	15 mL
1 Tbsp.	chopped garlic	15 mL
½ tsp.	mustard seed	2 mL
½ tsp.	cracked black peppercorns	2 mL
½ tsp.	ground cumin	2 mL
¼ tsp.	turmeric	1 mL
	Pinch cayenne pepper	
	Pinch saffron	
2 cups	cherry tomatoes, washed & halved	500 mL
½	finger-hot chili, sliced with seeds	½
2	scallions, trimmed & thinly sliced	2
2 Tbsp.	chopped fresh coriander leaves	25 mL

In a large bowl, mix sugar and salt with vinegar until sugar is dissolved. Set aside.

Heat oil in a heavy skillet until hot but not smoking. Add ginger and garlic, being careful not to spatter hot oil, and stir in mustard seed, peppercorns, cumin, turmeric, cayenne and saffron. Remove from heat, and carefully add to vinegar mixture. Stir in tomatoes and chili. When mixture is cool, stir in scallions and coriander.

Serves 4

YAM WOON SEN (Glass Noodle Salad)

The influence of Chinese cuisine is evident in this substantial salad. Red curry paste, however, identifies this recipe as a Thai interpretation. Bean, bean-thread and bean-curd vermicelli noodles are also known as cellophane, transparent and glass noodles. They are made from mung-bean flour, and because they are tough, these noodles should be soaked in water for several minutes before using.

1 Tbsp.	peanut oil	15 mL
1 lb.	pork, minced	500 g
4 Tbsp.	chopped shallots	50 mL
2	small onions, sliced	2
1	red bell pepper, diced	1
1/3 cup	chicken stock (*see Basic Stock, page 46*)	75 mL
3 Tbsp.	lemon juice	45 mL
2 Tbsp.	fish sauce	25 mL
1 Tbsp.	red curry paste (*see page 129*)	15 mL
7 oz.	bean-curd vermicelli noodles, soaked & drained	200 g
	Coarse salt & freshly ground black pepper	
4 Tbsp.	chopped fresh coriander leaves	50 mL
4 Tbsp.	chopped fresh mint leaves	50 mL

In a heavy-bottomed saucepan, heat oil, and add pork, browning meat quickly. Remove pork from pan with a slotted spoon, leaving pan juices behind. Set pork aside.

Add shallots, onions and red pepper to pan, and sauté to soften. Deglaze pan with stock, lemon juice and fish sauce. Reduce heat, and stir in red curry paste.

Stir noodles into pan, and cook over medium heat for 5 minutes. Season with salt and pepper to taste. When liquid has been absorbed, stir in pork. Toss gently with coriander and mint. Serve chilled or at room temperature.

Serves 4 to 6

THAI BEEF SALAD

This is an excellent main-course salad for anyone who enjoys the flavors of Thai cooking.

BEEF

¼ cup	soy sauce	50 mL
¼ cup	sake	50 mL
1	fresh chili, chopped	1
1	clove garlic, chopped	1
2 tsp.	brown sugar	10 mL
1 lb.	beef sirloin	500 g

Mix together soy sauce, sake, chili, garlic and sugar in a bowl. Add beef, cover, and marinate in refrigerator overnight. The next day, preheat oven to 500°F (260°C). Heat a large ovenproof skillet over medium-high heat. Remove beef from marinade, and sear on both sides. Place pan in oven for 8 minutes, cooking the meat rare. Let cool, and slice thinly. Set aside.

NUOC CHAM

1¼ cups	water	300 mL
½ cup + 2 Tbsp.	fish sauce	150 mL
½ cup	lemon juice	125 mL
½ cup	sugar	125 mL
7	fresh Thai chilies, chopped	7
6	cloves garlic, chopped	6
	Juice & pulp of 3 limes	

Mix ingredients together, and refrigerate until needed.
Makes 3 cups (750 mL)

SALAD

8 oz.	bean-curd vermicelli noodles	250 g
1 Tbsp.	vegetable oil	15 mL
½	medium onion, chopped	½
	Lettuce, washed & torn	
	Fresh coriander sprigs	
	Fresh mint sprigs	
1 cup	bean sprouts	250 mL
1	cucumber, sliced or julienned	1
¼ cup	crushed unsalted peanuts	50 mL

Soak noodles in warm water until soft. Drain, and reserve liquid. In a large skillet over medium heat, warm oil, and sauté onion until brown. Add noodles and about ½ cup (125 mL) soaking liquid. Cook for 5 minutes. Allow to cool. Dress with 2 tablespoons (25 mL) nuoc cham. Arrange lettuce on a serving platter. Top with noodles, beef, bean sprouts, cucumber, coriander and mint. Sprinkle with peanuts, and lightly drizzle with nuoc cham.
Serves 8

Thai Chicken Salad

THAI CHICKEN SALAD

This is one of the most popular dishes on our menu.
The combination of greens and marinated chicken with glass noodles, mint
and coriander, all topped with nuoc cham, is a satisfying meal in itself.

CHICKEN

1 cup	sake	250 mL
1/4 cup	Japanese soy sauce	50 mL
2 Tbsp.	mushroom soy sauce	25 mL
1/2	small fresh Thai chili, chopped	1/2
1	clove garlic, chopped	1
1/4 cup	brown sugar	50 mL
8	boneless, skinless chicken breasts	8

Mix together sake, soy sauces, chili, garlic and sugar in a bowl. Add chicken, and marinate for 2 hours.

Preheat oven to 400°F (200°C). Place chicken and marinade in a roasting pan, and cook in oven for 8 minutes or until done. Let cool, and slice thinly. Set aside.

SALAD

8 oz.	bean-curd vermicelli noodles	250 g
1 Tbsp.	vegetable oil	15 mL
½	medium onion, chopped	½
	Nuoc cham (*see page 87*)	
	Lettuce, washed & torn	
	Fresh coriander sprigs	
	Fresh mint sprigs	
1 cup	bean sprouts	250 mL
1	cucumber, sliced or julienned	1
¼ cup	crushed unsalted peanuts	50 mL

Soak noodles in warm water until soft. Drain, and reserve liquid. In a large skillet over medium heat, warm oil, and sauté onion until brown. Add noodles and about ½ cup (125 mL) soaking liquid. Cook for 5 minutes. Allow to cool. Dress with 2 tablespoons (25 mL) nuoc cham. Arrange lettuce on a serving platter. Top with noodles, chicken, bean sprouts, cucumber, coriander and mint. Sprinkle with peanuts, and lightly drizzle with nuoc cham.

Serves 8

MARINATED EGG NOODLE SALAD

This salad is an excellent companion to satays and grilled or barbecued meats.

½ lb.	fresh egg noodles	250 g
¼ cup	peanut oil	50 mL
¼ cup	sesame oil	50 mL
2½ Tbsp.	Japanese soy sauce	35 mL
2½ Tbsp.	rice-wine vinegar	35 mL
4 tsp.	lemon juice	20 mL
1 tsp.	chili sauce	5 mL
3 Tbsp.	sugar	45 mL
2 tsp.	black sesame seed	10 mL
½ tsp.	coarse salt	2 mL
3	scallions, chopped	3
	Zest of 1 lemon	

Cook noodles briefly in boiling salted water, then cool under cold running water. Drain, and set aside.

In a bowl, mix together oils, soy sauce, vinegar, lemon juice, chili sauce, sugar, sesame seed and salt. Add noodles, scallions and lemon zest, and toss. Let stand for 1 hour.

Serves 4

BRAISED LEEKS

The braising process caramelizes the sugar in the vegetables,
bringing out the natural sweetness and eliminating any tartness in the leeks.
When preparing this dish, make sure the leeks are thoroughly rinsed—sand has
a way of getting in between each of the growth layers.

8	leeks, trimmed of hairy roots & dark green leaves	8
6	cloves garlic, chopped	6
1 cup	olive oil	250 mL
2 Tbsp.	balsamic vinegar	25 mL
	Course salt & freshly ground black pepper	

Preheat oven to 375°F (190°C). Cut leeks in half lengthwise, and thoroughly rinse to remove sand. Mix together garlic, oil and vinegar, and season with salt and pepper to taste. Place leeks in a roasting pan, coat with dressing, cover, and bake for 25 minutes.

Serves 8 to 12

BRAISED FENNEL

Braised fennel is a completely addictive treat that takes little time or fuss to prepare.
Serve with veal dishes such as Vitello Tonnato (see page 142) or with chicken breaded
with Parmesan or as an appetizer with fresh bread.

3	large fennel bulbs, trimmed of leaves, woody stalks & outer layer, if bruised	3
12	cloves garlic	12
½ cup	white wine	125 mL
¾ cup	olive oil	175 mL
3 Tbsp.	tomato paste	45 mL
	Coarse salt & freshly ground black pepper	
	Juice of ½ lemon	

Preheat oven to 375°F (190°C). Cut fennel into quarters. (Young and tender summer bulbs are sometimes small enough that they can be cooked whole or in halves.) Arrange fennel and garlic in a casserole. Mix wine, oil and tomato paste together in a bowl, and season lightly with salt and pepper to taste. Coat fennel with wine mixture, and drizzle with lemon juice. Bake, covered, for 45 minutes, turning fennel after 20 minutes.

Serves 8 to 12

SOUSCAILLE (Caribbean Mango Salad)

For a sweet, full taste, use ripe mangoes in this Caribbean salad.

2	mangoes, peeled & sliced	2
¼	red bell pepper, finely diced	¼
½ cup	lime juice	125 mL
1	clove garlic, chopped	1
1	small fresh Thai chili, finely chopped	1
½ cup	water	125 mL
¼ tsp.	coarse salt	1 mL
	Fresh mint sprigs for garnish	

Toss mangoes and red pepper with lime juice, garlic, chili, water and salt. Cover, and refrigerate for 2 hours. Garnish with mint.

Serves 4

BANANA PAPAYA SALAD

This sweet fruit salad makes a refreshingly cool accompaniment to many spicy Caribbean meat dishes. Serve it immediately, or the bananas will become discolored.

4	bananas, peeled & sliced	4
2	papayas, peeled & sliced	2
2 tsp.	honey	10 mL
1 Tbsp.	amber rum	15 mL
1 Tbsp.	lime juice	15 mL

In a large bowl, gently toss bananas and papayas with honey, rum and lime juice. Serve immediately.

Serves 6

BLACK BEAN SALAD

Not a wimpy bean salad, this recipe gets a kick from fresh chilies. The key to using black beans in a salad is not to overcook the beans. They should be cooked to just tender.

1 cup	dried black beans, sorted & rinsed	250 mL
6	cloves garlic	6
1 Tbsp.	coarse salt	15 mL
1 tsp.	cumin seed	5 mL
1	bay leaf	1
¼ cup	diced red onion	50 mL
¼ cup	diced green bell pepper	50 mL
4	tomatoes, diced	4
2	finger-hot chilies, minced	2
¼ cup	chopped fresh coriander leaves	50 mL
½ cup	lime juice	125 mL
2 Tbsp.	lemon zest	25 mL
2 Tbsp.	lime zest	25 mL
2 Tbsp.	orange zest	25 mL
¼ cup	olive oil	50 mL

Coarse salt & freshly ground black pepper

Place beans in a pot, and cover with water. Chop 2 cloves garlic, and add to pot along with salt, cumin and bay leaf. Simmer until beans are soft. Do not overcook. Drain and rinse in cold water to cool. Remove bay leaf.

Place beans in a large bowl. Chop remaining 4 cloves garlic, and combine with remaining ingredients, seasoning with salt and pepper to taste. Add to beans, and toss. Chill.

Serves 4 to 6

BROWN RICE & ADZUKI BEAN SALAD

This mild-tasting salad is a grain lover's delight that relies
on the familiar combination of peas (or beans) and rice.
The addition of miso, tamari, sesame seed and oil lend it a Japanese flavor.
Mirin is a sweetened rice wine used for cooking.

1¼ cups	dried adzuki beans, sorted & rinsed	300 mL
1¾ cups	brown rice	425 mL
2½ cups	water	625 mL
2¼ tsp.	miso	11 mL
2 Tbsp.	light sesame oil	25 mL
3 Tbsp.	grated fresh ginger	45 mL
3	cloves garlic, chopped	3
¼ cup	rice-wine vinegar	50 mL
¼ cup	diced celery	50 mL
¼ cup	diced carrot	50 mL
¼ cup	diced red bell pepper	50 mL
¼ cup	diced red onion	50 mL
¾ cup	sliced scallions	175 mL
½ cup	chopped fresh coriander leaves	125 mL
2 Tbsp.	rice syrup	25 mL
½ cup	tamari	125 mL
¼ cup	toasted sesame oil	50 mL
¼ cup	sesame seed	50 mL
1½ tsp.	mirin	7 mL
	Coarse salt & freshly ground black pepper	

Fill a large pot with salted water, and bring to a boil. Reduce heat, add beans, and cook until tender. Drain and chill.

Rinse rice. Place water in a pot, and bring to a boil. Add rice and miso. Return to a boil, then reduce heat, cover, and simmer for 35 minutes. Let cool, then chill.

Heat light sesame oil in a large heavy-bottomed skillet, and add ginger, garlic and vinegar. Cook for 1 to 2 minutes, then add celery, carrot, red pepper, onion and scallions. Cook until tender. Toss vegetables with beans and rice. Combine remaining ingredients, and toss with bean mixture. Season with salt and pepper to taste.

Serves 8

CALYPSO BEAN SALAD

The beans in this salad were chosen largely because of their color,
but feel free to substitute other varieties, such as Mexican red or pinto beans.
Cooking the beans in separate batches is important to ensure that each is done just right.

½ cup	dried black beans, sorted & rinsed	125 mL
½ cup	dried white beans, sorted & rinsed	125 mL
½ cup	dried pigeon peas, sorted & rinsed	125 mL
1 cup	diced peeled sweet potato	250 mL
½	red onion, diced	½
½	red bell pepper, diced	½
½	green bell pepper, diced	½
1	ripe mango, peeled & diced	1
⅓ cup	olive oil	75 mL
2	jalapeños, chopped	2
2	cloves garlic, chopped	2
½ cup	chopped fresh coriander leaves	125 mL
4 Tbsp.	lime juice	50 mL
½ tsp.	allspice	2 mL
½ tsp.	coarse salt	2 mL
	Freshly ground black pepper	

In separate saucepans filled with cold water, soak beans overnight. In the morning, drain and rinse each batch, and refill with fresh, cold, salted water. Bring each pot to a boil. Reduce heat, and simmer until beans are tender, skimming top, if necessary. Drain, rinse, and cool each batch after it cooks. Set aside.

Cook sweet potato in boiling salted water until tender. Drain and cool.

In a large bowl, combine beans with sweet potato, onion, red and green peppers and mango. Set aside.

In a small skillet, barely heat oil, and add jalapeños and garlic. Do not fry or brown. Pour the warmed, spicy oil over the bean mixture. Add coriander, lime juice, allspice and salt. Season with pepper to taste.

Makes 5 cups (1.25 L)

SHREDDED PORK SALAD
WITH MANGO & JICAMA

The tropical flavor of mango adds a fruity, juicy taste to this salad, while the jicama has the texture and mild flavor of a water chestnut. Peel and cut up the jicama at the last possible moment before adding it, because it tends to discolor once it has been peeled. We serve this salad with fried corn tortillas.

PORK

2 lb.	boneless pork loin	1 kg
½ cup	sugar	125 mL
2 Tbsp.	coarse salt	25 mL
5	sprigs fresh thyme	5
2	bay leaves, crushed	2
1 tsp.	coarsely ground black pepper	5 mL
1 tsp.	dried oregano	5 mL
2 Tbsp.	crushed dried chilies	25 mL
4	allspice berries	4
4	cloves	4
1	stick cinnamon	1
4-6 cups	water	1-1.5 L

SALAD

1	mango, peeled & finely diced or julienned	1
1	jicama, peeled & finely diced or julienned	1
½ cup	coarsely chopped fresh coriander leaves	125 mL
	Juice of 6 limes	
½ cup	extra-virgin olive oil	125 mL
	Coarse salt & freshly ground black pepper	

Place pork in a deep bowl. In a separate bowl, whisk together sugar, salt, thyme, bay leaves, pepper, oregano, chilies, allspice, cloves, cinnamon and 4 cups (1 L) water. Pour over pork, adding more water, if necessary, to cover meat completely. Cover bowl, and refrigerate overnight.

The next day, remove pork from marinade, and place in a roasting pan. Let stand at room temperature for approximately 1 hour.

Preheat oven to 400°F (200°C). Roast pork, uncovered, for 45 to 60 minutes, or until internal temperature reaches 170°F (77°C). Let pork cool enough to be handled easily. Shred meat into thin strips with your fingers.

Place pork in a large bowl, and toss with salad ingredients, seasoning with salt and pepper to taste.

Serves 10

RATATOUILLE

This Mediterranean vegetable stew can be prepared several ways, but we find that it is especially tasty in the summer, when field tomatoes, tender zucchini and fresh herbs are readily available. We frequently serve ratatouille as an accompaniment to our main courses, but it is also an excellent omelette filling or pasta sauce.

½ cup	olive oil	125 mL
1	medium eggplant, diced small	1
3	medium onions, diced small	3
3	zucchini, cut into rounds	3
2	green bell peppers, diced small	2
1	red bell pepper, diced small	1
5	whole tomatoes, diced small	5
4	large cloves garlic, diced small	4
1 cup	dry red wine	250 mL
1 tsp.	minced fresh oregano	5 mL
	or ½ tsp. (2 mL) dried	
1 tsp.	minced fresh basil	5 mL
	or ½ tsp. (2 mL) dried	
1 tsp.	minced fresh fennel tops	5 mL
	or ½ tsp. (2 mL) dried	
½ cup	chopped fresh parsley	125 mL
	Coarse salt & freshly ground black pepper	

Heat oil over medium heat in a large skillet or a broad-bottomed pot, and fry eggplant until tender. Add onions, and cook for 5 minutes. Stir in zucchini, and sauté until tender. Add green and red peppers, tomatoes and garlic, and gently heat through. Add wine and herbs, and season with salt and pepper to taste. Cook for 30 minutes. Serve tepid for best flavor.

Serves 8

RATATOUILLE VINAIGRETTE

A sassy variation on stewed ratatouille, this wonderfully aromatic mélange
of the traditional ingredients is tossed with fresh tomatoes and capers in white-wine vinegar.
It is a good summer accompaniment to cold chicken breasts or sliced lamb.

2	red onions, sliced	2
1	red bell pepper, cut into chunks	1
1	green bell pepper, cut into chunks	1
4	cloves garlic, chopped	4
½ cup	olive oil	125 mL
1	eggplant, diced small	1
2	zucchini, diced small	2
8	tomatoes, diced small	8
¼ cup	capers	50 mL
¼ cup	white-wine vinegar	50 mL
1 tsp.	lemon juice	5 mL
3 Tbsp.	chopped fresh chervil, parsley, basil or thyme or a combination	45 mL
	Coarse salt & freshly ground black pepper	

Sauté onions and red and green peppers with garlic in ¼ cup (50 mL) oil
for 5 minutes. Add eggplant, and continue to cook over low temperature for
5 minutes. Add zucchini, and cook for 5 minutes. Let sautéed vegetables cool,
and toss with tomatoes, capers, vinegar, lemon juice, herb(s) and remaining
¼ cup (50 mL) oil. Season with salt and pepper to taste.
Serves 12 to 14 as a side dish

PARSLEY SALAD

Parsley moves from garnish to featured ingredient in this delightfully addictive salad.
Flat-leaf Italian parsley, rather than the more common curly variety,
gives this recipe a milder taste. Serve immediately, because it does not keep well.

2	bunches Italian flat-leaf parsley, coarsely chopped	2
2	scallions, chopped	2
2 Tbsp.	olive oil	25 mL
	Juice of 1 lemon	
	Coarse salt & freshly ground black pepper	

In a large bowl, combine parsley, scallions, oil and lemon juice. Season with
salt and pepper to taste.
Serves 6

Pass da Pasta

Pasta is a regular feature on our menu, and Chez Piggy customers love it. While we don't make our own noodles, we rely on a good-quality imported dried pasta, cooked "al dente" in lots of boiling salted water. Cream sauces like Sun-Dried Tomato Cream Sauce have become the centerpiece of our pasta repertoire, and we make them the authentic way, by reducing heavy cream. The result is unbelievably rich—and unbelievably delicious. We also make more simple, traditional sauces such as Aglio Olio, Basil Pine-Nut Pesto, Anne's Puttanesca and Salsa Verde, and summertime visitors savor pasta tossed in Tomato, Bocconcini & Basil in Balsamic Vinaigrette.

Pasta comes in a multitude of shapes and sizes, but in the recipes that follow, we generally do not specify a type or shape. Match the thickness and ingredients of the sauce to the noodle. Cavatappi or penne can hold a hearty sauce such as our Funky Tomato Sauce With Hot Italian Sausage, but save light or simple sauces for a delicate noodle such as capellini or linguine.

Pasta is not complete without Parmesan cheese, and imported Italian Parmesan is the best. With nothing more than freshly ground black pepper or a few dried chili flakes for spice, pasta dressed with a good olive oil and a bit of freshly grated Parmesan, such as Parmigiano-Reggiano, succeeds on its own.

OF BAGUETTES AND
BANQUETTES, from left
to right: Pan Chancho
treats bakery and
restaurant customers
to "pain extraordinaire";
time-out for staff meal on
second floor; basil, garlic,
tomatoes and bocconcini
make pasta perfecto;
spirited service from
bartender Virginia Clark.

AGLIO OLIO SAUCE

This extremely easy garlic-and-oil sauce lends itself to a main-course, an appetizer or a side-dish pasta. The success of the recipe relies on the addition of a flavorful olive oil. But don't turn your back on the garlic—it burns easily.

3 Tbsp.	butter	45 mL
½ cup	olive oil	125 mL
4	cloves garlic, finely chopped	4
2 tsp.	coarse salt	10 mL
1 lb.	pasta, cooked & drained	500 g
	Freshly ground black pepper	
	Freshly grated Parmesan cheese for garnish	

Gently warm butter, oil, garlic and salt over low heat in a double boiler until the butter is melted. Toss with hot pasta, and garnish with pepper and cheese.
Serves 4

BLACK-OLIVE THYME BUTTER WITH CHERRY TOMATOES

An olive lover's recipe, this pasta sauce combines kalamata olives with fragrant thyme and sweet bite-size cherry tomatoes.

¼ lb.	butter, room temperature	125 g
2 tsp.	chopped fresh thyme	10 mL
15	kalamata olives, pitted	15
½ pint	cherry tomatoes, washed & halved	250 mL
1 lb.	pasta, cooked & drained	500 g
	Freshly grated Parmesan cheese for garnish	

Blend butter, thyme and olives in a food processor. Heat 1 tablespoon (15 mL) olive-butter mixture in a large skillet, and sauté tomatoes. Toss in hot pasta and remaining olive-butter mixture, and warm through. Be careful not to overheat and separate the butter. Garnish with cheese.
Serves 4

Anne's Puttanesca Sauce

ANNE'S PUTTANESCA SAUCE

Anne Linton's variation of this sauce emphasizes olives over tomatoes
and has a slight sweetness from the raisins. Toast the pine nuts
in a dry skillet over medium heat until browned.

¼ cup	golden raisins	50 mL
1 cup	olive oil	250 mL
15	green colossal olives, pitted & chopped	15
12	kalamata olives, pitted & chopped	12
½ cup	pine nuts, toasted & chopped	125 mL
3	cloves garlic, chopped	3
2	anchovies, chopped (optional)	2
	Pinch cayenne pepper	
3	ripe tomatoes, seeded & diced	3
4 Tbsp.	capers	50 mL
2 Tbsp.	chopped fresh dill or parsley	25 mL
	Freshly ground black pepper	
1½-2 lb.	pasta, cooked & drained	750 g-1 kg
	Freshly grated Parmesan cheese for garnish	

Soak raisins in hot water for 15 minutes until soft, then drain and chop.
Warm oil in a large skillet, and stir in all ingredients, except pasta and cheese.
Heat through. Toss with hot pasta, and garnish with cheese.
Serves 6 to 8

TAPENADE FOR PASTA

The addition of onion to this basic tapenade lightens the olive flavor,
making it more suitable as a pasta sauce than the traditional rich appetizer tapenade.

¼ cup	olive oil	50 mL
1	medium onion, diced	1
1 lb.	kalamata olives, pitted & coarsely chopped	500 g
¼ cup	chopped rinsed capers	50 mL
2-3	anchovies, rinsed & chopped	2-3
4	cloves garlic, chopped	4
½ tsp.	dried thyme	2 mL
2 tsp.	brandy	10 mL
1 Tbsp.	Dijon mustard	15 mL
2 lb.	pasta, cooked & drained	1 kg
	Freshly grated Parmesan cheese for garnish	

Heat oil in a large skillet over low heat, and sauté onion until soft and translucent. Let cool, then mix in a large bowl together with olives, capers, anchovies, garlic, thyme, brandy and mustard. Toss hot pasta with tapenade, and garnish with cheese.

Serves 6

TOMATO, BOCCONCINI & BASIL
IN BALSAMIC VINAIGRETTE

This dish should be made only when fresh basil and vine-ripened tomatoes are abundant.
Bocconcini is a soft, unripened mozzarella that is packaged in whey.
The addition of balsamic vinegar makes a flavorful light dressing.

¾ cup	olive oil	175 mL
1 Tbsp.	red-wine vinegar	15 mL
¼ cup	balsamic vinegar	50 mL
4	cloves garlic, chopped	4
4	fresh tomatoes, cut into wedges	4
1¼ cups	coarsely chopped, loosely packed fresh basil	300 mL
½ lb.	bocconcini cheese, sliced	250 g
1¼ lb.	pasta, cooked & drained	625 g
	Coarse salt & freshly ground black pepper	

Warm the oil, vinegars and garlic in a heavy skillet over low heat. Add tomatoes, basil, cheese and hot pasta, and gently toss to warm through. Season with salt and pepper to taste. Serve as cheese begins to melt.

Serves 4

CARAMELIZED ONIONS
& KALE IN BALSAMIC VINAIGRETTE

*In this ideal winter pasta, lightly cooked kale is mixed with the aromatic flavors
of balsamic vinegar and Madeira. Balsamic vinegar is a mild vinegar
from the Italian province of Modena. Aged in casks for up to 25 years,
it is available at various prices, with the most expensive being the oldest.
The caramelized onions add a distinctive sweetness to the entire dish.*

³/₄ cup	olive oil	175 mL
3	small red onions, thinly sliced	3
1 heaping Tbsp.	brown sugar	15 mL
	Pinch mace	
2 Tbsp.	balsamic vinegar	25 mL
¹/₈ tsp.	coarse salt	0.5 mL
¹/₈ tsp.	freshly ground black pepper	0.5 mL
³/₄ cup	Madeira	175 mL
1	bunch kale	1
1 lb.	pasta, cooked & drained	500 g
	Freshly grated Parmesan cheese for garnish	

Preheat oven to 350°F (180°C). Heat oil in an ovenproof skillet, and add
onions, sugar, mace, vinegar, salt, pepper and Madeira. Stir to mix. Bake,
uncovered, for about 1½ hours, stirring occasionally. The onions should be
soft, and there should still be some liquid left.

While onions are cooking, wash, trim and coarsely chop kale. Bring a large
pot of water to a boil, and blanch kale by immersing it for 1 minute. Remove
kale, and refresh in a cold-water bath. Set aside.

Toss kale with hot pasta and hot onions. Garnish with cheese.

Serves 4

Tomato, Bocconcini
& Basil in Balsamic
Vinaigrette

BOLOGNESE SAUCE

This basic tomato-meat pasta sauce has a subtle orange taste.

2 Tbsp.	olive oil	25 mL
1	onion, finely diced	1
2	cloves garlic, minced	2
1	finger-hot chili, minced	1
1	carrot, finely diced	1
1	stalk celery, finely diced	1
1 lb.	ground beef, veal or pork or a combination	500 g
2	chicken necks or backs	2
1 tsp.	orange zest	5 mL
	Juice of 1 orange	
½ tsp.	ground cumin	2 mL
¼ tsp.	dried thyme	1 mL
2 tsp.	dried oregano	10 mL
1 tsp.	coarse salt	5 mL
½ tsp.	freshly ground black pepper	2 mL
½ cup	dry red wine	125 mL
2	28 oz. (796 mL) cans whole tomatoes	2
2 lb.	pasta, cooked & drained	1 kg

In a heavy-bottomed pot, heat oil over medium heat, and sauté onion, garlic, chili, carrot and celery for about 15 minutes, until vegetables are tender but not browned. Add meat, and cook over medium-high heat. Stir in orange zest, orange juice, cumin, thyme, oregano, salt, pepper, wine and tomatoes. Simmer, partially covered, for up to 2 hours, stirring occasionally. Remove chicken necks or backs. Spoon sauce over hot pasta.

Serves 6

FUNKY TOMATO SAUCE
WITH HOT ITALIAN SAUSAGE

For no good reason, people usually wince when they hear the word "anchovies."
So we obscured the presence of these tiny fish in our tomato sauce by
calling it "Funky." Our deception has paid off over the years,
because this is one of our most popular pasta sauces.

½ lb.	spicy Italian sausages	250 g
1	medium onion, diced	1
4	cloves garlic, minced	4
1	fresh chili, chopped	1
½	carrot, finely diced	½
½	stalk celery, finely diced	½
½	green bell pepper, diced	½
¼ cup	olive oil	50 mL
¼ cup	red wine	50 mL
3	anchovies, minced	3
½ tsp.	dried oregano	2 mL
1	bay leaf	1
1 tsp.	dried basil	5 mL
1 tsp.	fennel seed, ground	5 mL
1	28 oz. (796 mL) can whole tomatoes, mushed	1
1½ lb.	pasta, cooked & drained	750 g
	Basil-flavored mayonnaise	
	Freshly grated Parmesan cheese for garnish	

Heat water in a skillet over medium heat, and partially cook sausages. Do not allow water to boil, or fat will separate in the sausages. Drain sausages, let cool, and cut into chunks. Set aside.

Sauté onion, garlic, chili, carrot, celery and green pepper in oil over low heat until tender, about 30 minutes. Add wine, sausages, anchovies, herbs and tomatoes. Simmer for 2 hours. Spoon over hot pasta, drizzle with mayonnaise, and garnish with cheese.

Serves 6

TOMATO CHORIZO SAUCE

*This hearty sauce, which gets its unique flavor from chorizo sausages and saffron,
is a Spanish variation of Funky Tomato Sauce With Hot Italian Sausage (see page 105).*

3	cloves garlic, minced	3
	Pinch saffron	
¼ cup	olive oil	50 mL
2	onions, finely diced	2
1	carrot, finely diced	1
½	stalk celery, finely diced	½
1	bay leaf	1
½ tsp.	dried thyme	2 mL
1 tsp.	dried basil	5 mL
1 tsp.	dried oregano	5 mL
2 cups	red wine	500 mL
16 inches	chorizo sausages, sliced	40 cm
2	28 oz. (796 mL) cans whole tomatoes, slightly crushed	2
2 lb.	pasta, cooked & drained	1 kg

In a mortar and pestle, grind garlic and saffron. Let stand for 15 minutes.
Heat oil in a heavy-bottomed pot, and sauté onions, garlic mixture, carrot
and celery over medium heat until vegetables are tender but not browned,
about 15 minutes. Stir in herbs, wine, sausages and tomatoes. Simmer, partially
covered, for up to 1½ hours, stirring occasionally. Spoon over hot pasta.
Serves 8

FRESH PEAS & HAM
IN WHITE-WINE BUTTER SAUCE

The flavors of fresh summer peas and ham shine through in this light summer pasta.

4 cups	white wine	1 L
½ lb.	butter	250 g
3	onions, sliced	3
⅛ tsp.	coarse salt	0.5 mL
	Pinch freshly ground black pepper	
2 cups	fresh peas	500 mL
1 lb.	cooked ham, julienned	500 g
1 lb.	pasta, cooked & drained	500 g

Boil wine in a small saucepan until it is reduced by half. Set aside.
Melt butter in a large skillet, and sauté onions over low heat until they are
soft and mushy. Add salt, pepper and reduced wine, and heat through. Add
peas and ham, and heat until just warm. Toss with hot pasta.
Serves 4

BASIL PINE-NUT PESTO

*Pesto is a seasonal treat when fresh sweet basil is readily available
and there are lots of vine-ripened field tomatoes to serve sliced on the side.
Adjust the amount of garlic to suit your taste. Toast pine nuts
in a dry skillet over medium heat until browned.*

8 cups	washed & trimmed fresh basil leaves	2 L
8-12	cloves garlic	8-12
1 cup	olive oil	250 mL
½ cup	pine nuts, toasted	125 mL
1 cup	freshly grated Parmesan cheese	250 mL
2 lb.	pasta, cooked & drained	1 kg

In a food processor, blend basil, garlic, oil, pine nuts and cheese to a smooth paste. Toss with hot pasta.

Serves 8

PESTO PLUS

*For a variation of
Basil Pine-Nut Pesto,
substitute toasted
California walnuts for the
pine nuts. Peppery-tasting
arugula leaves are also an
excellent substitute for
basil. Both basil and
arugula pesto are delicious
dressings on cold pasta
or boiled potatoes.*

FRESH CORIANDER PESTO

*The word pesto originated with the process of grinding a combination of herbs
with a mortar and pestle. The distinctive taste of coriander cut with parsley
produces a pungent variation on a classic sauce. Pine nuts, or pignolia,
are flavorful little nuts that come from the cone of the umbrella pine.*

6	cloves garlic	6
½ cup	pine nuts, toasted	125 mL
3 cups	fresh coriander leaves	750 mL
1 cup	fresh parsley leaves	250 mL
1 cup	olive oil	250 mL
1 cup	freshly grated Parmesan cheese	250 mL
	Coarse salt & freshly ground black pepper	
1 lb.	pasta, cooked & drained	500 g

In a food processor, coarsely chop garlic, pine nuts, coriander and parsley. Continue processing, and slowly drizzle in oil. Stir in cheese by hand, and season with salt and pepper to taste. Toss with hot pasta.

Serves 4

ROMESCO SAUCE

*Romesco is a thick, nutty Spanish sauce. Think of it as pesto
made with peppers and almonds instead of basil and pine nuts.*

½ cup	olive oil	125 mL
2	red bell peppers	2
1	tomato, halved	1
5	cloves garlic	5
2	finger-hot chilies	2
1½ cups	blanched almonds, toasted	375 mL
1 tsp.	red-wine vinegar	5 mL
	Pinch coarse salt	
1 lb.	pasta, cooked & drained	500 g
	Freshly grated Parmesan cheese for garnish	

Preheat oven to 350°F (180°C). Warm 1 teaspoon (5 mL) oil in an ovenproof pan. Place tomato in pan, coat with oil, and roast in oven for 20 minutes
or until browned. Set aside.

Roast red peppers over a gas flame or the coils of an electric stove until skin
blisters and chars. Allow peppers to steam in a paper bag or a bowl covered
with plastic wrap. After 15 minutes, peel off skin and remove stems and seeds.

Place remaining oil, roasted peppers, tomato, garlic, chilies, almonds and
vinegar in a food processor, and blend to a paste. Season with salt to taste.
Toss with hot pasta, and garnish with cheese.

Serves 4

SPAGHETTI ALLA CARBONARA

*This dish features cream, egg yolks, cheese and prosciutto, which is salt-cured,
air-dried Italian ham. The prosciutto and onion can be cooked in advance
and heated with the cream just before serving. It is important to drain the pasta
well and to keep tossing it so that the eggs don't "cook" to a rubbery texture.*

1 Tbsp.	olive oil	15 mL
4 Tbsp.	diced onion	50 mL
¼ lb.	prosciutto, diced	125 g
5 Tbsp.	35% B.F. cream	65 mL
¼ cup	freshly grated Parmesan cheese	50 mL
5	egg yolks	5
1 lb.	spaghetti, cooked & drained	500 g

Heat oil in a skillet over low heat, and sauté onion. When onion is almost
translucent, add prosciutto, and cook until it turns an even coral color. Stir in
cream and cheese, and warm gently. In a serving dish, beat egg yolks, and add
hot pasta, tossing to coat well. Toss with prosciutto mixture. Serve immediately.

Serves 4

SUN-DRIED TOMATO CREAM SAUCE

The success of this extremely rich and creamy sauce—one of the most popular at the restaurant—is based on the intensified flavor of sun-dried tomatoes. If you use tomatoes packed in oil, there is no need to rehydrate them before cooking.

½ cup	sun-dried tomatoes, rehydrated & chopped	125 mL
1½ cups	35% B.F. cream	375 mL
½ cup	brandy	125 mL
	Coarse salt & freshly ground black pepper	
3 Tbsp.	butter, chilled & chopped (optional)	45 mL
1 lb.	pasta, cooked & drained	500 g

Mix tomatoes, cream and brandy in a heavy-bottomed saucepan. Simmer over medium heat until reduced by half. Season with salt and pepper to taste.

For an extra-rich sauce, whisk in butter just before serving. Spoon over hot pasta.

Serves 4

CHICKEN LIVERS
IN GRAINY-MUSTARD CREAM SAUCE

This is a rich pasta sauce with butter, cream and chicken livers, seasoned with the tangy flavor of seed mustard. When preparing the chicken livers for cooking, carefully cut the liver away from the green bile sac. Do not puncture the sac, or it will give the livers a bitter taste.

¾ lb.	chicken livers	375 g
2 Tbsp.	butter	25 mL
2 Tbsp.	flour	25 mL
2 cups	half-and-half	500 mL
1 Tbsp.	grainy mustard	15 mL
	Coarse salt & freshly ground black pepper	
1 Tbsp.	olive oil	15 mL
1 lb.	pasta, cooked & drained	500 g

Rinse livers, and remove fat and glistening green bile sacs. Cut livers into chunks, and set aside.

Melt butter in a saucepan over medium heat, and sprinkle in flour. Cook for about 5 minutes. Gradually add cream, and stir in mustard. Cook for about 10 minutes, until sauce thickens. Season with salt and pepper to taste. Keep warm.

Sauté liver chunks in oil until cooked. Arrange over hot pasta, and spoon sauce on top.

Serves 4

PORCINI PANCETTA CREAM SAUCE

Pancetta and porcini are both available at Italian food markets, and there are no substitutes for their flavors. Pancetta is salt-cured pork belly that is prepared with the fat wrapped around the lean meat. Porcini are dried Boletus mushrooms. Their smoky flavor is intensified by drying.

½ oz.	dried porcini mushrooms	15 g
¼ cup	warm water or white wine	50 mL
10 oz.	fresh button mushrooms, sliced	300 g
3 Tbsp.	butter	15 mL + 25 mL
2 oz.	pancetta, chopped	50 g
2 Tbsp.	flour	25 mL
2 cups	35% B.F. cream or half-and-half	500 mL
	Coarse salt & freshly ground black pepper	
1 lb.	pasta, cooked & drained	500 g

Soak porcini mushrooms in water or wine until soft, about 20 minutes. Drain, and set aside, reserving mushroom liquid.

Sauté button mushrooms in 1 tablespoon (15 mL) butter. Remove with a slotted spoon, and set aside, reserving mushroom liquid.

Fry pancetta, and set aside.

Add remaining 2 tablespoons (25 mL) butter to pan drippings. When butter has melted, sprinkle in flour. Cook for 2 minutes over medium heat to make a roux. Stir in pancetta, sautéed mushrooms and porcini mushrooms, and heat through. Slowly add cream while stirring, and add enough reserved mushroom liquid to thin sauce slightly. Simmer until cream coats the back of a wooden spoon. Season with salt and pepper to taste. Spoon over hot pasta.

Serves 4

SALSA VERDE (Green Sauce)

*Thinner and oilier than a pesto and with a strong parsley taste, this sauce can also
be served as a condiment with fresh seafood or used to fill mushroom caps for broiling.
Individually, the ingredients have a distinctive flavor, but in combination,
they gently complement each other. Use only the leafy parts of the parsley.*

3	cloves garlic	3
3 cups	parsley leaves	750 mL
1	2 oz. (50 g) can anchovies in oil	1
1 cup	capers	250 mL
½ cup	olive oil	125 mL
	Freshly ground black pepper	
1 lb.	pasta, cooked & drained	500 g

Place garlic, parsley, anchovies and capers in a food processor, and coarsely
chop. Continue to process, and slowly drizzle in oil, mixing until smooth.
Add pepper to taste, and toss with hot pasta.
Serves 4

CLAMS IN WHITE WINE

*We recommend using a long noodle in this simple and subtle pasta dish
that allows the clams to stand on their own. Mussels can be substituted
for the clams but do not require as long a steaming time.*

4 dozen	littleneck clams, scrubbed	4 dozen
2 cups	white wine	500 mL
⅓ cup	butter	75 mL
2	medium onions, finely diced	2
2	cloves garlic, minced	2
	Coarse salt & freshly ground black pepper	
1 lb.	pasta, cooked & drained	500 g
	Freshly grated Parmesan cheese for garnish	

Heat a large empty pot over medium-high heat until a drop of water dances
across the surface. Carefully add clams and wine. Cover, and cook until clams
open. Remove clams with a slotted spoon, and set aside. Discard any clams
that do not open fully during cooking.

Strain cooking liquid through a coffee filter to remove any sand. Return to
pot, and boil to reduce liquid to 1½ cups (375 mL). Set aside.

Heat butter in a large skillet, and slowly simmer onions and garlic until
onions are translucent. Add clams and reduced cooking liquid to warm. Season
with salt and pepper to taste. Toss with hot pasta, and garnish with cheese.
Serves 4

OPEN FOR BUSINESS

*Store fresh clams
or mussels in the
refrigerator in a bowl
covered with a cold,
damp cloth. Soak clams
or mussels in clear, cold
water for a few hours
so that they expel any
grit. Scrub the exterior
shells with a vegetable
brush to remove sand.
Always discard clams or
mussels with cracked or
chipped shells and any
that do not open fully
during cooking.*

LEMON ANCHOVY CREAM SAUCE

The distinctive flavors of onion, garlic, anchovies, lemon and cream
blend harmoniously in this rich, thick sauce.

1 Tbsp.	butter	15 mL
4 Tbsp.	lemon juice	50 mL
1	small onion, sliced	1
1	clove garlic, minced	1
4	anchovies, chopped	4
½ tsp.	lemon zest	2 mL
4 cups	35% B.F. cream	1 L
	Pinch coarse salt	
	Pinch freshly ground black pepper	
1 lb.	pasta, cooked & drained	500 g

Melt butter in a small pan, add lemon juice, onion, garlic, anchovies and
lemon zest, and cook over low heat until onion is tender. In a large pot, boil
cream over medium-high heat until it is reduced by half. Add reduced cream
to anchovy mixture, and heat through. Season with salt and pepper to taste.
Toss with hot pasta.
Serves 4

ORRECHIETTE WITH SPINACH, CHICKPEAS & SHAVED PARMESAN

Zal stole this fabulous pasta dish from Massimo Capra. It combines three starches—noodles,
potatoes and chickpeas. Somehow, it works, and the result is like a warm pasta salad.

8 oz.	piece Parmesan cheese	250 g
8 oz.	spinach, cleaned & stems removed	250 g
⅓ cup	olive oil	75 mL
2	potatoes, peeled, cut into medium dice & parboiled	2
½	medium onion, finely diced	½
2	cloves garlic, minced	2
1	19 oz. (540 mL) can chickpeas, drained (reserve 1 cup/250 mL chickpea juice)	1
1 lb.	orrechiette pasta, cooked & drained	500 g

Using a potato peeler, shave cheese into curls, and set aside.
Blanch spinach in boiling salted water. Drain, and set aside.
Heat oil in a large skillet, and sauté potatoes, onion and garlic for 10 minutes,
or until potatoes are cooked. Add chickpeas and reserved juice to the pan,
and heat through. Toss with hot pasta and spinach. Serve pasta layered with
cheese in bowls.
Serves 4

CHILLED BUCKWHEAT NOODLES
WITH SHIITAKE MUSHROOMS

This Japanese-inspired dish features the distinctive flavor
of buckwheat noodles in a light vinaigrette.

4 oz.	dried shiitake mushrooms	125 g
	Coarse salt	
8 oz.	buckwheat noodles	250 g
1 Tbsp.	sesame oil	15 mL
2 Tbsp.	rice-wine vinegar	25 mL
2 Tbsp.	mushroom soy sauce	25 mL
¼ cup	chicken stock (*see Basic Stock, page 46*)	50 mL
1 tsp.	sugar	5 mL
3	scallions, julienned	3
½	English cucumber, julienned	½

Soak mushrooms in hot water for 20 minutes. Drain, and wash well. Cut off and discard stems. Julienne caps.

Bring a large pot of water to a boil. Add salt and noodles, and cook. Watch carefully, because these noodles cook quickly. Drain, and rinse in cold water. Toss noodles with oil, then refrigerate.

In a small saucepan, mix together vinegar, soy sauce, stock and sugar. Add mushrooms, and simmer for 5 minutes. Chill mixture. Toss with noodles, and garnish with scallions and cucumber.

Serves 6

Gone Fishin'

"Fish, like eggs, should be cooked quickly and lightly and served at once in its own odorous heat," observed M.F.K. Fisher. We don't always follow Fisher's advice to the letter, but whether our fish is baked, poached, braised or grilled, we aim to abide by the spirit of her wisdom.

Fish is one of our favorite things to eat. Sometimes, we like it plain, as in Salmon With Citrus Glaze; other times, we like it simmered in a savory Moroccan stew, as in Fish Tajine With Tomatoes & Sweet Potatoes. Chef Cuong Ly's expertise with seafood has enabled us to expand our repertoire. In this chapter, we have fish fare that reflects appetites from around the world. From Atlantic Canada, we offer salt-cod-based Newfie Fish Cakes; from Spain, Shrimp Basque; from the Mediterranean, Garides Me Feta; from Thailand, Pad Prik Hoi; and from New Orleans, Turbot en Papillotte.

LOVIN' SPOONFULS,
from left to right: Chef
Cuong Ly (foreground)
works magic during the
dinner rush with help from
brother Ngan Ly; Chez
Piggy's garden of dining
delights; Karen Linton
totes steaming plates
posthaste; Sarah Wynn
serves lunch to summer
patrons on the patio.

GRILL HAPPY

*Both of these recipes
will make enough
to glaze or garnish
six 6-ounce (175 g)
salmon fillets.
To cook the salmon,
rub both sides of the fillet
with olive oil,
then grill or pan-fry
until cooked.*

SALMON WITH CITRUS GLAZE

*This glaze is a perfect match for the taste and texture of pan-fried salmon
and can be prepared a day in advance and stored in the refrigerator.*

2 Tbsp.	orange zest	25 mL
1 Tbsp.	lime zest	15 mL
1¼ cups	dry white wine	300 mL
¾ cup	orange juice	175 mL
¼ cup	lime juice	50 mL
¼ cup	lemon juice	50 mL
¼ cup	brown sugar	50 mL
1	1-inch (2.5 cm) piece fresh ginger, sliced	1
6	salmon fillets (each 6 oz./175 g), grilled or pan-fried	6

Blanch zest in boiling water, then remove from water and set aside.

To make citrus glaze, place remaining ingredients, except salmon, in a small saucepan, and cook over medium heat until reduced to one-third. Strain through a fine sieve.

If salmon is pan-fried, remove it from pan. Pour off excess oil, and deglaze pan with citrus glaze. Pour glaze over salmon, and garnish with zest.

Serves 6

SALMON WITH HORSERADISH CREAM SAUCE

This rich, creamy horseradish sauce gives the salmon a spicy bite.

1½ cups	dry white wine	375 mL
1	medium onion, cut in half	1
6	cloves	6
2 cups	35% B.F. cream	500 mL
2	cloves garlic	2
2	bay leaves	2
2 Tbsp.	prepared horseradish	25 mL
6	salmon fillets (each 6 oz./175 g), grilled or pan-fried	6

Heat wine in a saucepan over medium-high heat, and reduce to 4 table-spoons (50 mL). Set aside.

Stud the onion with cloves, and place in a pot with cream, garlic and bay leaves. Heat over medium-high heat until cream is reduced to ¾ cup (175 mL). Strain out onion, garlic and bay leaves. Add reduced wine, and stir in horseradish. Pour warm sauce over salmon.

Serves 6

Salmon With Citrus Glaze
and Souscaille

MACHLI KI TIKKA (Indian Curried Sole)

*Although this Indian dish calls for sole, the onion-and-dill sauce also works
well with other kinds of mild white fish, such as turbot or cod. At the
restaurant, we serve the sole with basmati rice and spiced lentils (see page 84).*

3 lb.	sole	1.5 kg
½ cup	lemon juice	125 mL
1 tsp.	coarse salt	5 mL
2 Tbsp.	butter	25 mL
2	medium onions, chopped	2
2	cloves garlic, chopped	2
1	1-inch (2.5 cm) piece fresh ginger, chopped	1
1	fresh chili, chopped	1
1 Tbsp.	turmeric	15 mL
⅓ cup	fish stock (see *Basic Stock, page 46*)	75 mL
	or water or dry white wine	
	Coarse salt & freshly ground black pepper	
¼ cup	fresh dill, chopped	50 mL

Marinate sole in lemon juice and 1 teaspoon (5 mL) salt for a few minutes or
up to 2 hours, but no longer (otherwise, lemon juice will start to "cook" the fish).

Preheat oven to 350°F (180°C). Melt butter in a large skillet, and sauté
onions, garlic, ginger, chili and turmeric over low heat until onions are
translucent. Add stock, water or wine, season with salt and pepper to taste,
and simmer for 5 minutes. Add dill, remove from heat, and set sauce aside.

On a greased baking sheet, bake sole for 8 to 10 minutes, or until fish is
flaky. If using a fish other than sole, you may need to cook for a few minutes
longer. Transfer to a serving dish, and spoon sauce on top.

Serves 6

LACQUERED HALIBUT
WITH SOBA NOODLE SALAD

This Japanese-style dish is simple to make and elegant to serve.
The hearty flavor of buckwheat noodles is lightened by rice-wine vinegar
and sugar and is a tasty accompaniment for the lacquered halibut.

SOBA NOODLE SALAD

4 oz.	dried shiitake mushrooms	125 g
	Coarse salt	
8 oz.	buckwheat noodles	250 g
1 Tbsp.	sesame oil	15 mL
2 Tbsp.	rice-wine vinegar	25 mL
2 Tbsp.	mushroom soy sauce	25 mL
1 tsp.	sugar	5 mL
3	scallions, julienned	3
1/2	English cucumber, julienned	1/2

Separate mushroom stems and caps. Discard stems. Place mushroom caps in a bowl, and add enough hot water to cover. Soak for 20 minutes. Strain through a coffee filter, and reserve liquid. Wash mushroom caps well, and julienne. Set aside.

Fill a large pot with water, and add a pinch of salt. Bring to a boil, and cook noodles, being careful not to overcook. Drain, and rinse in cold water. Toss noodles with oil, and refrigerate.

Place reserved mushroom liquid in a small saucepan over medium-high heat, and reduce to 2 tablespoons (25 mL). Add vinegar, soy sauce and sugar. Add mushrooms, and simmer for 5 minutes. Let mixture cool, and toss with chilled noodles. Garnish with scallions and cucumber.

SWEET SOY SAUCE

1 cup	light soy sauce	250 mL
1/3 cup	dark soy sauce	75 mL
1/3 cup	dry sherry	75 mL
1 tsp.	sesame oil	5 mL
4 tsp.	brown sugar	20 mL
2	slivers fresh ginger	2
2	cloves	2
1	clove garlic	1
1	star anise	1
1	1-inch (2.5 cm) stick cinnamon	1
1 tsp.	Szechuan peppercorns	5 mL
1/2 tsp.	aniseed	2 mL
1/2 tsp.	fennel seed	2 mL

Place all ingredients in a saucepan, and bring to a boil. Continue boiling to reduce by half. Strain sauce, and set aside.

HALIBUT

	Peanut oil for frying	
6	halibut steaks (each 6 oz./175 g)	6
½	red bell pepper, julienned, for garnish	½
4	scallions, julienned, for garnish	4
	Fresh coriander sprigs for garnish	

Heat oil in a large skillet over medium heat, and fry halibut for about 4 minutes per side, until fish is opaque on the inside. Arrange fish on a serving platter. Drain excess oil from pan, and deglaze with sweet soy sauce. Pour sauce over fish. Garnish with red pepper, scallions and coriander. Serve with soba noodle salad on the side.

Serves 6

NEW ORLEANS TURBOT EN PAPILLOTTE

Baking in parchment paper preserves moisture and the natural aroma of the food.

SPICED BUTTER

½ cup	butter, softened	125 mL
1 tsp.	tomato paste	5 mL
2 tsp.	dried thyme	10 mL
½ tsp.	cayenne pepper	2 mL
2	cloves garlic, minced	2
	Coarse salt & freshly ground black pepper	

TURBOT

1	stalk celery, julienned	1
1	carrot, julienned	1
1	leek, julienned	1
1	red bell pepper, julienned	1
3 lb.	turbot fillets	1.5 kg
	Parchment paper, cut into six 12-inch (30 cm) circles	

Mix spiced-butter ingredients together in a large bowl, adding salt and pepper to taste. Mound on wax paper, and roll into a tight cylinder. Refrigerate until firm.

Partially fill a saucepan with water, and bring to a boil. Blanch vegetables together, drain, and refresh under cold water. Drain again, and set aside.

Preheat oven to 350°F (180°C). Divide fish, spiced butter and vegetables into six equal portions. To make one serving, place one fillet on one half of a parchment circle. Season with salt and pepper to taste, and top with one portion of vegetables and one portion of butter. Fold parchment circle in half. Starting at one end, seal the parchment by crimping a ¼-inch (6 mm) seam all around the edges. Repeat for other servings.

Bake for 8 to 10 minutes. Serve in parchment paper, opening the packages at the table to release the aromas.

Serves 6

FISH TAJINE
WITH TOMATOES & SWEET POTATOES

The heady aromas of garlic, cumin and coriander combine with
the saffron-yellow to make this Moroccan dish.

CHARMOULA

2 Tbsp.	white-wine vinegar	25 mL
⅓ cup	lemon juice	75 mL
½ cup	chopped fresh coriander leaves	125 mL
½ cup	chopped fresh parsley	125 mL
5	cloves garlic	5
1½ tsp.	coarse salt	7 mL
1 tsp.	paprika	5 mL
¼ tsp.	ground cumin	1 mL
	Cayenne pepper to taste	

Place all ingredients in a food processor, and blend into a paste. Set aside.

FISH

2 lb.	monkfish, cut into ¾-inch (2 cm) chunks	1 kg
2 lb.	shrimp, peeled	1 kg
¼ cup	vegetable oil	50 mL
2	onions, diced	2
2	cloves garlic, chopped	2
2	carrots, cut into chunks	2
2	large sweet potatoes, cut into chunks	2
3	tomatoes, diced	3
2	green bell peppers, sliced	2
1	red bell pepper, sliced	1
	Pinch saffron	
1 tsp.	ground cumin	5 mL
1½ tsp.	tomato paste	7 mL
⅓ cup	lemon juice	75 mL
	Coarse salt	
6 cups	steamed couscous	1.5 L

Rub fish and shrimp with charmoula, and let marinate for 30 minutes.
Meanwhile, in a large skillet, heat oil, and sauté onions, garlic, carrots and
sweet potatoes until they are almost cooked. Add tomatoes and green and red
peppers, and continue to cook until vegetables soften. Stir in saffron, cumin,
tomato paste and lemon juice. Cover, and cook over low heat for 15 minutes.
Add fish and shrimp, and cook, covered, stirring occasionally, for 15 minutes,
or until fish is done. Season with salt to taste, and serve over couscous.
Serves 6

Robalo en Cazuela

ROBALO EN CAZUELA

*"Robalo" is Spanish for haddock, and "cazuela" is an individual dish
in which you prepare the haddock. In the absence of a cazuela,
however, you can bake all the fish pieces together in one casserole.*

4	haddock fillets (each 4-6 oz./125-175 g)	4
4 cups	cooked white rice	1 L
4	scallions, julienned	4
1	red bell pepper, julienned	1
1	jalapeño, sliced in rings (seeds in)	1
¼ cup	chopped fresh parsley	50 mL
¾ cup + 2 Tbsp.	extra-virgin olive oil	200 mL
1⅔ cups	dry white wine	400 mL
	Coarse salt & freshly ground black pepper	
	Juice of 2 limes	

Preheat oven to 400°F (200°C). Place one fillet in the center of each cazuela.
Arrange 1 cup (250 mL) rice around each fillet. Sprinkle with scallions, red
pepper, jalapeño and parsley. Drizzle with oil and wine. Season with salt and
pepper to taste.

Bake for 15 to 17 minutes, or until fish is cooked. Garnish with lime juice,
and serve in the cazuelas.

Serves 4

NEWFIE FISH CAKES
WITH TOMATO-CAPER MAYONNAISE

Salt cod is part of the unique taste in this enhanced fish-cake recipe. Bacon is added in deference to the Newfoundland dish called "scrunchions," in which bits of fried salt pork are used to garnish "fish and brewis," a mash of salt cod and hardtack. Depending on the thickness of the cod, the amount of soaking time will vary from 8 to 14 hours. The only way to know for sure that the fish is ready is to sample it. Do not oversoak the fish, or it will taste like flannel. Cooking the cod in milk somewhat neutralizes the remaining salt. Vicki's mom always cooks salt cod in milk, so it must be right.

TOMATO-CAPER MAYONNAISE

1	egg	1
2 tsp.	lemon juice	10 mL
½ tsp.	red-wine vinegar	2 mL
½ tsp.	Dijon mustard	2 mL
1	clove garlic	1
	Coarse salt & freshly ground black pepper	
1½-2 cups	vegetable oil	375-500 mL
2 Tbsp.	tomato paste	25 mL
4 tsp.	capers	20 mL

Place egg, lemon juice, vinegar, mustard, garlic and salt and pepper to taste in a blender, and mix. Slowly drizzle in oil while continuing to blend until thick. Stir in tomato paste and capers by hand. Store in a covered jar in the refrigerator.

FISH CAKES

1 lb.	boneless salt cod	500 g
1½-2 cups	milk	375-500 mL
2 lb.	potatoes, peeled & cooked	1 kg
5	slices bacon, diced & fried crispy	5
1	stalk celery, finely diced	1
1	onion, finely diced	1
¼ cup	chopped fresh parsley	50 mL
	or 1 Tbsp. (15 mL) summer savory	
2	eggs	2
	Juice of ½ lemon	
3 cups	breadcrumbs	750 mL
	Vegetable oil for frying	

Place cod in a deep roasting pan, and cover with cold water. Soak cod until the extremely salty taste is gone, changing water twice, if possible. Check saltiness before cooking by tasting a bit from the center of the thickest portion. If sufficient salt has leached out, drain fish.

In a pot, heat milk over medium-high heat, and add cod. Cook until fish flakes apart. Drain cod, and discard milk.

In a large bowl, mash together cod and potatoes. Stir in bacon, celery, onion, parsley, eggs, lemon juice and 1 cup (250 mL) breadcrumbs. Chill mixture.

Form into patties. Roll patties in remaining 2 cups (500 mL) breadcrumbs. Heat oil in a skillet over medium-high heat, and fry patties, turning to brown evenly. Serve hot with tomato-caper mayonnaise.

Makes 10 to 12 fish cakes

LOBSTER RISOTTO
WITH BASIL & ROASTED TOMATOES

This creamy risotto is rich with the taste of lobster. Make the stock using fresh water, not the water used to cook the crustacean. The tomalley (and coral, if you are lucky enough to have it) can be stirred into the onion and added to the recipe. To avoid conflicts over oven time, you should prepare the tomatoes in advance and set them aside.

4	whole tomatoes	4
1 Tbsp.	balsamic vinegar	15 mL
½ cup	olive oil	125 mL
	Pinch coarse salt	
	Pinch freshly ground black pepper	
4	cloves garlic	4
1-1½ lb.	lobster, cooked, meat removed & chopped (retain shell)	500-750 g
1	large onion, finely diced	1
2 cups	arborio rice	500 mL
1 cup	dry white wine	250 mL
3 cups	lobster or shrimp stock (see Basic Stock, page 46)	750 mL
2 cups	coarsely chopped, loosely packed fresh basil	500 mL
¾ cup	freshly grated Parmesan cheese	175 mL

Preheat oven to 250°F (120°C). Carefully remove tomato stems. Cut tomatoes in half horizontally. Gently squeeze out seeds without breaking the skin. Place tomato halves on a baking sheet, cut side up, and sprinkle with vinegar, ¼ cup (50 mL) oil, salt and pepper. Bake for 5 to 6 hours, until tomatoes are dry. Cut into quarters, and set aside.

Preheat oven to 350°F (180°C). Place garlic in a piece of aluminum foil with a few drops of remaining oil. Bake for 15 minutes. Set aside.

Slightly crush lobster shells, place in a roasting pan, and bake for 20 minutes. Partially fill a large stockpot with water, and bring to a boil. Reduce heat, add roasted shells, and simmer for 45 minutes. Strain and reserve stock.

In a large pot, warm remaining oil (about ¼ cup/50 mL), and sauté onion until translucent. Stir in rice, and continue cooking, uncovered. Add wine, and continue stirring. Gradually add stock in small amounts until rice achieves desired texture. Stir in lobster meat, basil, roasted tomato and roasted garlic. Add ½ cup (125 mL) cheese. Garnish with remaining ¼ cup (50 mL) cheese.

Serves 4

VATAPA DE CAMARAÕ WITH COCONUT RICE & LIME HOT SAUCE

This Brazilian dish is distinctive for the combined flavors of shrimp with ginger and a pestolike almond-and-cashew paste that are cut by the lime hot sauce. The coconut rice complements other dishes, such as skewered chicken with peanut sauce or stir-fried meat and vegetables.

LIME HOT SAUCE

1 cup	lime juice	250 mL
½ cup	water	125 mL
1	red onion, finely diced	1
1	fresh chili, seeded & chopped	1
1	clove garlic, chopped	1
	Pinch coarse salt	

Mix all ingredients together in a bowl, and set aside.

COCONUT RICE

2 cups	short-grain rice	500 mL
3 cups	water	750 mL
1¾ cups	coconut milk	425 mL
	Pinch coarse salt	
2 tsp.	butter	10 mL

Place all ingredients in a pot. Bring to a boil, and reduce heat. Stir, then cover, and simmer over low heat until rice is cooked, approximately 20 minutes. Put rice into individual molds, and turn out onto plates. Serve surrounded by shrimp.

SHRIMP

¼ cup + 3 Tbsp.	olive oil	50 mL + 45 mL
2	medium onions, puréed	2
4	cloves garlic, chopped	4
2	fresh chilies, seeded & chopped	2
1	1-inch (2.5 cm) piece fresh ginger, peeled & chopped	1
1 cup	dried shrimp	250 mL
½ cup	shrimp stock (see *Basic Stock, page 46*)	125 mL
1¾ cups	coconut milk	425 mL
1 cup	cashews	250 mL
1 cup	blanched almonds	250 mL
2½ lb.	large shrimp, peeled	1.1 kg
	Fresh coriander leaves for garnish	

To make vatapa sauce, heat ¼ cup (50 mL) oil in a pot over medium heat, and sauté onions, garlic, chilies and ginger. Place in a food processor, add dried shrimp, and purée. Return to pot, add stock and coconut milk, and heat for

10 minutes. Grind cashews and almonds in a mortar and pestle, and add to pot. Heat through, and set aside.

Heat remaining 3 tablespoons (45 mL) oil over medium-high heat, and cook shrimp. Add vatapa sauce, and heat through. Garnish with coriander, and serve with coconut rice, with lime hot sauce on the side.

Serves 6 to 8

SHRIMP BASQUE

Chorizo sausage, which is totally addictive, is the important ingredient in this dish. It is available at Portuguese specialty-food stores.

5 Tbsp.	olive oil	65 mL
1	6-to-8-inch (15-20 cm) chorizo sausage, sliced	1
1	medium onion, finely diced	1
6	cloves garlic, minced	6
½	red bell pepper, finely diced	½
1	fresh chili, chopped	1
1	28 oz. (796 mL) can tomatoes	1
½ cup	dry red wine	125 mL
½ tsp.	paprika	2 mL
	Pinch saffron	
1 tsp.	dried thyme	5 mL
	Coarse salt & freshly ground black pepper	
2½ lb.	large shrimp, peeled	1.1 kg
6 cups	cooked rice	1.5 L
	Chopped fresh parsley for garnish	

Heat 1 tablespoon (15 mL) oil in a heavy-bottomed skillet, and fry sausage. Remove from pan, and set aside.

Sauté onion, garlic, red pepper and chili in 2 tablespoons (25 mL) oil until vegetables are tender. Stir in tomatoes, wine, paprika, saffron, thyme and salt and pepper to taste. Simmer over low heat for up to 2 hours, or until sauce thickens. Add sausage, and heat through.

Sauté shrimp in remaining 2 tablespoons (25 mL) oil until they turn pink.

Partially fill bowls with rice, then ladle sauce over rice. Top with shrimp, and garnish with parsley.

Serves 6

GARIDES ME FETA (Shrimp With Feta Cheese)

*Garides me Feta is a combination of several Greek classics—sweet, rich black beans,
tart tomato and dill sauce and skordalia (garlic paste)—in one fabulous dish that was
developed at the restaurant by Anne Linton. The sweetened black beans can also be
served as a side dish with other savory courses, such as gambas or cooked chicken breast,
while the skordalia can be used as a spread on bread or as a vegetable dip.*

HONEYED BLACK BEANS

2 cups	dried black beans, sorted & rinsed	500 mL
1	whole onion, peeled	1
1	whole carrot, unpeeled	1
2	bay leaves	2
	Pinch coarse salt	
½ cup	olive oil	125 mL
¼ cup	honey	50 mL
2	cloves garlic, minced	2
½ tsp.	freshly ground black pepper	2 mL

Place beans in a pot, cover with cold water, and soak overnight. In the
morning, drain, rinse, and cover with fresh water. Add onion, carrot, bay leaves
and salt. Bring to a boil, then reduce heat, and simmer until beans are cooked,
adding more water as necessary. Drain beans, and remove onion, carrot and
bay leaves. Place beans in a bowl, and set aside.

In a separate pan, heat oil, honey, garlic and pepper over medium heat, then
pour over beans. Gently toss, and season with salt and pepper to taste.

Makes 4 cups (1 L)

SKORDALIA

6	medium white potatoes, peeled, boiled & mashed	6
¾ cup	blanched almonds, finely ground	175 mL
6	cloves garlic, minced	6
1 tsp.	sugar	5 mL
1 tsp.	coarse salt	5 mL
¼ cup	white-wine vinegar	50 mL
⅓ cup	olive oil	75 mL

In a large bowl, mix together potatoes, almonds, garlic, sugar and salt. Stir
in vinegar, then slowly drizzle in oil, mixing constantly by hand or with an
electric mixer. The finished mixture should be a thick paste but can be thinned
slightly with a little warm water if it is too dry. Skordalia will keep for up to
6 days in the refrigerator.

Makes 7-8 cups (2 L)

SHRIMP

4 Tbsp.	olive oil	50 mL
1	onion, diced	1
2 Tbsp.	dry mustard	25 mL
1	28 oz. (796 mL) can tomatoes	1
3 Tbsp.	chopped fresh dill	45 mL
1½ lb.	medium shrimp, peeled	750 g
4 cups	honeyed black beans	1 L
2 cups	crumbled feta cheese	500 mL
2 Tbsp.	fresh dill for garnish	25 mL
1 cup	skordalia for garnish	250 mL

Heat 2 tablespoons (25 mL) oil in a large skillet, and sauté onion until translucent. Add mustard and tomatoes, and simmer, uncovered, for 20 minutes. Stir in chopped dill, and keep sauce warm.

In another pan, heat remaining 2 tablespoons (25 mL) oil, and sauté shrimp until just pink. Set aside, but keep warm.

In individual ovenproof dishes, place a layer of black beans, then tomato sauce, then shrimp. Sprinkle with feta, and broil until cheese is melted and lightly browned.

Garnish with dill, and serve with a generous spoonful of skordalia.

Serves 4 to 6

GARLIC-FRIED SHRIMP

Don't let the oil and pan drippings go to waste. Mop them up with a piece of crusty bread while you enjoy a glass of red wine.

½ cup	olive oil	125 mL
1 lb.	medium shrimp, peeled (leave tails on)	500 g
6	cloves garlic, minced	6
2 Tbsp.	dry sherry	25 mL
1 Tbsp.	lemon juice	15 mL
2 Tbsp.	chopped fresh parsley	25 mL
¼ tsp.	sweet paprika	1 mL
	Coarse salt & freshly ground black pepper	
	Black Bean Salad (*see page 92*)	

Heat oil in a heavy-bottomed pan. When oil is hot but not smoking, fry shrimp until just pink. Stir in garlic, sherry, lemon juice, parsley and paprika, and toss shrimp. Season with salt and pepper to taste. Serve with Black Bean Salad.

Serves 4

PAD PRIK HOI (Scallops With Chilies & Basil)

The subtle layering of flavors in our homemade red curry paste is the centerpiece of this dish. Together with the holy basil, which has a dark angular leaf and a strong licorice flavor, the curry paste sets off the delicate taste of the scallops.

4 Tbsp.	red curry paste (*recipe follows*)	50 mL
16	large fresh sea scallops	16
2 Tbsp.	vegetable oil	25 mL
2	cloves garlic, finely chopped	2
2	red finger-hot chilies, slivered	2
1 Tbsp.	sugar	15 mL
2 Tbsp.	fish sauce	25 mL
	Coarse salt & freshly ground black pepper	
¼ cup	fresh holy basil leaves	50 mL

Place red curry paste in a large bowl, and add scallops. Toss, and marinate for no more than 15 minutes. In a wok, heat oil until hot but not smoking. Add garlic and chilies, and heat until garlic is golden but not brown. Remove scallops from marinade with a slotted spoon, and toss into pan. Sear the outside. Stir in marinade, sugar and fish sauce. Cook until scallops are crisp on the outside and translucent inside. Season with salt and pepper to taste. Stir in basil just before serving.
Serves 4

KRUANG KAENG DANG (Red Curry Paste)

While the ingredients may be hard to find and it is time-consuming to make, homemade curry paste is well worth the effort. In commercial blends, it is difficult to discern the flavors of individual ingredients. With homemade, however, each ingredient retains its integrity, making its taste subtly apparent in the mix. If coriander root is not available, substitute additional stems. Kapi is a pungent shrimp paste made from sun-dried prawns and salt. Use sparingly.

1 Tbsp.	coriander seed	15 mL
2 tsp.	cumin seed	10 mL
1 tsp.	black peppercorns	5 mL
2 tsp.	shrimp paste (kapi)	10 mL
10	red finger-hot chilies, chopped	10
½ cup	small purple shallots, chopped	125 mL
1 Tbsp.	chopped garlic	15 mL
¼ cup	finely sliced lemongrass	50 mL
	or thinly peeled rind of 1 lemon	
1 Tbsp.	chopped fresh galangal	15 mL
	or 1 Tbsp. (15 mL) powdered galangal	
1 Tbsp.	chopped fresh coriander roots	15 mL
1 Tbsp.	chopped fresh coriander stems	15 mL
1 tsp.	finely grated kaffir lime rind	5 mL
4	kaffir lime leaves, midribs removed	4
2 Tbsp.	vegetable oil	25 mL
2 tsp.	paprika	10 mL
1 tsp.	turmeric	5 mL

In a small, dry saucepan, toast coriander seed until golden and fragrant; remove from pan. Lightly toast cumin seed, and remove from pan. Then toast peppercorns, and remove from pan. Grind all three to a powder in a mortar and pestle or a spice grinder. Set aside.

Place shrimp paste in foil, and wrap, flattening it to make a small pocket. Place under a hot broiler, and cook for 2 to 3 minutes on each side. Set aside.

Place chilies, shallots, garlic, lemongrass or lemon rind, galangal, coriander roots and stems, lime rind and lime leaves in a blender. Add oil, and blend to a smooth paste. Add ground toasted spices, shrimp paste, paprika and turmeric. Blend.

Store in a clean, dry bottle in the refrigerator, where it will keep for 3 to 4 weeks, or divide into portions, wrap, and freeze.

Makes 1½ cups (375 mL)

SEARED SCALLOPS WITH CITRUS VINAIGRETTE & ONION CONFIT

Sweet caramelized onions provide a nice contrast to the citrus vinaigrette in this delicately flavored warm seafood salad.

ONION CONFIT

3	red onions, peeled & cut into wedges	3
1 cup	dry red wine	250 mL
½ cup	chicken stock (*see Basic Stock, page 46*)	125 mL
⅓ cup	olive oil	75 mL
3	cloves garlic, chopped	3
	Pinch coarse salt	
	Pinch freshly ground black pepper	

Preheat oven to 350°F (180°C). Mix all ingredients together, and place in a baking dish. Bake, uncovered, for about 2 hours, stirring occasionally, until onions are cooked and almost dry. Set aside.

CITRUS VINAIGRETTE

1 cup	olive oil	250 mL
¾ cup	orange juice	175 mL
2 Tbsp.	white-wine vinegar	25 mL
2 Tbsp.	lemon juice	25 mL
1 Tbsp.	lime juice	15 mL
1 Tbsp.	chopped orange zest	15 mL
2 tsp.	sugar	10 mL
	Pinch coarse salt	
	Pinch freshly ground black pepper	

Place all ingredients in a shaker or a blender, and mix until sugar dissolves. Set aside.

Makes 2 cups (500 mL)

SCALLOPS

4	carrots, julienned	4
½ lb.	snow peas	250 g
½ cup	citrus vinaigrette	125 mL
2 lb.	sea scallops	1 kg
	Mixed salad greens & lettuces for 6, washed & drained	

Partially fill a large pot with water, and bring to a boil. In separate batches, blanch carrots and snow peas. Refresh under cold water. Drain, and set aside.

Pour vinaigrette in a large skillet, and increase heat to high. When pan is hot, carefully add scallops, and sear until liquid evaporates and scallops are cooked. Remove from heat immediately.

Place a mound of greens in the center of each plate. Arrange carrots and snow peas to radiate out from greens in a sunburst pattern. Place a few wedges of onion confit on greens. Spoon scallops on top, and dress lightly with some vinaigrette.

Serves 4 to 6

MUSSELS WITH SAFFRON CREAM SAUCE

Saffron colors this creamy rich yet simple seafood dish.

2 tsp.	butter	10 mL
4 tsp.	finely diced shallots	20 mL
2 cups	dry white wine	300 mL + 175 mL
4 cups	35% B.F. cream	1 L
	or 1¼ cups (300 mL) crème fraîche (*see page 110*)	
1 tsp.	saffron	5 mL
	Coarse salt & freshly ground black pepper	
2 lb.	mussels, scrubbed & debearded	1 kg

In a medium saucepan, melt butter over low heat, and gently cook shallots for 3 to 4 minutes. Increase heat to high, add 1¼ cups (300 mL) wine, and reduce liquid to 3 tablespoons (45 mL). Set aside.

In a medium saucepan, heat cream or crème fraîche and saffron over high heat, and reduce to about 1¼ cups (300 mL). Reduce heat, add shallot mixture, and simmer for 5 minutes. Season with salt and pepper to taste.

In a large pot, heat remaining ¾ cup (175 mL) wine until steaming. Add mussels, and cook, covered, until shells open, discarding any that do not open fully. Remove mussels with a slotted spoon, and place on a serving dish.

Pour a little cooking liquid into the dish, and pour piping-hot saffron sauce over mussels.

Serves 4 as an appetizer or 2 for lunch

AMEIJOAS LA CATAPLANA
(Clams With Sausage & Prosciutto)

This smoky seafood dish features the tastes of rich sausage and spicy wine broth and offers a different combination of flavors in each bite. Chorizo— smoked Portuguese sausage—is available at specialty-food stores.

PIRI PIRI

½ cup	olive oil	125 mL
4	bay leaves	4
1 Tbsp.	lemon zest	15 mL
¼ cup	lemon juice	50 mL
¼ cup	crushed dried chilies	50 mL
6	cloves garlic, julienned	6

Mix all ingredients together in a small bowl, and set aside.

SAUSAGE-TOMATO SAUCE

¼ cup	olive oil	50 mL
6	cloves garlic, chopped	6
4	onions, chopped	4
1	12-to-14-inch (30-35 cm) chorizo sausage, sliced	1
½ lb.	prosciutto, cubed	250 g
½ lb.	cooked ham, cubed	250 g
2	28 oz. (796 mL) cans tomatoes, chopped, with liquid	2
	Coarse salt & freshly ground black pepper	
30	littleneck or cherrystone clams	30
1 cup	white wine	250 mL
6 cups	cooked long-grain rice, colored with a few threads of saffron	1.5 L

Heat oil in a deep heavy-bottomed skillet, and sauté garlic and onions over low heat until onions are translucent, but do not allow garlic to brown.

Add chorizo, prosciutto and ham, and warm over low heat. Add tomatoes, and increase heat to medium-high to reduce liquid until thick and glossy. Season with salt and pepper to taste. Keep warm over low heat.

Soak clams so that they will expel grit, and scrub shells with a vegetable brush to remove sand. Discard any clams with broken or cracked shells. Heat wine in a large pot until steaming. Add clams, cover, and cook until shells open, discarding any that do not open fully. Drain.

Arrange each serving of rice on a plate, and spoon sausage-tomato sauce on top. Stud with steamed clams. Pass piri piri at the table.

Serves 4 to 6

SEAFOOD SUCCOTASH

*The Chez Piggy seafood succotash is a traditional New England-style
down-home dish that combines corn, lima beans and bacon and is enlivened by
four kinds of seafood as well as leeks, carrots and red pepper.*

¾ cup	dried lima beans	175 mL
	Pinch coarse salt	
2 dozen	littleneck or cherrystone clams (or more)	2 dozen
1 cup	white wine	250 mL
½ lb.	bacon, diced	250 g
1	leek, diced	1
1	stalk celery, diced	1
2	carrots, diced	2
3	cloves garlic, minced	3
3 Tbsp.	dried thyme	45 mL
1	red bell pepper, diced	1
	Kernels from 6 ears of fresh corn	
3	large tomatoes, diced	3
	or one 28 oz. (796 mL) can, drained & diced	
	Coarse salt & freshly ground black pepper	
½ lb.	sea scallops	250 g
½ lb.	red snapper, cut into chunks	250 g
½ lb.	cod, cut into chunks	250 g
1 cup	35% B.F. cream	250 mL
3	scallions, chopped, for garnish	3

Place beans in a large pot, cover with water, and soak overnight. In the
morning, drain, then cover with fresh water, and add salt. Bring to a simmer,
and cook until tender, about 1½ hours. Drain, and set aside.

Soak clams to expel grit, and scrub shells with a vegetable brush to remove
sand. Bring a heavy-bottomed pot to high heat, then toss in clams and wine.
Cover, and cook until shells open. Discard any that do not open fully. Remove
clams with a slotted spoon, and set aside. Strain cooking liquid through a
coffee filter to remove sand, and reserve liquid.

In a large skillet, fry bacon until crisp. Add leek, celery, carrots, garlic and
thyme, and sauté until vegetables are tender. Stir in red pepper, corn, tomatoes
and reserved clam liquid, and heat through. Season with salt and pepper to
taste. Add beans, scallops, red snapper and cod, and heat over medium heat
until fish is fully cooked. Stir in cream, and add clams to warm. Spoon into
bowls, and garnish with scallions.

Serves 6 to 8

For Meat's Sake

Zal's first professional cooking gig took place at The Golden Apple in Gananoque, Ontario, under the guidance of an old-style eastern European chef who aged his own beef and was a master of the meat-and-potatoes tradition. To this day, Zal and Rose both prefer cuts that are big on flavor—dark, lean meats like lamb and veal shanks, rich-tasting duck or chicken legs and thighs. Chez Piggy's favorite dishes tend to be those which simmer for hours in their own juices or in strong, savory sauces until they are fall-off-the-bone tender.

Chez Piggy cannot be accused of being a fan of light cuisine, a fact that is especially true of its main-course meats. Regulars count on the aged rib steak, Ly's ribs and beef tenderloin for a satisfying hit of red meat, but diners are also treated to tasty Moroccan and Peruvian lamb stews, Indonesian Grilled Chicken and Asian Duck Leg Confit.

SLICE OF LIFE, from left to right: Chez Piggy's mouth-watering rack of lamb; summer in the lime-stone city; mincing work; Chef Vicki Newbury, her son Nate (center) and a handful of the restaurant's staff of 100.

BEEF TENDERLOIN WITH SHALLOT SAUCE & MUSHROOM-HORSERADISH PÂTÉ

Beef, mushrooms and horseradish blend together beautifully
in this elegant presentation. Make the pâté the day before.

PÂTÉ

¼ cup	dried porcini mushrooms	50 mL
	Marsala, warmed	
2 tsp.	butter	10 mL
1	small onion, diced	1
1	clove garlic, minced	1
1 cup	sliced button mushrooms	250 mL
	Coarse salt & freshly ground black pepper	
½ lb.	cream cheese, softened	250 g
¼ cup	prepared horseradish, drained & squeezed dry	50 mL
¼ cup	mixed chopped fresh mild herbs (such as parsley, thyme, chervil)	50 mL

Place porcini mushrooms in a bowl, and pour Marsala over to cover. Allow mushrooms to soften for a few minutes, then remove and set aside, reserving Marsala.

Melt butter over medium heat in a large skillet, and sauté onion, garlic and button mushrooms. Season with salt and pepper to taste. Increase heat to medium-high, and deglaze pan with reserved Marsala, cooking until moisture evaporates. Add porcini mushrooms, and stir, then transfer mixture to a food processor, and blend to a paste. Cool.

Beat cream cheese with an electric mixer until fluffy, and mix in horseradish. Slowly add mushroom mixture. Add herbs, but do not overmix. Season with salt and pepper to taste. Mound at one end of parchment paper, and roll into logs. Chill overnight. Unwrap and slice when ready to serve.

BROWN SAUCE

12 cups	brown stock (*see page 47*)	3 L

One of the following for flavor:
1 cup (250 mL) brandy
or zest of 1 lemon
or 3-inch (8 cm) piece fresh ginger, sliced,
or flavoring of your choice

Skim fat from chilled stock. Add your choice of flavoring, and boil stock until it is reduced to 2 cups (500 mL), approximately 5 to 6 hours. When hot, the sauce should be thick like syrup, and when chilled, it should firm up like fudge.

BEEF

3 Tbsp.	olive oil	15 mL + 25 mL
1 cup	sliced shallots	250 mL
¼ cup	Madeira	50 mL
2 Tbsp.	brown sugar	25 mL
	Coarse salt & freshly ground black pepper	
2 cups	brown sauce	500 mL
2 tsp.	prepared horseradish	10 mL
3 lb.	beef tenderloin	1.5 kg

In a large skillet, warm 1 tablespoon (15 mL) oil over low heat. Add shallots, Madeira, sugar and salt and pepper to taste. Cook until Madeira is almost evaporated and shallots are soft and have a caramelized glaze. Add brown sauce, and stir in horseradish. Set shallot sauce aside, and keep warm.

Preheat oven to 450°F (230°C). Trim excess fat from meat, and bring meat to room temperature. Rub with remaining 2 tablespoons (25 mL) oil and salt and pepper to taste. Heat a cast-iron frying pan over medium-high heat, and sear meat on all sides. Transfer pan to oven to complete cooking, allowing 12 to 15 minutes per pound for rare, 20 minutes per pound for medium. For well done, reduce heat to 350°F (180°C) and cook for 25 minutes per pound. Slice tenderloin into steaks, top each with a slice of pâté, and spoon on some shallot sauce before serving.

Serves 6

BEEF TENDERLOIN
WITH ANCHOVY BUTTER

Beef tenderloin is straightforward to prepare and is guaranteed to taste delicious.

1 cup	dry red wine	250 mL
2 Tbsp.	tomato paste	25 mL
½ lb.	butter, softened	250 g
2 Tbsp.	cumin seed, toasted & ground	25 mL
12	anchovies, chopped	12
3 lb.	beef tenderloin	1.5 kg

Place wine and tomato paste in a saucepan over high heat, and boil until reduced by half. Cool to room temperature. Blend butter with wine mixture, cumin and anchovies. Mound butter mixture onto a sheet of wax paper, and roll into a cylindrical shape. Chill until firm.

Preheat oven to 450°F (230°C). Trim excess fat from meat, and bring meat to room temperature. Heat a cast-iron frying pan over medium-high heat, and sear meat on all sides. Transfer pan to oven to complete cooking, allowing 12 to 15 minutes per pound for rare, 20 minutes per pound for medium. For well done, reduce heat to 350°F (180°C) and cook for 25 minutes per pound. Slice tenderloin into steaks, and serve with a pat of chilled anchovy butter on top.

Serves 6

BEEF TENDERLOIN
WITH BLACK-OLIVE TAPENADE

The saltiness of the olives, anchovies and capers in this Mediterranean tapenade complements the beef. The leftover tapenade makes an excellent appetizer when served on garlic crostini or tossed with warm pasta. It's also an enticing garnish on tomato soup.

5 Tbsp.	olive oil	45 mL + 25 mL
1 lb.	kalamata olives, pitted & coarsely chopped	500 g
4 Tbsp.	chopped capers	50 mL
2	anchovies, rinsed & chopped	2
4	cloves garlic, chopped	4
	Pinch dried thyme	
1 Tbsp.	brandy	15 mL
1 Tbsp.	Dijon mustard	15 mL
3 lb.	beef tenderloin	1.5 kg
2 Tbsp.	olive oil	25 mL
	Coarse salt & freshly ground black pepper	

Mix 3 tablespoons (45 mL) oil with olives, capers, anchovies, garlic, thyme, brandy and mustard in a bowl. Set tapenade aside. (Makes 4 cups/1 L.)

Preheat oven to 450°F (230°C). Trim excess fat from meat, and bring meat to room temperature. Rub with remaining 2 tablespoons (25 mL) oil and salt and pepper to taste. Heat a cast-iron frying pan over medium-high heat, and sear meat on all sides. Transfer pan to oven to complete cooking, allowing 12 to 15 minutes per pound for rare, 20 minutes per pound for medium. For well done, reduce heat to 350°F (180°C) and cook for 25 minutes per pound. Slice tenderloin into steaks, and top each with a generous helping of tapenade.

Serves 6

BEEF KURMAH

This Indonesian dish is part of a traditional rijsttafel, or rice table. We serve it on a platter with more than a dozen exotic delicacies and rice. Kurmah powder makes an interesting substitute for curry powder in any curry recipe. Toast cardamom in a dry skillet over medium heat until fragrant. Cool, and grind in a clean coffee grinder or a spice blender. The same technique can be used to toast nuts.

KURMAH POWDER

3 Tbsp.	cardamom, toasted & ground	45 mL
2 tsp.	turmeric	10 mL
2 tsp.	fennel seed, ground	10 mL
1 tsp.	black peppercorns, ground	5 mL
1 tsp.	white peppercorns, ground	5 mL
1 tsp.	ground coriander	5 mL
½ tsp.	cinnamon	2 mL
½ tsp.	ground nutmeg	2 mL

Mix all ingredients together, and store in a jar.

BEEF

2 lb.	beef shoulder, cubed	1 kg
2	cloves garlic, julienned	2
⅓ cup	julienned shallots	75 mL
1	medium onion, sliced	1
1 Tbsp.	julienned fresh green chilies	15 mL
1 Tbsp.	julienned fresh red chilies	15 mL
1¾ cups	coconut milk	425 mL
2 Tbsp.	ground toasted cashews	25 mL
2 Tbsp.	ground toasted almonds	25 mL
1 tsp.	poppy seed, ground	5 mL
2 tsp.	Kurmah powder	10 mL
2	tomatoes, cored & cut into wedges	2
5 cups	steamed white rice	1.25 L
½ cup	chopped fresh coriander leaves	125 mL

Place beef, garlic, shallots, onion, green and red chilies and coconut milk in a heavy-bottomed pot, and cook over medium heat for 25 minutes, or until beef is tender. Add cashews, almonds, poppy seed and kurmah powder, and simmer for 25 minutes. Add tomatoes, and heat through, but do not let tomatoes disintegrate. Spoon over rice, and garnish with coriander.
Serves 6

MALAYSIAN RED CURRY BEEF

This sweet-hot beef dish gives off the exotic aromas of lemongrass and cloves as it cooks. Soy sauce, cinnamon and beef combine to produce a rich auburn color. Serve with steamed rice.

10	dried chilies, ground	10
1	stalk lemongrass	1
½ cup	sultana raisins	125 mL
10	shallots, minced	10
1	1-inch (2.5 cm) piece ginger, chopped	1
1 tsp.	freshly ground black pepper	5 mL
2 Tbsp.	vegetable oil	25 mL
4 lb.	shank or stewing beef, cubed	1.8 kg
1	1-inch (2.5 cm) stick cinnamon	1
3	cloves	3
4	cloves garlic, chopped	4
4	shallots, chopped	4
1¾ cups	coconut milk	425 mL
1 tsp.	dark soy sauce	5 mL
	Coarse salt	

In a bowl, blend chilies, lemongrass, raisins, minced shallots, ginger and pepper with oil to make a marinade. Place beef in a shallow roasting pan, cover with half of the marinade, and let marinate for 1 hour.

In a dry skillet, heat cinnamon, cloves, garlic and chopped shallots over low heat until fragrant. Add remaining half of marinade, and cook for a few minutes. Add beef, coconut milk and soy sauce, and season with salt to taste. Simmer over medium heat for 1 to 2 hours, until beef is tender.

Serves 6 to 8

CHEZ PIGGY RIB STEAK

At Chez Piggy, we use rib steak cut from a whole rib that has been aged for up to 20 days. To give the cut extra flavor, we marinate the meat an additional two or three days before preparing it.

4	cloves garlic, chopped	4
2½ Tbsp.	black peppercorns, coarsely ground	35 mL
¼ cup	olive oil	50 mL
6	rib steaks	6

Mix garlic, peppercorns and oil together in a small skillet, and warm over low heat to allow the garlic flavor to infuse the oil. Cool, and brush onto both sides of steak. Grill or fry to desired doneness.

Serves 6

BOFFO BURGERS WITH CHILI SAUCE

Over the years, we have varied the dressing to give our signature burger a new taste.
This chili sauce is a rich, spicy tomato mixture that is delicious on other cuts of beef
and even spices up barbecued hot dogs. It keeps refrigerated in a jar for up to a month.
If you have a crop of unripened tomatoes in your garden at the end of the season, try this
recipe using green tomatoes. They'll give the chili sauce a slightly tart taste.

CHILI SAUCE

9	tomatoes, cored & coarsely chopped	9
3	onions, diced	3
1¼ cups	white vinegar	300 mL
1¼ cups	sugar	300 mL
1½ tsp.	freshly ground black pepper	7 mL
1½ tsp.	ground ginger	7 mL
1¼ tsp.	coarse salt	6 mL
½ tsp.	cayenne pepper	2 mL
½ tsp.	allspice	2 mL
½ tsp.	ground cloves	2 mL
½ tsp.	cinnamon	2 mL

Combine all ingredients in a large pot. Bring to a boil, reduce heat, and cook for 2 hours, or until sauce thickens.

Makes approximately 4 cups

BURGERS

2 lb.	ground chuck	1 kg
2	cloves garlic, finely chopped	2
1	medium onion, finely chopped	1
2	eggs	2
1 Tbsp.	Dijon mustard	15 mL
1 Tbsp.	ground cumin	15 mL
1½ tsp.	chili powder	7 mL
1½ tsp.	coarse salt	7 mL
	Small handful of ground rolled oats	
6	crusty white rolls	6

Place all ingredients except rolls in a bowl, and mix thoroughly. Shape into patties, and fry, broil or grill to your liking. Serve with chili sauce on warmed rolls.

Makes 6 burgers

LOIN OF VEAL
WITH SAMBUCA CREAM SAUCE

*The sambuca-flavored cream sauce deliciously enhances the mild taste
of the veal, while the green peppercorns provide a piquant contrast.*

4 lb.	veal loin, rolled	1.8 kg
3 Tbsp.	olive oil	45 mL
4	cloves garlic, chopped	4
1 tsp. + 1 Tbsp.	canned green peppercorns, drained & crushed	5 mL + 15 mL
1 tsp.	black peppercorns, crushed	5 mL
1 tsp.	mustard seed	5 mL
1 tsp.	coarse salt	5 mL
2 tsp.	red-wine vinegar	10 mL
2 cups	35% B.F. cream	500 mL
¼ cup	sambuca, flamed (*see* "Light My Fire," *page* 26)	50 mL
1 Tbsp.	Dijon mustard	15 mL

Rub veal with oil. In a small bowl, mix together garlic, 1 teaspoon (5 mL)
green peppercorns, black peppercorns, mustard seed, salt and vinegar. Place
veal in a shallow pan, and press marinade onto outside. Cover, and let marinate
overnight in the refrigerator.

The next day, preheat oven to 375°F (190°C), and bake veal 10 to 12
minutes per pound for rare, up to 20 minutes per pound for well done.
Transfer veal to serving platter.

In a small saucepan, boil cream until reduced to 1½ cups (375 mL).
Deglaze roasting pan with reduced cream, sambuca, mustard and remaining
1 tablespoon (15 mL) green peppercorns, incorporating the pan drippings
into the sauce as it cooks. Strain the sauce.

Slice veal, and top with cream sauce.

Serves 8

VITELLO TONNATO

*This light veal dish is served cold with tuna-flavored mayonnaise. The secret to the tasty
mayonnaise is the gelatin from the veal bones (don't forget to bring them home
from the butcher). This recipe takes a day and a half to prepare.*

8 cups	water	2 L
3 cups	white wine	750 mL
2 Tbsp.	black peppercorns	25 mL
2	stalks celery	2
2	carrots	2
1	large onion	1
	Veal bones	
4 lb.	veal loin, boned & rolled	1.8 kg

TUNA-ANCHOVY MAYONNAISE

1	egg	1
1	clove garlic, minced	1
3	anchovies	3
1½ tsp.	Dijon mustard	7 mL
1½ tsp.	lemon juice	7 mL
½ tsp.	red-wine vinegar	2 mL
1¾ cups	vegetable oil	425 mL
½ cup	olive oil	125 mL
1½ oz.	canned or cooked fresh tuna	40 g
¼ cup	gelatin from veal poaching liquid	50 mL

Place water, wine, peppercorns, celery, carrots, onion and veal bones in a heavy-bottomed pot that is large enough to hold the roast. Cover, and bring to a boil. Add veal, reduce heat to a simmer, and poach veal for 1½ to 2 hours, turning to ensure that veal cooks evenly. When the meat is cooked, cool and chill veal in cooking liquid overnight. Remove veal from cooking liquid. Cover veal, and return to refrigerator until ready to serve.

Put cooking liquid in a pot, bring to a boil, and cook until reduced to 2 cups (500 mL). Strain liquid into a bowl through a fine-mesh sieve. Cool and chill to form a gelatin; reserve to enrich mayonnaise.

To make mayonnaise, mix egg, garlic, anchovies, mustard, lemon juice and vinegar together with a hand blender. Gradually add vegetable oil. Drizzle in olive oil. Once mixture has thickened, blend in tuna. Thin slightly with the gelatin. Refrigerate mayonnaise until ready to serve.

Thinly slice veal, and serve with tuna-anchovy mayonnaise.

Serves 8

Roasted Garlic

OSSO BUCO

This traditional Italian dish is a flavorful treatment of an inexpensive cut of veal. Allow the meat to cook for several hours so that it will be completely tender and have a gelatinous texture. True connoisseurs scoop the marrow from the shanks and spread it on bread.

GREMOLATA

1 Tbsp.	chopped lemon zest	15 mL
3 Tbsp.	chopped fresh parsley	45 mL
2	cloves garlic, chopped	2
1 tsp.	freshly ground black pepper	5 mL

STEW

1½ cups	flour	375 mL
	Coarse salt & freshly ground black pepper	
2-3 lb.	veal shanks	1-1.5 kg
¼ cup	olive oil	50 mL
2	medium onions, sliced	2
3	cloves garlic, chopped	3
2 tsp.	dried basil	10 mL
1 tsp.	dried thyme	5 mL
1 cup	red wine	250 mL
1½ cups	canned whole tomatoes, crushed	375 mL
1 cup	veal stock (*see Basic Stock, page 46*)	250 mL
2	carrots, sliced	2
	Saffron risotto (*see "Risotto Milano-Style," page 42*)	

Combine gremolata ingredients, and set aside.

Place flour in a large bowl, and season with salt and pepper to taste. Dredge veal in flour mixture. Heat oil in a large heavy-bottomed pot over low heat, and brown veal on all sides. Remove veal from pan with a slotted spoon. Add onions, garlic, basil and thyme to the pan, and cook until onions are translucent. Add wine, tomatoes, stock and carrots. Return veal to pot, and cook for about 2 hours, until meat is tender and readily pulls away from the bone. Garnish with gremolata, and serve with risotto.

Serves 4

KALE NYAMA (Lamb With Chilies & Mint)

Chefs have dubbed this recipe "Call Me Mama," but the name of the African lamb dish actually means "angry hot meat," denoting the spices in the marinade. Serve with Citrus Chutney (recipe below), rice and sautéed or quick-fried okra. Lamb tenderloins are only two ounces (50 g) each, so don't be alarmed by the number you will use.

½ cup	chopped fresh mint	125 mL
4	fresh green chilies, finely chopped	4
½ tsp.	crushed dried chilies	2 mL
2	cloves garlic, finely minced	2
1 tsp.	cloves, coarsely ground	5 mL
½ tsp.	finely chopped fresh ginger	2 mL
18	lamb tenderloins	18
	Vegetable oil for frying	

In a shallow pan, combine mint, chilies, garlic, cloves and ginger. Marinate lamb in this mixture for 2 days in the refrigerator, stirring occasionally.

Lightly coat a large skillet with oil, and fry lamb over high heat for about 3 minutes per side, until medium rare.

Serves 6

CITRUS CHUTNEY

Serve this sassy chutney as an accompaniment to Kale Nyama (recipe above) or other lamb dishes. It will keep for up to one week in an airtight container in the refrigerator.

3	fresh tomatoes, diced	3
1	small onion, finely diced	1
2	oranges, thinly sliced	2
2	lemons, thinly sliced	2
1 Tbsp.	finely chopped ginger in syrup	15 mL
1 Tbsp.	brown sugar	15 mL
½ cup	golden raisins, coarsely chopped	125 mL
¼ cup	white vinegar	50 mL

Combine all ingredients in a large saucepan, and cook over medium heat for 15 minutes. Cool and serve.

Makes 5 cups (1.25 L)

LAMB TENDERLOINS
WITH FRESH MINT CHUTNEY

Marinated and then pan-fried, these lamb tenderloins take very little time to prepare.

½ cup	white wine	125 mL
¼ cup	white-wine vinegar	50 mL
2 cups	fresh mint leaves, chopped	500 mL
1	fresh chili, chopped	1
2	cloves garlic, minced	2
12	lamb tenderloins	12
	Vegetable oil for frying	

In a shallow pan, mix together wine, vinegar, mint, chili and garlic. Add lamb, and refrigerate for a minimum of 2 hours.

Lightly coat a heavy skillet with oil, and place over high heat. For medium rare, fry lamb for about 3 minutes on each side.

Serve with Mint Chutney (*recipe below*).

Serves 4

MINT CHUTNEY

This fresh mint chutney is unbelievably simple to prepare and is the perfect cool complement for the spicy taste of marinated, pan-fried lamb tenderloins. It is delicious with any curried dish. Vary by adding coriander leaves instead of mint.

4 cups	fresh mint leaves	1 L
1 cup	golden raisins	250 mL
½	small sweet onion	½
6	½-inch (1 cm) pieces candied ginger	6
1 Tbsp.	lemon juice	15 mL
	Coarse salt	

In a food processor, blend all ingredients to a paste, seasoning with salt to taste. Serve chilled or at room temperature. Store in the refrigerator.

Makes 2½ cups (625 mL)

Rack of Lamb
With Ethiopian
Red Lentil Salad

RACK OF LAMB WITH LENTIL SALAD

This recipe features a combination of perfectly matched flavors:
grilled lamb, spicy seasoned red lentils and a tart salad of cherry tomatoes.

4	racks of lamb, trimmed of fat or Frenched	4
	Coarse salt & freshly ground black pepper	
	Vegetable oil	
	Ethiopian Red Lentil Salad (*see page 84*)	
	Fresh baby greens	
	Chez Piggy House Dressing (*see page 71*)	
	Spiced Cherry Tomatoes (*see page 8ɔ*)	

Preheat oven to 450°F (230°C). Season lamb with salt and pepper to taste. Heat oil in a large skillet, and brown lamb on both sides. Place lamb in an ovenproof pan in the oven for 16 minutes for medium rare, 25 minutes for well done. Let stand for 3 minutes, then cut into individual chops.

To serve, mound lentils in the center of a platter. Top with greens dressed lightly with Chez Piggy House Dressing, and encircle with tomatoes. Arrange lamb chops around the outside.

Serves 4

SECO DE CARNERO (Peruvian Lamb Stew)

The tart citrus juice offsets the strong flavor of lamb to make this a surprisingly light-tasting stew. For a tangy variation, substitute two-thirds cup (150 mL) fresh orange juice and one-third cup (75 mL) fresh lime juice for the Seville orange juice.

1 cup	Seville orange juice	250 mL
4 lb.	cubed lamb	1.8 kg
1 cup	chopped fresh coriander leaves	250 mL
3	fresh chilies, seeded & chopped	3
8	cloves garlic	8
2	medium onions, diced	2
½ cup	olive oil	125 mL
	Coarse salt & freshly ground black pepper	
2 lb.	potatoes, peeled & sliced	1 kg
1 lb.	fresh or frozen green peas	500 g

Pour orange juice into a shallow pan. Add lamb, and marinate in refrigerator for 2 to 3 hours.

In a food processor, blend coriander, chilies and garlic. In a large skillet, sauté garlic mixture and onions in oil. Drain lamb, reserving the marinade, and add lamb to onion mixture. Cook over medium heat for 30 minutes. Season with salt and pepper to taste. Add marinade, and simmer for about 1½ hours, or until meat is tender.

Place potatoes in a large pot, cover with water, add a pinch of salt, and bring to a boil. Cook until tender, and drain. Mix potatoes with peas, and add to simmering stew immediately before serving.

Serves 6 to 8

MOUSSAKA

A good recipe for using up leftover cooked lamb, this Greek casserole has layers of tomato sauce, creamy béchamel, ground meat and seasoned eggplant. In Chez Piggy's early days, Zal made this in large quantities as a lunch special. It was a delicious main course but, to our surprise, was even more delicious the next day when used as a filling for an omelette.

TOMATO SAUCE

⅓ cup	olive oil	75 mL
2	medium onions, sliced	2
1	red bell pepper, sliced	1
1	green bell pepper, sliced	1
8	cloves garlic, minced	8
2	28 oz. (796 mL) cans whole tomatoes, undrained	2
½ cup	red wine	125 mL
1 Tbsp.	ground cumin	15 mL
	Coarse salt & freshly ground black pepper	

EGGPLANT

1	egg, beaten	1
1 ½ cups	milk	375 mL
3	eggplants, cut into ½-inch (1 cm) rounds	3
1 ½ cups	breadcrumbs	375 mL

LAMB

1 ½ lb.	ground lamb	750 g
3 Tbsp.	olive oil	45 mL
1	medium onion, minced	1
3	cloves garlic, minced	3
	Coarse salt & freshly ground black pepper	

BÉCHAMEL

4 Tbsp.	butter	50 mL
4 Tbsp.	flour	50 mL
4 cups	half-and-half	1 L
½ cup	white wine	125 mL
	Coarse salt & freshly ground black pepper	

To make tomato sauce, heat oil in a pot, and sauté onions, red and green peppers and garlic. Add tomatoes, wine, cumin and salt and pepper to taste. Simmer, uncovered, for 1 hour until thick. Set aside.

To prepare eggplant, preheat oven to 350°F (180°C). Beat egg together with milk. Dip eggplant slices into egg mixture, and coat with breadcrumbs. Bake on a greased cookie sheet for 30 minutes. Set aside.

To prepare lamb mixture, brown lamb in oil in a large skillet with onion and garlic. Season with salt and pepper to taste, and set aside.

To make béchamel, melt butter in a saucepan over medium heat, add flour, and cook, stirring, for 5 minutes. Add cream, wine and salt and pepper to taste, and heat, stirring constantly, until sauce thickens slightly. Set aside.

To assemble the moussaka, spread lamb mixture in the bottom of a square casserole, layer with tomato sauce, then eggplant slices, and top with béchamel. (If the pan is smaller and deep, you can do this layering twice.) Bake at 350°F (180°C) for 45 minutes, or until top is browned and crispy.

Serves 8 to 12

LAMB TAJINE (Moroccan Lamb Stew)

In Morocco, tajine describes either an earthenware pot with a conical lid or the stew you cook in it. Of the different tajines that we make at the restaurant, such as vegetable, chicken and fish, this particular version, with its warmed cinnamon and lemon aromas, is a special favorite. Serve over steamed couscous or rice.

4	cloves garlic, minced	4
1 Tbsp.	ground ginger	15 mL
1 tsp.	ground coriander	5 mL
1 tsp.	paprika	5 mL
1	½-inch (1 cm) stick cinnamon	1
½ tsp.	saffron	2 mL
¼ cup	lemon juice	50 mL
1¼ lb.	cubed lamb	625 g
1½ cups	lamb stock or water	375 mL
1	onion, chopped	1
½ cup	chopped fresh parsley or coriander leaves	125 mL
	Chopped rind from ½ preserved lemon	
	(see page 176)	
12	green colossal olives	12
	Coarse salt	

Mix together garlic, ginger, ground coriander, paprika, cinnamon, saffron and lemon juice in a shallow pan. Add lamb, and marinate for a minimum of 3 hours.

Remove lamb from marinade. Boil stock or water in a heavy-bottomed pot. Add lamb, cover, and cook for 1½ hours. Remove lamb with a slotted spoon, and continue simmering stock until it is reduced to the consistency of heavy cream. Add onion, parsley or coriander, preserved lemon and olives, and return lamb to pot. Cook over low heat for 30 minutes, until sauce clings to meat. Season with salt to taste.

Serves 4

LAMB TAJINE KAMMAMA

*Subtly sweet caramelized onions and tomatoes create the background flavors
for this Moroccan dish. Serve over steamed couscous.*

1	onion, grated	1
1 Tbsp.	ground ginger	15 mL
2	cloves garlic, minced	2
1 tsp.	saffron	5 mL
2 Tbsp.	olive oil	25 mL
3 lb.	cubed lamb	1.5 kg
3 cups	lamb or chicken stock (*see Basic Stock, page 46*)	750 mL
½ tsp.	coarse salt	2 mL
6	tomatoes, thickly sliced	6
¼ cup	sugar	50 mL
2 tsp.	cinnamon	10 mL
2	onions, thickly sliced	2

Mix grated onion, ginger, garlic, saffron and oil in a large bowl. Add lamb,
and marinate for a minimum of 2 hours. In a large pot, bring stock to a boil,
add lamb and salt. Simmer, uncovered, for 1½ hours.

In the meantime, preheat oven to 350°F (180°C). Place tomatoes in a roasting pan, sprinkle with sugar and cinnamon, and layer with sliced onions. Bake,
uncovered, for 1 hour, ladling stock from simmering lamb over vegetables to
keep them moist.

After 1½ hours, place lamb in a large roasting pan, and cover with tomato-
onion mixture. Bake, uncovered, at 350°F (180°C) for 30 minutes.

Serves 8

BOBOTIE (South African Ground Lamb Curry)

*Bobotie is somewhat complicated to prepare, but the result is a delectable layered casserole
of seasoned ground lamb topped with custard lightly flavored with nutmeg.
It is also a favorite among Chez Piggy cooks as a cold leftover.*

2 oz.	unsliced crusty white bread, crust removed	50 g
2¼ cups	milk	550 mL
2 lb.	ground lamb	1 kg
2	medium onions, sliced	2
3 Tbsp.	butter	45 mL
1	bay leaf	1
4 Tbsp.	brown sugar	50 mL
3 Tbsp.	curry powder	45 mL
	Coarse salt & freshly ground black pepper	
½ cup	sliced almonds	125 mL
2 Tbsp.	lemon juice	25 mL
1	apple, diced	1
½ cup	sultana raisins	125 mL
2	eggs	2
¾ tsp.	ground nutmeg	4 mL

GARNISH

1	medium onion, sliced	1
½ cup	sultana raisins	125 mL
½ cup	sliced almonds	125 mL
2 Tbsp.	butter	25 mL

Preheat oven to 375°F (190°C). Soak bread in 1¼ cups (300 mL) milk until
soft. Squeeze out milk, and reserve. Set bread aside.

In a large skillet, brown lamb and onions in butter over medium heat. Add
bay leaf, sugar and curry powder, and season with salt and pepper to taste.
Continue to cook for 15 minutes. Remove from heat, and let cool. In a large
bowl, use your hands to mix lamb mixture together with softened bread,
almonds, lemon juice, apple and raisins. Press firmly into a casserole dish.

Lightly beat eggs and nutmeg together with the reserved bread milk, adding
as much of the remaining 1 cup (250 mL) milk as necessary to make 2 cups
(500 mL) liquid. Pour over lamb mixture in casserole. Bake for 1 hour.

To make garnish, fry onion, raisins and almonds in butter until lightly
browned. Sprinkle on top of baked casserole.

Serves 6

OBGUSHT
(Azerbaijani Lamb Shanks With Mashed Chickpeas)

The strong flavor of lamb is intensified in the shank, which has a gelatinous texture.
When cooked to fall-off-the-bone tender, lamb shanks make a wonderfully rich stewed dish.
Serve with lots of pita bread to mop up the savory juices.

1 tsp.	turmeric	5 mL
3	cloves garlic, chopped	3
5 Tbsp.	vegetable oil	45 mL + 25 mL
4	lamb shanks	4
½ cup	dried navy beans, sorted & rinsed	125 mL
	Coarse salt	
2	medium potatoes, peeled & diced	2
2½ cups	lamb stock (*see Basic Stock, page 46*)	625 mL
1	28 oz. (796 mL) can whole tomatoes, undrained	1
1	carrot, peeled & diced	1
2	medium onions, diced	2
½ tsp.	cinnamon	2 mL
¼ tsp.	ground fenugreek	1 mL
1 tsp.	allspice	5 mL
	Coarse salt & freshly ground black pepper	
1	19 oz. (540 mL) can chickpeas, drained (reserve 1 cup/250 mL liquid)	1
¾ cup	crumbled feta cheese	175 mL

In a large bowl, mix together turmeric, garlic and 3 tablespoons (45 mL) oil.
Add lamb shanks, cover, and marinate in the refrigerator overnight.

Place beans in a pot, cover with water, and soak for 1½ hours. Drain beans,
cover with fresh water, and bring to a boil. Add a dash of salt, and simmer
for 1½ hours, skimming off foam as beans cook. Drain, and set aside.

Blanch potatoes in boiling salted water, drain, and set aside.

Brown lamb in a deep heavy-bottomed pot. Add stock and tomatoes, and
bring to a boil. Reduce heat, and simmer for at least 2 hours, or until meat is
tender enough to fall off the bone.

When lamb is nearly ready, sauté carrot and onions with cinnamon,
fenugreek and allspice in remaining 2 tablespoons (25 mL) oil. Stir in beans
and potatoes. Season with salt and pepper to taste. Add to lamb pot, and
heat through.

In a saucepan, heat chickpeas with reserved liquid and cheese. Purée in
a food processor. Make a mound of the warm chickpea mash on individual
plates, and spoon lamb-and-bean ragout over top.

Serves 4

SUSAN NEWBURY'S
TUNISIAN LAMB PIE

Cumin, citrus zest and mint give the filling of lamb chunks, carrots and white beans
a fresh, exotic flavor, which is complemented by the cinnamon in the pie crust.
At the restaurant, Sue painstakingly carves the shapes of grapes, vines and leaves
out of the leftover pastry to decorate the top of the pie. The result is spectacular.

CRUST

1	egg, unbeaten	1
	Sour cream	
2½ cups	flour	625 mL
¼ tsp.	coarse salt	1 mL
¼ tsp.	cinnamon	1 mL
½ lb.	lard or shortening	250 g

Before you start, chill all ingredients thoroughly.

Put egg in a measuring cup, and add enough sour cream to measure ½ cup (125 mL). Set aside.

Mix flour, salt and cinnamon in a large bowl. Cut in lard or shortening with knives or a pastry cutter to produce pea-size lumps. Add egg and sour cream, and blend together. Chill for 15 minutes. Roll out into two 9-inch (23 cm) crusts.

LAMB FILLING

1 cup	dried white beans, sorted & rinsed	250 mL
1 tsp.	coarse salt	5 mL
¼ cup	olive oil	50 mL
2 lb.	cubed lamb	1 kg
3	small onions, diced	3
3	cloves garlic, chopped	3
2 Tbsp.	ground cumin	25 mL
¼ tsp.	freshly ground black pepper	1 mL
⅛ tsp.	crushed dried chilies	0.5 mL
	Juice of 3 oranges	
	Zest of 1 orange	
3	large carrots, cut into rounds	3
¼ cup	chopped fresh mint	50 mL
1	egg yolk	1
3 Tbsp.	water	45 mL

Place beans in a large pot, cover with cold water, and soak overnight. Drain, and cover with fresh water. Add salt, and bring to a boil. Reduce heat, and simmer, uncovered, for 1 hour, or until beans are tender. Drain, and set aside.

In a heavy pan, heat oil over medium heat, and brown lamb. Remove lamb with a slotted spoon, and set aside.

Add onions, garlic, cumin, pepper and chilies to the pan, and sauté over low heat for 15 minutes. Add orange juice and orange zest, return lamb to the pan, and cook for 30 minutes. Add carrots and beans, and cook over medium heat for 15 minutes. Stir in mint just before filling pie shell.

Preheat oven to 425°F (220°C). Beat egg yolk and water together to make an egg wash. Place the lower crust in a pie plate, and brush with egg wash. Spoon in lamb filling, and cover with top crust. Brush top of pie with egg wash. Bake for 10 minutes. Reduce heat to 350°F (180°C), and bake for 40 minutes. Serve hot.

Serves 6 to 8

BRAISED LAMB SHANKS

Lamb shanks braised in stock with vegetables is a perfect winter dish.

	Olive oil for frying	
6	lamb shanks	6
3	medium carrots, peeled & cut into	3
	2-inch (5 cm) pieces	
2	medium onions, cut into thick slices	2
2	stalks celery, cut into 2-inch (5 cm) pieces	2
4	cloves garlic	4
1 tsp.	dried thyme or rosemary or a few fresh sprigs	5 mL
2	bay leaves	2
3 cups	chicken stock (*see Basic Stock, page 46*)	750 mL
2 cups	canned tomatoes, squeezed to break up	500 mL
2 cups	dry red wine	500 mL

Preheat oven to 350°F (180°C). Over medium-high heat, warm oil in a large sauté pan. Add lamb shanks, and sauté until browned on all sides. Remove shanks, and set aside.

Add carrots, onions, celery, garlic, thyme or rosemary and bay leaves to the pan, and sauté until vegetables are slightly softened.

Place shanks, vegetables, stock, tomatoes and wine in a large roasting pan. Place pan over two burners on top of the stove, and bring to a boil. Cover pan with foil, transfer to the oven, and braise shanks for 1½ hours. Turn each shank, and continue braising until meat is fall-off-the-bone tender. Remove shanks with a slotted spoon, and arrange on a platter. Reduce braising liquid by half, and drizzle some over shanks.

Serves 6

LAMB WITH CORN-CRUSTED ARTICHOKES, BLACK-OLIVE JUS & ROUILLE

*With its subtle seasonings and whole presentation, this dish appeals to
mainstream lamb lovers. The artichokes complement the lamb flavors.
Ask your butcher to French the lamb.*

ROUILLE

½ tsp.	saffron	2 mL
3	cloves garlic	3
1	fresh cayenne	1
2 Tbsp.	lemon juice	25 mL
1	egg plus 2 yolks	1
1½ cups	vegetable oil	375 mL
1 cup	olive oil	250 mL
1 Tbsp.	tomato paste	15 mL
¼	pimiento or roasted red bell pepper	¼

Grind saffron, garlic, cayenne and lemon juice together with a mortar and
pestle, and let stand for 20 minutes. Place egg, egg yolks and saffron-garlic
mixture in a blender. Gradually pour in oils, and blend until rouille is thick.
Continue to blend, adding tomato paste and pimiento or roasted pepper. Wrap
and refrigerate. The rouille will keep for up to 2 weeks in the refrigerator.

BLACK-OLIVE JUS

6 cups	brown stock (*see page 47*)	1.5 L
8	kalamata olives, pitted & chopped	8

Heat stock in a saucepan, and reduce by half. Add olives. Set aside.

ARTICHOKES

2	eggs, lightly beaten	2
1½ cups	milk	375 mL
1½ cups	flour	375 mL
	Pinch freshly ground black pepper	
10	canned artichoke hearts, cut into quarters	10
2 cups	cornmeal	500 mL
	Vegetable oil for deep-frying	

Beat eggs and milk together in a large bowl. In another bowl, mix flour with
pepper. Dredge artichokes in seasoned flour, dip in egg mixture, and roll in
cornmeal. Heat oil in a skillet, and deep-fry artichokes for 1 minute or until
golden brown. Drain on paper towels. The artichokes can be precooked and
kept warm in the oven.

LAMB

4	racks of lamb trimmed of fat or Frenched	4
	Coarse salt & freshly ground black pepper	
	Vegetable oil	

Preheat oven to 450°F (230°C). Season lamb with salt and pepper. Heat oil in a large skillet, and brown lamb on both sides. Finish cooking by placing lamb in an ovenproof pan in the oven and cooking for 16 minutes for medium rare, 25 minutes for well done. Let stand for 3 minutes, then cut into individual chops. Serve with black-olive jus and corn-crusted artichokes drizzled with rouille.

Serves 4 to 6

PORK SATAY (Balinese Marinated Skewered Pork)

Lightly spiced cubes of pork shoulder or butt, flavored with the sweet richness of coconut milk, make a wonderful appetizer or main course. Serve over rice with spicy peanut sauce. If you prefer, you can substitute cubed breast of chicken to make chicken satay.

12	bamboo skewers	12
½ cup	coconut milk	125 mL
¼ cup	soy sauce	50 mL
1	clove garlic, minced	1
2 tsp.	finely chopped fresh ginger	10 mL
1 tsp.	coriander seed, crushed	5 mL
1 tsp.	ground white pepper	5 mL
½ tsp.	turmeric	2 mL
½ tsp.	coarse salt	2 mL
3 lb.	pork shoulder, cubed	1.5 kg

Soak skewers in water for 30 minutes to make them flame-resistant.

Mix together coconut milk, soy sauce, garlic, ginger, coriander, pepper, turmeric and salt in a shallow pan. Add pork, and marinate for a minimum of 3 hours.

Preheat oven to 400°F (200°C). Skewer meat, and bake for 30 minutes, or grill on a barbecue until done.

Serves 6 to 8

LY'S GRILLED FIRE RIBS

Dry and spicy, thanks to the exotic taste of the oyster sauce, these ribs are reminiscent of Asian cuisine. We use baby back ribs and allow the racks to cook evenly.

¹/₄ cup	lemon juice	50 mL
1 cup	water	250 mL
4 lb.	pork spareribs	1.8 kg
1 cup	ketchup	250 mL
¹/₄ cup	beer	50 mL
¹/₄ cup	molasses	50 mL
2 Tbsp.	oyster sauce	25 mL
1 Tbsp.	Worcestershire sauce	15 mL
¹/₄ cup	brown sugar	50 mL
2 Tbsp.	chopped fresh ginger	25 mL
2 Tbsp.	chopped garlic	25 mL
2 Tbsp.	chopped fresh chilies	25 mL

Preheat oven to 300°F (150°C). Mix together lemon juice and water, and set aside. Arrange ribs in a broiling pan, and bake, uncovered, for 2 hours, brushing them every 30 minutes with the lemon-and-water mixture. In the meantime, mix remaining ingredients together in a saucepan, and simmer for 8 minutes. Brush hot cooked ribs with sauce. Return ribs to oven for 20 minutes.
Serves 4

Ly's Grilled Fire Ribs
With Green Cabbage Salad

JAMAICAN JERK PORK

This spicy, dry barbecued pork is infused with the flavors of allspice, cinnamon and nutmeg.

1 cup	tamarind water (see "Tips for Jerks," right)	250 mL
24	finger-hot chilies	24
1 cup	chopped shallots	250 mL
1 cup	chopped scallions	250 mL
¼ cup	peanut oil	50 mL
1 Tbsp.	lime juice	15 mL
1 Tbsp.	vinegar	15 mL
1 Tbsp.	allspice	15 mL
1 tsp.	coarse salt	5 mL
1 tsp.	cinnamon	5 mL
1 tsp.	freshly ground black pepper	5 mL
½ tsp.	ground nutmeg	2 mL
3 lb.	pork butt, cubed & skewered	1.5 kg

Combine all ingredients, except pork, in a blender, and process until mixed. Arrange pork in a shallow pan, and cover with marinade. Cover, and marinate in the refrigerator overnight.

The next day, barbecue pork for 10 to 15 minutes per side until done in the center but still juicy. Serve with Fiesta Chutney (*recipe below*).

Serves 6 to 8

TIPS FOR JERKS

For jerk stews, a fatty cut such as the butt is best. If you are a lean-is-for-me person, pork tenderloin will do, but add a bit more oil, or the finished result will be dry.

TAMARIND WATER
In a saucepan over low to medium heat, soften 2 ounces (50 g) tamarind pulp in 4 cups (1 L) water for about 20 minutes. When seeds and pulp are softened and volume of liquid is reduced by half, strain, pushing as much pulp as possible through the sieve. Reserve liquid.

FIESTA CHUTNEY

This sweet-tart chunky chutney tastes great with roast pork or barbecued chops.

3	green apples, unpeeled, cored & diced	3
½ cup	golden raisins	125 mL
1	small red onion, diced	1
1	finger-hot chili, chopped	1
1 tsp.	chopped garlic	5 mL
1 Tbsp.	chopped candied ginger	15 mL
½ tsp.	black mustard seed or poppy seed	2 mL
¾ cup	brown sugar	175 mL
¾ cup	tequila	175 mL
½ cup	toasted sunflower seed	125 mL
2	limes, peeled & cut into wedges	2
2	oranges, peeled & cut into wedges	2

In a heavy saucepan, combine all ingredients, except lime and orange wedges, and bring to a boil. Reduce heat, and simmer for 1 hour. While the chutney is still hot, add lime and orange wedges. Cool, cover, and store in the refrigerator.

Makes 4 cups (1 L)

PORK TENDERLOIN WITH PINEAPPLE GREEN-PEPPERCORN SAUCE

Easy to prepare, this recipe for tenderloins is a tart and sweet combination of pineapple and tender pork.

1 ½ cups	white wine	375 mL
¼ cup	white-wine vinegar	50 mL
4	cloves garlic, chopped	4
3	pork tenderloins	3
2 Tbsp.	peanut oil	25 mL
1	medium onion, coarsely chopped	1
1	pineapple, peeled, cored & cut into chunks	1
3 Tbsp.	canned green peppercorns	45 mL
2 cups	pineapple juice	500 mL
	Coarse salt & freshly ground black pepper	

Mix together ½ cup (125 mL) wine, vinegar and garlic in a shallow pan. Add tenderloins, cover, and marinate for 6 to 8 hours or overnight.

In a large saucepan, heat oil, and sauté onion and pineapple until onion is translucent. Add peppercorns, pineapple juice and remaining 1 cup (250 mL) wine, and season with salt and pepper to taste. Simmer for 20 minutes to reduce liquid by one-quarter. While sauce is still warm, use a hand blender to purée. Set aside.

Preheat oven to 350°F (180°C). Turn tails under, and bake tenderloins in marinade for 25 to 30 minutes. Slice, and serve topped with sauce.

Serves 6

PORK PICATTA

This simple dish is essentially scaloppine with pork.
Serve it with garlic-flavored mashed potatoes.

1 cup	flour	250 mL
½ tsp.	coarse salt	2 mL
⅛ tsp.	freshly ground black pepper	0.5 mL
1	egg	1
1 cup	milk	250 mL
1 cup	breadcrumbs	250 mL
1 Tbsp.	chopped lemon zest	15 mL
1 Tbsp.	chopped fresh sage	15 mL
8	pork cutlets (each 4 oz./125 g)	8
2 Tbsp.	butter	25 mL
2 Tbsp.	olive oil	25 mL
2	cloves garlic, sliced	2
	Lemon juice	
½ cup	chopped fresh parsley for garnish	125 mL
2	lemons, cut into wedges	2

In a large bowl, mix flour with salt and pepper. In a separate bowl, mix egg with milk. In a third bowl, mix breadcrumbs with lemon zest and sage.

Pound cutlets until ¼ inch (6 mm) thick, then coat with flour mixture, dip into egg mixture, and coat with breadcrumbs.

Heat butter, oil and garlic in a skillet over medium heat, being careful not to brown garlic. Remove garlic, add cutlets, and cook until brown on both sides.

Remove cutlets to a serving platter, and sprinkle with lemon juice. Garnish with parsley, and serve with lemon wedges.

Serves 4 to 6

MAIALE ALLA TUSCANA (Tuscan-Style Pork)

*The taste of roast pork is enhanced by the aromatic mixture of allspice,
pepper and garlic seasoning. The centerpiece of this recipe, however,
is the navy beans, which have a rich olive-oil-and-garlic flavor.*

13	cloves garlic, minced	13
²/₃ cup + ¼ cup	olive oil	150 mL + 50 mL
2 Tbsp.	black peppercorns, crushed	25 mL
1 Tbsp.	allspice berries, crushed	15 mL
½ tsp.	coarse salt	2 mL
3 lb.	rolled pork loin roast (with fat on top)	1.5 kg
1¼ cups	dried navy beans, sorted & rinsed	300 mL
1	bay leaf	1
1	ham bone or chunk of pork fat	1
	Coarse salt & freshly ground black pepper	
	Chopped fresh Italian parsley for garnish	

Mix together one-quarter of the garlic, ⅓ cup (75 mL) oil, peppercorns, allspice and salt. Rub marinade over pork, and let stand overnight.

Place beans in a large saucepan, cover with water, and soak overnight.

The next day, roast pork at 375°F (190°C) for 1 to 1½ hours, or until juices run clear.

In the meantime, drain beans, and cover with fresh salted water. Add bay leaf, ham bone or pork fat and ¼ cup (50 mL) oil. Simmer beans until nearly done. Remove and discard bay leaf and ham bone or pork fat, drain beans, and set aside. In a large saucepan, heat remaining ⅓ cup (75 mL) oil with remaining garlic. Add beans, and heat through. Season with salt and pepper to taste. Place pork on a serving platter, and surround with beans. Garnish with parsley.

Serves 6 to 8

CHEZ PIGGY CASSOULET

A hearty winter dish, cassoulet is a way of making the most of preserved meats. Cooks adapt their interpretation of the basic recipe to the ingredients available in their region, which can vary from pork chops to smoked pork or duck sausages. Cassoulet is a time-consuming, somewhat complicated dish that you will need to start a day in advance. The consolation: It improves with age, so you can make lots.

3 cups	dried white beans, sorted & rinsed	750 mL
¼ lb.	salt pork	125 g
1	whole head garlic	1
¼ cup	duck fat from confit	50 mL
1½ lb.	pork shoulder, trimmed & cut into strips	750 g
4	onions, sliced	4
4	carrots, sliced	4
5-6	cloves garlic, chopped	5-6
1 Tbsp.	tomato paste	15 mL
3 cups	chicken stock (*see Basic Stock, page 46*)	750 mL
½ cup	chopped fresh parsley	125 mL
4 oz.	prosciutto, julienned	125 g
1 tsp.	dried thyme	5 mL
1	bay leaf	1
4	Toulouse sausages	4
2	duck legs confit (*see page 184*)	2
3	smoked duck sausages	3
1½ cups	breadcrumbs	375 mL

Soak beans in cold water for at least 2 hours, then drain. Cover with fresh water, and cook with salt pork and head of garlic until beans are nearly done. Remove salt pork, and reserve. Drain beans, and discard garlic. Set aside.

Heat duck fat in a large pot. Add pork shoulder, and fry until brown. Add onions, carrots, chopped garlic and tomato paste, and sauté over medium-low heat for 15 to 20 minutes to brown vegetables and cook tomato paste. Stir in stock, parsley, prosciutto, thyme and bay leaf. Simmer for 25 to 30 minutes, then stir in beans.

Trim fat from reserved salt pork, and mince in a food processor. Stir into bean mixture. Set aside.

Preheat oven to 350°F (180°C). In a medium-size saucepan, bring a little water to a boil, and steam Toulouse sausages until they are cooked, then slice. Strip meat from duck legs, and slice. Slice duck sausages. In a casserole dish, layer Toulouse sausages, duck sausages, duck meat and bean mixture, adding any liquid. Top with breadcrumbs, and bake for 1 to 1½ hours. Serve with a fresh green salad topped with Chez Piggy House Dressing (*see page 71*).

Serves 8 to 10

PORK RUBDOWN

The garlic, allspice berries, peppercorns and salt mixture featured in Maiale alla Tuscana makes a great marinade for pork chops and spareribs too. Rub the meat with a little olive oil and the garlic mixture. Fry pork chops in a generous amount of olive oil, turning the meat only once. For ribs, bake at 375°F (190°C) for 1 hour. Then squeeze fresh lime juice over them, and serve.

MEE KROB (Deep-Fried Crispy Rice Noodles)

*This Thai dish is unusual for the simple reason that it is a meal unto itself.
The meat can be served hot or cold over rice noodles (sen mee),
which achieve a puffed texture when deep-fried.*

1 lb.	rice noodles	500 g
	Vegetable oil for deep-frying	
¼ cup	peanut oil	50 mL
4	scallions, chopped	4
3	cloves garlic, minced	3
6 oz.	pork tenderloin, julienned	175 g
1	boneless, skinless chicken breast, julienned	1
4 oz.	medium shrimp, peeled	125 g
1	tofu cake, sliced	1
1 cup	white bean sprouts	250 mL
2 Tbsp.	sugar	25 mL
4 Tbsp.	rice-wine vinegar	50 mL
4 Tbsp.	fish sauce	50 mL
1 Tbsp.	lime juice	15 mL
1 Tbsp.	orange zest	15 mL
5	eggs, lightly beaten	5
	Chopped fresh coriander leaves for garnish	

Deep-fry noodles in batches in hot vegetable oil, and set aside on paper towels to drain.

Heat peanut oil in a wok, and add scallions and garlic. Fry until soft. Add pork, chicken, shrimp, tofu and bean sprouts, and stir-fry until meat is cooked. Add sugar, vinegar, fish sauce, lime juice and orange zest, and mix well. Stir in eggs, and cook until set.

Arrange noodles on a serving platter, and spoon meat mixture on top. Garnish with coriander.

Serves 4

10ᵀᴴ ANNIVERSARY CHILI

Vicki Newbury developed this chili recipe for our 10th anniversary celebration in February 1989, part of the restaurant's all-day complimentary chili-and-champagne party. While the recipe contains many familiar chili ingredients, we think that the added depth of flavor comes from the combination of cocoa and cumin. The addition of ground pork and cubed beef gives it a hearty texture. Be sure to remove the cinnamon stick before you store the chili, because it will continue to release its flavor.

½ cup	dried black beans, sorted & rinsed	125 mL
½ cup	dried Mexican red or pinto beans	125 mL
½ cup	olive oil	125 mL
2	onions, diced	2
1	green bell pepper, diced	1
½	stalk celery, diced	½
5	cloves garlic, minced	5
6	fresh chilies, chopped	6
½ lb.	ground beef	250 g
½ lb.	ground pork	250 g
1 lb.	cubed beef	500 g
2 Tbsp.	chili powder	25 mL
1 Tbsp.	cumin seed, ground	15 mL
1	½-inch (1 cm) stick cinnamon	1
2	28 oz. (796 mL) cans tomatoes	2
1	12 oz. (341 mL) bottle of beer	1
2 tsp.	cocoa powder	10 mL
2 cups	finely chopped onions for garnish	500 mL
2 cups	grated Cheddar cheese for garnish	500 mL

The night before you plan to prepare the chili, put black beans and red or pinto beans in separate bowls, and cover with water. The next day, drain beans, place in separate saucepans, and cover with fresh salted water. Bring to a boil, reduce heat, and cook until tender. Drain and rinse. Set aside.

Heat oil in a large heavy-bottomed pot over medium heat, and sauté onions, green pepper, celery, garlic and chilies. Add meats, and cook until brown. Stir in chili powder, cumin, cinnamon, tomatoes, beer and cocoa. Add beans. Simmer for 1 to 2 hours, until thickened. Remove cinnamon stick. Serve in bowls topped with chopped onions and cheese.

Serves 8

SUSAN NEWBURY'S PORK TOURTIÈRE

This tourtière is Susan's Christmas special at the bakery. The potato pastry is a Chez Piggy favorite for savory pies. We serve the hot tourtière with homemade applesauce.

POTATO PASTRY

1½ cups	flour	375 mL
1 tsp.	baking powder	5 mL
½ tsp.	coarse salt	2 mL
½ cup	chilled butter, cubed	125 mL
1 cup	cold mashed potatoes	250 mL
3-4 Tbsp.	milk	45-50 mL

With a pastry cutter, blend flour, baking powder, salt and butter into pea-size lumps. Using your hands, mix in potatoes and milk. Chill for 30 minutes. Roll into two 9-inch (23 cm) pastry circles.

TOURTIÈRE

1½ lb.	lean ground pork	750 g
2	small onions, diced	2
1	stalk celery, diced	1
2	cloves garlic, minced	2
1 Tbsp.	olive oil	15 mL
1	apple, peeled & diced	1
1 cup	sliced mushrooms	250 mL
1 Tbsp.	clarified butter	15 mL
1 cup	mashed potatoes	250 mL
2 tsp.	white-wine vinegar	10 mL
1 tsp.	ground nutmeg	5 mL
½ tsp.	ground cloves	2 mL
½ tsp.	cinnamon	2 mL
1 tsp.	freshly ground black pepper	5 mL
1 tsp.	coarse salt	5 mL
1	egg yolk	1
¼ cup	cold water	50 mL

Fry pork, onions, celery and garlic in oil until meat is brown. Stir in apple, and fry until soft. Remove ingredients from pan, and set aside in a large bowl.

In the same pan, sauté mushrooms in butter until they are brown and liquid has evaporated. Stir mushrooms, potatoes, vinegar, nutmeg, cloves, cinnamon, pepper and salt into pork mixture, and let cool.

Mix egg yolk and water together to make egg wash, and set aside.

Preheat oven to 425°F (220°C). Place one pastry circle in the bottom of a 9-inch (23 cm) pie plate. Lightly press pork mixture into bottom crust, and cover with second crust. Brush top with egg wash, and cut vent holes with a sharp knife. Bake for 10 minutes, then reduce temperature to 350°F (180°C), and bake for 45 minutes. Serve hot or cold.

Serves 8 to 10

CHANCHO ADOBADO

This South American pork stew is infused with the delectable taste
of sweet potato. As the citrus juices are cooked together
with the meat, their tart flavor mellows.

8	cloves garlic, chopped	8
2	fresh chilies, seeds removed, chopped	2
2 Tbsp.	annatto, ground	25 mL
4 tsp.	cumin seed, ground	20 mL
3 lb.	cubed pork	1.5 kg
5 Tbsp.	vegetable oil	65 mL
2	onions, sliced	2
1¼ cups	orange juice	300 mL
	Juice of 6 limes	
2	medium sweet potatoes, cubed	2
	Coarse salt & freshly ground black pepper	
	Chopped fresh coriander leaves for garnish	

Mix garlic, chilies, annatto and cumin. Dredge pork in these seasonings, cover, and marinate in refrigerator overnight.

Heat oil in a skillet, and sauté onions until translucent and soft. Add pork, and brown. Pour in orange and lime juices, and simmer over medium heat for 1½ to 2 hours, or until meat is tender. Add sweet potatoes, season with salt and pepper to taste, and simmer for 20 minutes, or until sweet potatoes are tender. Serve stew garnished with lots of coriander.

Serves 4

BEWARE THE BERBERE

Niter kebbeh imparts a subtle exotic taste and color to any simple dish and can be used as a substitute for oil to fry meats or cook vegetables. In addition to flavoring Doro Wat, berbere can be used to give life to hamburgers, steak tartare or stews, but it is fairly potent, so use sparingly.

DORO WAT
(Ethiopian Chicken Stew With Spiced Split Peas)

Known for its combination of strong, aromatic spices, Ethiopian cuisine emphasizes paprika and cardamom. This thick, spicy chicken stew, for instance, has a brick-red gravy heavily seasoned with paprika. There are a few basic steps you must take before you can make the main course. Prepare the niter kebbeh (spiced butter) and berbere (spice mixture) first. The cooking process for the spiced split peas can take up to two hours, so allow yourself some time to prepare this dish.

NITER KEBBEH

1 lb.	unsalted butter	500 g
½	onion, coarsely chopped	½
2	cloves garlic	2
2 tsp.	coarsely chopped fresh ginger	10 mL
1 tsp.	turmeric	5 mL
1	cardamom pod	1
	Sliver of cinnamon stick	
1	clove	1
	Pinch freshly grated nutmeg	

In a skillet, heat butter over medium heat until it bubbles. Add remaining ingredients, and simmer, uncovered, until butter fat separates. Do not allow solids to burn. Skim butter fat off top, and chill. Discard milk solids and spices.
Makes 1¼ cups (300 mL) oil

BERBERE

½ tsp.	ground ginger	2 mL
¼ tsp.	ground cardamom	1 mL
¼ tsp.	ground coriander	1 mL
½ tsp.	ground fenugreek	2 mL
¼ tsp.	freshly grated nutmeg	1 mL
	Pinch ground cloves	
	Pinch cinnamon	
	Pinch allspice	
2 Tbsp.	grated onion	25 mL
	Vegetable oil	
1 Tbsp.	cayenne pepper	15 mL
1 cup	paprika	250 mL
2 Tbsp.	dry red wine	25 mL
¾ cup	water	175 mL

In a dry cast-iron frying pan, lightly toast ginger, cardamom, coriander, fenugreek, nutmeg, cloves, cinnamon and allspice until their fragrance is released. Stir in onion, and moisten with oil. Continue to cook for 10 minutes. Stir in cayenne and paprika. Thin mixture with wine and water. Cook over extremely low heat, stirring constantly, until mixture forms a thick paste. Cool, and refrigerate in a jar.
Makes 1 cup (250 mL)

SPICED SPLIT PEAS

¼ cup	niter kebbeh	50 mL
1	onion, finely diced	1
4	cloves garlic, minced	4
1	fresh chili, chopped	1
1	2-inch (5 cm) piece fresh ginger, chopped	1
1 tsp.	ground mace	5 mL
1 tsp.	ground fenugreek	5 mL
½ tsp.	turmeric	2 mL
1 Tbsp.	ground cardamom	15 mL
2 cups	dried yellow split peas, sorted	500 mL
3-4 cups	water	750 mL-1 L
	Coarse salt	

Heat niter kebbeh in a skillet over low heat. Add onion, garlic, chili, ginger and spices, and cook until onion is soft. Stir in peas. Increase heat to medium, and add 3 cups (750 mL) water. Cover, and cook until peas disintegrate to the consistency of mashed potatoes. Stir frequently to prevent sticking, and add up to 1 cup (250 mL) more water as needed. Season with salt to taste.

STEW

2	4 lb. (1.8 kg) roasting chickens, cut into pieces, with breasts deboned	2
⅓ cup	lemon juice	75 mL
2 tsp.	coarse salt	10 mL
¾ cup	niter kebbeh	175 mL
2	onions, finely diced	2
2	finger-hot chilies, minced	2
3	cloves garlic, minced	3
1	2-inch (5 cm) piece fresh ginger, minced	1
1 tsp.	fenugreek, ground	5 mL
2 tsp.	ground cardamom	10 mL
½ tsp.	ground nutmeg	2 mL
¼ cup	berbere	50 mL
2 Tbsp.	paprika	25 mL
1 cup	red wine	250 mL
½ cup	chicken stock (*see Basic Stock, page 46*)	125 mL
6	hard-cooked eggs, peeled & left whole	6

Place chicken pieces in a shallow pan, and coat with lemon juice and salt. Marinate for 30 minutes at room temperature.

Melt niter kebbeh in a large skillet over medium heat, and cook onions, chilies, garlic, ginger, fenugreek, cardamom and nutmeg until onions are soft. Add berbere, paprika, wine and stock, and heat for 5 minutes to thicken. Add chicken pieces to skillet, and simmer, covered, for 20 minutes. Add eggs, and simmer, uncovered, for 20 minutes, or until chicken is cooked.

To serve, remove eggs and cut into wedges. Spoon chicken and sauce over spiced split peas, and garnish with eggs.

Serves 6 to 8

POLLO VERDE ALMENDRADO
(Green Chicken With Almonds)

An unusual sauce of puréed romaine lettuce and almonds dresses this Mexican chicken dish.

½ cup	olive oil	125 mL
2	medium onions, grated	2
6	fresh chilies, chopped	6
4	cloves garlic, minced	4
1 cup	ground blanched almonds	250 mL
1	head Romaine lettuce, coarsely chopped	1
½ cup	coarsely chopped fresh coriander leaves	125 mL
⅓ cup	coarsely chopped fresh parsley	75 mL
1 Tbsp.	ground coriander	15 mL
2	whole chickens, cut into pieces, with breasts deboned	2
2 cups	chicken stock (*see Basic Stock, page 46*)	500 mL
	Coarse salt	

Heat oil in a large skillet, and sauté onions, chilies and garlic until onions are soft. Mix ½ cup (125 mL) almonds into onion mixture.

In a food processor, purée lettuce, and mix with fresh coriander, parsley and ground coriander. Add one-third lettuce mixture to onion mixture, and heat through.

Preheat oven to 375°F (190°C). Place chicken in a baking pan, and coat with onion mixture. Bake for 1 hour. Remove chicken to a serving platter. Add stock and remaining two-thirds lettuce mixture to baking dish. Cook on top of stove for 10 minutes. Thicken with remaining ½ cup (125 mL) almonds, and season with salt to taste.

Serves 6

CHICKEN MOLE

Mole has many variations. While commercially prepared mole is available in grocery stores, no premixed brand can compare to the flavor of homemade. You can adjust the individual flavors—chilies, raisins, chocolate, cinnamon, anise and cloves—to suit your own taste. Leftover mole can be used in empanadas.

2 Tbsp.	ground coriander	25 mL
1 tsp.	ground cumin	5 mL
2	cloves garlic, chopped	2
3 Tbsp.	olive oil	45 mL
8	chicken legs	8
8	chicken thighs	8
1	dried ancho chili or 3 finger-hot chilies, seeds removed, chopped	1
2	medium onions	2
4	cloves garlic	4
2 Tbsp.	chicken fat or olive oil	25 mL
1 cup	almonds	250 mL
¾ cup	sultana raisins	175 mL
2 Tbsp.	pepitas	25 mL
1 tsp.	sesame seed	5 mL
¼ tsp.	aniseed, ground	1 mL
¼ tsp.	cloves, ground	1 mL
1	28 oz. (796 mL) can whole tomatoes	1
1 oz.	semisweet chocolate	25 g
1	½-inch (1 cm) stick cinnamon	1
	Vegetable oil	
	Sesame seed for garnish	

Mix together 1 tablespoon (15 mL) coriander, cumin, chopped garlic and 3 tablespoons (45 mL) olive oil in a small bowl, and rub over chicken pieces. Set aside.

If using ancho chili, remove stem and seeds, cover with warm water, and soak until soft. In a food processor, grind together onions, garlic cloves and chili(es), then fry over low heat in chicken fat or olive oil.

Grind almonds, raisins, pepitas and sesame seed together in a food processor, and add to onion mixture. Add aniseed, remaining 1 tablespoon (15 mL) coriander and cloves. Stir in tomatoes, chocolate and cinnamon, and simmer sauce for 15 minutes.

Preheat oven to 350°F (180°C). Brown chicken in vegetable oil in a separate skillet. Place in a casserole, and cover with sauce. Bake for 40 to 50 minutes, or until chicken is cooked. Garnish with sesame seed.

Serves 4 to 6

CHICKEN MOLE EMPANADAS

Empanadas are small, crispy pastry turnovers that we stuff with chicken moistened with mole sauce. There will be about one cup (250 mL) of extra sauce that can be frozen for future use.

FILLING

3	guajillo chilies, stemmed & seeded	3
1	ancho chili, stemmed & seeded	1
1	pasilla chili, stemmed & seeded	1
1	small onion, chopped into chunks	1
2	cloves garlic	2
1	medium tomato, peeled & chopped	1
¼ cup	sultana raisins, soaked in water overnight	50 mL
¼ cup	ground almonds	50 mL
1 tsp.	chopped fresh oregano	5 mL
1 tsp.	chopped fresh thyme	5 mL
	Pinch ground cloves	
⅛ tsp.	ground canella or cinnamon	0.5 mL
1	whole chicken breast, bone in	1
2 oz.	unsweetened chocolate, coarsely chopped	50 g
	Coarse salt & freshly ground black pepper	

Place chilies in a saucepan with onion and garlic. Cover with water, and simmer over low heat for about 1 hour, or until chilies are soft. Cool slightly, then purée mixture in a food processor until smooth. Add tomato, raisins, almonds, oregano, thyme, cloves and canella or cinnamon, and blend until sauce is smooth.

Preheat oven to 375°F (190°C). Brush chicken with sauce. Place in an uncovered roasting pan, and bake for 20 minutes or until cooked. Remove from oven, and cool. Tear or chop chicken into small pieces.

Heat remaining mole sauce in a saucepan over low heat, and add chocolate. Heat until chocolate melts and sauce thickens, about 20 minutes. Remove from heat, and mix enough sauce with the chicken to bind meat together. Season with salt and pepper to taste. Refrigerate filling until needed.

PASTRY

3 cups	flour	750 mL
½ tsp.	coarse salt	2 mL
¾ cup	chilled unsalted butter, cut into small pieces	175 mL
1	egg plus 1 egg yolk, lightly beaten	1
6 Tbsp.	water	75 mL
1	egg yolk beaten with a little water to make egg wash	1

Place flour and salt in a food processor, and blend. Add butter, and pulse intermittently until dough forms a coarse meal. Transfer to a mixing bowl. Mix in lightly beaten egg and egg yolk with a fork, and gradually add water while mixing to form a soft (but not sticky) dough. Cover, and refrigerate for 1 hour.

Preheat oven to 350°F (180°C). Turn dough onto a floured surface, and roll to ¹⁄₁₆-inch (1.5 mm) thickness. Cut into 3-inch-diameter (8 cm) circles or 3-inch (8 cm) squares. Place 1 tablespoon (15 mL) filling in center of each pastry, and fold over. Crimp edges, and brush tops with egg wash. Bake for 15 minutes or until golden.

Makes 30 empanadas

POLLO EN PEPITORIA

Delicious served over couscous, this mild Spanish-inspired chicken is prepared in a thick sauce flavored with saffron and dry sherry.

2	cloves garlic, chopped	2
1 tsp.	loosely packed saffron	5 mL
3 Tbsp.	pine nuts for garnish	45 mL
4 Tbsp.	olive oil	50 mL
2	onions, thinly sliced	2
3-4 lb.	chicken, cut into pieces, with breasts deboned	1.5-1.8 kg
½ cup	chicken stock (*see Basic Stock, page 46*)	125 mL
1 cup	dry sherry	250 mL
	Coarse salt & freshly ground black pepper	
4 cups	steamed couscous (keep warm)	1 L
2	hard-cooked eggs, peeled & chopped, for garnish	2

Grind garlic and saffron together in a mortar and pestle, and let sit for 1 hour.

Preheat oven to 350°F (180°C). Spread pine nuts on a baking sheet, and roast for 5 to 10 minutes, tossing occasionally. Set aside.

In a skillet, heat oil over medium heat, and sauté onions and garlic-saffron mixture for 20 to 30 minutes, until onions are translucent. Add dark-meat chicken pieces, and cook for 20 minutes. Stir in stock, sherry and white-meat chicken pieces. Cover, and simmer over medium heat for 30 to 45 minutes, or until chicken is cooked, turning occasionally to coat with sauce. The sauce should achieve the consistency of thick cream. Season with salt and pepper to taste. Serve over couscous, and garnish with eggs and toasted pine nuts.

Serves 4

POLLO BORACCHO

The taste of wine is evident in this Mexican dish, dubbed "drunken chicken."
The recipe lends itself to dark meat that matches the rich seasonings. Serve with short-grain
rice to soak up the gravy and with a simple sautéed vegetable like zucchini.

5 Tbsp.	flour	65 mL
1 tsp.	ground cumin	5 mL
1 tsp.	ground coriander	5 mL
6	chicken legs, thighs attached	6
1 Tbsp.	butter	15 mL
1 Tbsp.	olive oil	15 mL
1 cup	white wine	250 mL
¼ cup	white-wine vinegar	50 mL
3	cloves garlic, finely chopped	3
2 oz.	cooked ham, cut into strips	50 g
6 cups	cooked short-grain white rice	1.5 L
	Sliced green olives for garnish	

Preheat oven to 350°F (180°C). Combine flour, cumin and coriander, and dredge chicken pieces in mixture. Heat butter and oil in a heavy-bottomed skillet, and brown chicken. Transfer to an ovenproof casserole, and set aside.

In a separate pot, bring wine and vinegar to a boil, and reduce by half. Add garlic and ham, and cook for 2 minutes. Pour over chicken. Bake until chicken is cooked, about 45 minutes. Spoon over rice, and garnish with olives.
Serves 6

AYAM PANGGANG WITH NASI GORENG
(Indonesian Grilled Chicken With Indonesian Fried Rice)

Fried bananas and green beans cooked with freshly grated ginger are also
great side dishes for this Indonesian chicken. Nasi Goreng is easy to prepare
and is a tasty way to use up leftover chicken, pork and vegetables,
if you have them on hand, although the dish can stand on its own.

CHICKEN

6	cloves garlic, minced	6
4	Thai chilies, chopped	4
1	2-inch (5 cm) piece fresh ginger, grated	1
2 Tbsp.	sesame or peanut oil	25 mL
2 tsp.	tamarind concentrate	10 mL
	dissolved in 4 tsp. (20 mL) water	
⅔ cup	Indonesian sweet soy sauce	150 mL
⅓ cup	coconut milk	75 mL
2	4 lb. (1.8 kg) chickens, cut into pieces,	2
	with breasts deboned	

Mix together garlic, chilies, ginger, oil, tamarind liquid, soy sauce and coconut milk in a shallow pan. (You can substitute 2 tablespoons/25 mL lime juice for the tamarind liquid.) Place chicken pieces in marinade, and refrigerate for at least 2 hours.

Grill or barbecue chicken for 30 to 45 minutes or until cooked. Keep hot until you are ready to serve.

INDONESIAN HOT SAUCE

2 Tbsp.	olive or peanut oil	25 mL
6	Thai chilies	6
2	cloves garlic	2
1	onion, cut into chunks	1
1 Tbsp.	lemon juice	15 mL
2	fresh tomatoes, cut into chunks	2
1 tsp.	brown sugar	5 mL

Heat oil in a large skillet over medium heat, and add chilies, garlic and onion. Fry for about 20 minutes, or until onion is soft and starting to brown. Stir in lemon juice, tomatoes and sugar. Cook until most of the liquid has evaporated. Let cool, then purée in a blender or a food processor. Set aside. Sauce can be stored, tightly sealed, for up to 1 month in refrigerator.

NASI GORENG

	Peanut oil	
2	medium onions, diced	2
2	leeks, julienned	2
2	carrots, peeled & julienned	2
1/4	small cabbage, thinly shredded	1/4
3	cloves garlic, minced	3
1	Thai chili, minced	1
1	1-inch (2.5 cm) piece fresh ginger, minced	1
1/4 lb.	chicken, cut into strips	125 g
1/4 lb.	pork, cut into thin strips	125 g
1/4 lb.	cooked ham, diced	125 g
18	medium shrimp, peeled	18
1/4 lb.	snow peas or green beans	125 g
1/4 cup	lime juice	50 mL
1/4 cup	mushroom soy sauce	50 mL
1/4 cup	Indonesian soy sauce	50 mL
6	eggs	6
3 cups	cooked rice (keep warm)	750 mL
2	scallions, chopped, for garnish	2

Heat oil in a large skillet over medium heat, and fry onions, leeks, carrots and cabbage until tender but still crisp. Add garlic, chili and ginger. Continue cooking, and stir in chicken, pork, ham, shrimp and snow peas or beans. When meat is cooked, add lime juice and soy sauces.

Fry eggs. Place rice on a large serving platter. Stir meat mixture into rice, and garnish with scallions and fried eggs. Serve with hot sauce and chicken.

Serves 6 to 8

CHICKEN TAJINE

*Slowly simmered and flavored with saffron, ginger and cinnamon,
this chicken is fall-off-the-bone tender and is best served over steamed couscous
and topped with harissa, a fiery Moroccan hot sauce. Preserved lemons are an essential
ingredient. You will need to make the lemons several weeks in advance.
After curing for about one month, the lemons have a surprisingly mild taste.
They will last a long time if stored refrigerated, immersed in the juice.*

PRESERVED LEMONS

6	whole lemons, washed	6
6 Tbsp.	coarse salt	75 mL
1	stick cinnamon	1
1 Tbsp.	coriander seed	15 mL
3-4	whole dried chilies	3-4
1 Tbsp.	black peppercorns	15 mL
2½ cups	lemon juice	625 mL

Carefully cut each lemon lengthwise into six sections to within ¼ inch (6 mm) of the stem so that the lemon will hold together. Gently pack the inside of each lemon with 1 tablespoon (15 mL) salt. Place lemons, cinnamon, coriander, chilies and peppercorns in a sterilized glass jar. Completely fill jar with lemon juice. Cover, and refrigerate for 1 month. Rinse lemons before using.

HARISSA

¼ cup	vegetable oil	50 mL
10	finger-hot chilies, whole stems removed	10
10	cloves garlic	10
2	onions, cut into chunks	2
6	tomatoes, cubed	6
2 Tbsp.	tomato paste or 1 roasted red bell pepper	25 mL
2 tsp.	ground cumin	10 mL
1 tsp.	caraway seed, ground	5 mL
	Coarse salt & freshly ground black pepper	

Heat oil in a skillet over medium-high heat, and add chilies, garlic, onions and tomatoes, frying until charred. Stir in tomato paste or roasted pepper, cumin and caraway seed, and continue cooking for 5 minutes. Remove from heat, and let cool. Place in a food processor, and blend. Season with salt and pepper to taste.

Makes 2 cups (500 mL)

CHICKEN

¼ cup + 2 Tbsp.	olive oil	50 mL + 25 mL
3 Tbsp.	lemon juice	45 mL
1 Tbsp. + 2 tsp.	ground ginger	15 mL + 10 mL
½ tsp.	saffron	2 mL
8	chicken pieces (thighs & legs)	8
2	medium onions, finely chopped	2
3	cloves garlic, finely chopped	3
1	1-inch (2.5 cm) stick cinnamon	1
½ tsp.	coarse salt	2 mL
3 cups	chicken stock (see Basic Stock, page 46)	750 mL
½ cup	chopped fresh coriander leaves	125 mL
½ cup	chopped fresh parsley	125 mL
2	preserved lemons, diced rind only	2
18	green colossal olives	18
4 cups	steamed couscous (keep warm)	1 L

Mix together ¼ cup (50 mL) oil, lemon juice, 1 tablespoon (15 mL) ginger and saffron in a large bowl. Thoroughly coat chicken pieces in oil mixture, and let stand for a minimum of 1 hour.

Heat remaining 2 tablespoons (25 mL) oil in a large skillet over medium heat, and sauté onions and garlic for about 15 minutes, being careful not to brown. Stir in remaining 2 teaspoons (10 mL) ginger, cinnamon, chicken pieces and salt. Coat chicken in sauce, and cook, uncovered, for 15 minutes. Add stock, and bring stew to a boil. Immediately reduce heat to low, cover, and cook chicken through, about 35 minutes.

Remove chicken, and set aside. Increase heat to medium-high, and reduce sauce to consistency of thick cream. Stir in coriander, parsley, preserved-lemon rind and olives. Return chicken to pan, and heat through. Spoon over couscous, and serve with harissa.

Serves 4

BISTEEYA

*This Moroccan pie is woven together with strips of light and crispy phyllo pastry.
Originally, Bisteeya was made with pigeon meat. Be sure to assemble the pie
on a baking sheet, because you will not be able to move it once it is finished.*

2	4-5 lb. (2 kg) roasting chickens, cut into pieces	2
5	cloves garlic	5
1	medium onion, grated	1
1 cup	chopped fresh parsley & coriander leaves	250 mL
½ tsp.	saffron	2 mL
1 tsp.	freshly ground black pepper	5 mL
¾ tsp.	ground ginger	4 mL
3	sticks cinnamon	3
1 cup	butter	250 mL
	Coarse salt	
3 cups	water	750 mL
¼ cup	vegetable oil	50 mL
¾ lb.	blanched almonds	375 g
⅓ cup	icing sugar	75 mL
1½ tsp.	cinnamon	7 mL
¼ cup	lemon juice	50 mL
10	eggs	10
1	1 lb. (500 g) pkg. phyllo pastry	1
	Cinnamon & icing sugar for garnish	

Place chicken pieces, garlic, onion, parsley and coriander, saffron, pepper,
ginger, cinnamon sticks, ½ cup (125 mL) butter, pinch of salt and water in
a stockpot. Bring to a boil, then reduce heat, and simmer for 1 hour.

In the meantime, heat oil in a skillet, and brown almonds. Drain and cool.
Grind almonds in a food processor. In a bowl, mix almonds with ⅓ cup
(75 mL) icing sugar and 1½ teaspoons (7 mL) cinnamon. Set aside.

Remove chicken, cinnamon sticks and any loose bones from the pot. Bring
to a boil, and reduce liquid to 1¾ cups (425 mL). Reduce heat to simmer, and
add lemon juice. Beat eggs in a mixing bowl, and stir into simmering sauce.
Stir until eggs cook and congeal. Drain through a fine-mesh sieve. Discard
liquid. Season egg mixture with salt to taste. Set aside.

Remove chicken from bones, and shred by hand. Set aside.

Preheat oven to 425°F (220°C). Clarify remaining ½ cup (125 mL) butter.
Cut phyllo pastry into 3-inch-wide (8 cm) strips, and arrange strips on a
baking sheet in a large pinwheel pattern, brushing each with clarified butter.
Lay chicken in center, and top with egg mixture. Fold half the strips over the
filling, brushing with butter as you go. Lay almond mixture in the center of
the pastry, and fold in remaining strips of phyllo. Brush top with butter.

Bake for 20 to 25 minutes, until pastry is browned. Dust pie with cinnamon
mixed with icing sugar. Cut into wedges.

Serves 6 to 8

CORN-CRUSTED CHICKEN WITH BLACK BEAN SALAD

Cornmeal makes a light, crispy coating for the chicken in this dish.

3 Tbsp.	olive oil	45 mL
2	cloves garlic, sliced	2
1 tsp.	chili powder	5 mL
½ tsp.	paprika	2 mL
1 tsp.	ground cumin	5 mL
½ tsp.	freshly ground black pepper	2 mL
¼ tsp.	coarse salt	1 mL
½ cup	cornmeal	125 mL
1 Tbsp.	chopped fresh parsley	15 mL
1 tsp.	dried thyme	5 mL
¼ cup	vegetable oil	50 mL
4	boneless chicken breasts, skin on	4
5 cups	Black Bean Salad (*see page 92*)	1.25 L
½ lb.	smoked Gruyère cheese, grated, for garnish	250 g
	Fresh greens or specialty lettuces for garnish	

Place olive oil in a bowl, and mix in garlic, chili powder, paprika, cumin, pepper and salt. In a separate bowl, combine cornmeal, parsley and thyme. Rub chicken with flavored oil, and coat with cornmeal mixture.

Heat vegetable oil in a large skillet over medium heat, and fry chicken until cooked, about 20 minutes, turning once.

To serve, spoon Black Bean Salad onto a plate, and top with sliced chicken. Garnish with cheese, and top with greens.

Serves 4

Corn-Crusted Chicken With Black Bean Salad

CURRIED CHICKEN PIE

This savory pie is filled with tender chunks of curried chicken, cauliflower, potatoes and sweet pepper, all simmered in rich coconut milk.

SUSAN'S SAVORY PIE CRUST

2½ cups	flour	625 mL
¼ tsp.	coarse salt	1 mL
½ lb.	lard or shortening	250 g
1	egg, unbeaten	1
	Sour cream	

Mix flour and salt in a large bowl. Cut in lard or shortening with knives or a pastry cutter until pea-size lumps form. Place egg in a measuring cup, and add enough sour cream to make ½ cup (125 mL). Stir into flour mixture, and blend together. Chill for 15 minutes. Roll out into two 9-inch (23 cm) crusts.

CURRY POWDER

½ cup	coriander seed	125 mL
¼ cup	cumin seed	50 mL
2 Tbsp.	black mustard seed	25 mL
2 Tbsp.	black peppercorns	25 mL
1 Tbsp.	fennel seed	15 mL
½ tsp.	cloves	2 mL
¼ cup	garam masala	50 mL
¼ cup	turmeric	50 mL
1½ tsp.	cinnamon	7 mL

Lightly toast coriander seed, cumin seed, black mustard seed, peppercorns, fennel seed and cloves together in a dry skillet until they begin to release their aroma. Grind in a spice or coffee grinder. Mix with garam masala, turmeric and cinnamon. Store in an airtight jar.

Makes 1 cup (250 mL)

FILLING

1	large stewing chicken, cut into pieces	1
2½ tsp.	curry powder	12 mL
4	onions, diced	4
1	1-inch (2.5 cm) piece fresh ginger, peeled & chopped	1
4	cloves garlic, chopped	4
2	finger-hot chilies, chopped	2
1 cup	coconut milk	250 mL
3	potatoes, peeled & cubed	3
½ cup	diced red bell pepper	125 mL
3 cups	cauliflower florets	750 mL
	Coarse salt & freshly ground black pepper	
1	egg yolk beaten with a little water to make egg wash	1

Place chicken pieces, curry powder, onions, ginger, garlic, chilies and coconut milk in a large pot over medium heat. Simmer until chicken is thoroughly cooked. Remove chicken from broth, and let cool. Remove meat from bones, and cut into small chunks. Set meat aside, and discard bones.

Add potatoes to broth, and simmer until tender. Add red pepper and cauliflower, and simmer for 5 minutes. Return chicken to pot, and simmer until broth is reduced to gravy thickness. Season with salt and pepper to taste. Remove from heat, and let cool for 1 hour.

In the meantime, preheat oven to 400°F (200°C). Line a 9-inch (23 cm) pie plate with bottom pie crust. Weight with another pie plate to prevent puffing, and bake for 12 minutes. Set aside to cool.

Fill bottom crust with filling. Cover with top crust. Cut vents, and brush with egg wash. Bake for 10 minutes. Reduce heat to 350°F (180°C), and bake for 45 minutes.

Serves 8

GAENG KEO NGAI (Green Chicken Curry)

This mild chicken curry is infused with the lemon-pepper flavor of galangal. The green curry paste can also be used to marinate meats that are to be grilled or barbecued.

GREEN CURRY PASTE

4	large (or 8 small) fresh green chilies, chopped	4
½ cup	chopped shallots or 1 medium onion, chopped	125 mL
1 Tbsp.	minced garlic	15 mL
½ cup	chopped fresh coriander	125 mL
	(roots, stems & leaves)	
¼ cup	finely sliced lemongrass or zest of 1 lemon	50 mL
1 Tbsp.	chopped fresh galangal	15 mL
2 tsp.	ground coriander	10 mL
1 tsp.	ground cumin	5 mL
1 tsp.	black peppercorns	5 mL
1 tsp.	turmeric	5 mL
1 tsp.	shrimp paste	5 mL
2 tsp.	vegetable oil	10 mL

Place all ingredients in a blender or a food processor, and blend to a smooth paste. Add an extra tablespoon (15 mL) oil or a little water, if necessary, to ease blending. Store in a clean, dry bottle in the refrigerator for 3 to 4 weeks, or divide into portions, wrap, and freeze.

Makes 3 cups (750 mL)

CURRY

2 cups	thick coconut milk	500 mL
2 Tbsp.	fish sauce	25 mL
3 Tbsp.	chopped fresh galangal	45 mL
3 lb.	chicken, boned & cut into small chunks	1.5 kg
3 Tbsp.	green curry paste	45 mL
2 cups	thin coconut milk	500 mL
3	pea eggplants, cut into chunks,	3
	or 1 cup (250 mL) chopped Japanese eggplant	
6	fresh lime leaves	6
½ cup	fresh sweet basil leaves	125 mL

Heat a wok over high heat. Add thick coconut milk, fish sauce, galangal and chicken, and poach until chicken is just cooked. Remove chicken with a slotted spoon. Cover, set aside, and keep warm.

Reduce liquid by half, add curry paste, and heat. The mixture should be smooth and fragrant. Add thin coconut milk, and continue to reduce for 5 to 10 minutes, until liquid is the thickness of heavy cream. Return chicken to wok, and add eggplant and lime leaves. Cook for 5 minutes. Stir in basil just before serving.

Serves 6 to 8

DUCK BREASTS WITH CALVADOS SAUCE

*Brown stock is made from bones that have been roasted in the oven, which produces
a stronger, richer flavor. Brown sauce is made from brown stock. The success of the
Calvados sauce in this recipe completely depends on the quality of your stock.
The whole process dictates that you start preparing this dish a day in advance.*

2	3-4 lb. (1.5-1.8 kg) Muscovy ducks	2
1	medium onion, cut into chunks	1
1	clove garlic	1
1	carrot, cut into chunks	1
1	stalk celery, cut into chunks	1
1 Tbsp.	tomato paste	15 mL
2	apples, cut into chunks	2
2 cups	red wine	500 mL
12 cups	water	3 L
¼ cup	Calvados	50 mL

Preheat oven to 375°F (190°C). Cut ducks into pieces. Refrigerate breasts
(save legs to use in Confit of Muscovy Duck Legs, *page 184*). Place wings and
carcasses in a roasting pan, and brown in oven, uncovered, for 40 minutes.
Remove from oven, and set aside.

Remove a few teaspoons of fat from roasting pan, and place in a large
stockpot. Over medium heat, sauté onion, garlic, carrot, celery, tomato paste
and apples until soft. Increase heat to medium-high, and add wine, water and
browned bones. Bring to a boil, reduce heat, and simmer, partially covered,
for 2 hours.

Cool and strain stock, discarding bones. Chill overnight.

The next day, skim off fat, and return stock to stove. Bring to a boil, and
reduce stock to 1 cup (250 mL) brown sauce—this may take 1 hour. Flame
Calvados in a ladle (*see "Light My Fire," page 26*), and pour into sauce. Keep warm
while frying duck breasts.

Preheat oven to 400°F (200°C). Heat a large ovenproof skillet over medium-
high heat, and lay breasts fat side down. Brown on both sides. Finish cooking
in oven, fat side down, roasting, uncovered, for 10 to 12 minutes. Slice breasts.
Pool sauce on plate, and serve duck on top.

Serves 4

CONFIT OF MUSCOVY DUCK LEGS

Confit is a slow, tenderizing method of cooking in oil or fat. It also preserves the meat—once the duck legs are prepared. At Chez Piggy, we serve these duck legs with White Bean & Spinach Purée (see facing page).

6	Muscovy duck legs	6
3	whole heads garlic	3
4 Tbsp.	coarse salt	50 mL
2 tsp.	black peppercorns	10 mL
1	whole nutmeg	1
2	bay leaves	2
2	sprigs fresh thyme or 1 tsp. (5 mL) dried	2
	Olive oil, bacon fat or chicken fat	

Heat a cast-iron frying pan until very hot but not smoking. Place duck legs in pan, skin side down, and fry until golden brown. Pour off and reserve fat as legs cook, turning to fry both sides.

Place garlic, salt, peppercorns, nutmeg, bay leaves, thyme and reserved fat in a pan large enough to hold the legs without layering. Place legs in pan, skin side down. If there is not enough fat to cover the legs, make up the difference with oil, bacon fat or chicken fat. Simmer, but do not boil, over medium-low heat for 2 to 2½ hours, or until meat is tender. Remove from heat, and let cool. Leave cooled duck completely covered with fat, and store in the refrigerator overnight.

Preheat oven to 400°F (200°C). Warm the fat to remove legs from pan, scraping off any residual fat. Heat an ovenproof pan over medium-high heat, and fry legs until skin is crispy. Transfer pan to oven for 10 to 15 minutes, until meat is hot.

Serves 6

Confit of Muscovy
Duck Legs
With White Bean
& Spinach Purée

WHITE BEAN & SPINACH PURÉE

*If you like hummus, you'll love this white bean purée. We make it as a warm side dish
for duck confit and braised cabbage, but it is suitable beside any grilled meat. For a lasting
vivid green color, chill the cooked ingredients in the refrigerator before you purée them.*

2 cups	dried white beans, sorted & rinsed	500 mL
2 tsp.	coarse salt	10 mL
1	onion, peeled & cut into quarters	1
3	cloves garlic	3
8 oz.	fresh spinach, washed	250 g
	Coarse salt & freshly ground black pepper	

Place beans in a large pot, cover with water, and soak overnight.

In the morning, drain beans, and cover with fresh water. Add salt, place pot
over high heat, and bring to a boil. Reduce heat, add onion and garlic, and
simmer until beans are very soft. Drain, and reserve cooking water. Cool both
reserved water and beans in the refrigerator.

In a food processor, purée beans with spinach, gradually adding as much
reserved water as necessary until mixture is the consistency of hummus. Season
with salt and pepper to taste.

Makes 4-5 cups (1-1.25 L)

ASIAN DUCK LEG CONFIT
WITH PICKLED RED CABBAGE

This interesting variation of the confit of duck uses Asian spices.
The pickled ginger, which is served as a condiment, adds a tangy sharpness,
but you'll need to marinate it for a week before serving.

PICKLED GINGER

1 lb.	fresh ginger, peeled	500 g
2⅓ cups	rice-wine vinegar	575 mL
⅓ cup	cider vinegar	75 mL
⅓ cup	white vinegar	75 mL
1 cup	sugar	250 mL
2 Tbsp. + 1 tsp.	coarse salt	30 mL

Cut ginger against the grain into paper-thin slices. Place in a bowl, cover with boiling water, and let stand for 2 minutes. Drain. In a small saucepan, bring remaining ingredients to a boil. Pour over ginger. Cover, let cool, and refrigerate for 1 week.

PICKLED RED CABBAGE

1 lb.	red cabbage, thinly shredded	500 g
1 cup	juice from pickled ginger	250 mL
2 Tbsp. + 1 tsp.	sugar	30 mL
1 Tbsp.	pickled ginger	15 mL
1½ tsp.	coarse salt	7 mL

Combine all ingredients in a bowl, and marinate for 24 hours.

SAUCE

2 cups	brown chicken stock or duck stock	500 mL
	(see Basic Stock, page 46)	
2 Tbsp.	rice wine or sherry	25 mL
1 Tbsp.	mushroom soy sauce	15 mL
3 Tbsp.	brown sugar	45 mL
1½ tsp.	tomato paste	7 mL
1 Tbsp.	Szechuan peppercorns	15 mL
1 tsp.	fennel seed	5 mL
1	star anise	1
½ tsp.	cumin seed	2 mL
1	1-inch (2.5 cm) stick cinnamon	1
	Pinch turmeric	
	Pinch cayenne pepper	
1	2-inch (5 cm) piece lemongrass, bruised	1

Heat all ingredients together in a saucepan, and simmer while cooking duck legs to infuse flavors. Strain, and keep warm.

DUCK

6	Muscovy duck legs	6
1	whole head garlic	1
¼ cup	coarse salt	50 mL
1 tsp.	fennel seed	5 mL
2	fresh lime leaves	2
4 tsp.	Szechuan peppercorns	20 mL
2	star anise	2
1 tsp.	coriander seed	5 mL
1 tsp.	cumin seed	5 mL
2	cloves	2
1	1-inch (2.5 cm) stick cinnamon	1
½ tsp.	turmeric	2 mL
	Olive oil, bacon fat or chicken fat	

Heat a cast-iron frying pan until very hot but not smoking. Place duck legs in pan, skin side down, and fry until golden brown. Pour off and reserve fat as legs cook, turning to fry both sides.

Place garlic, salt, fennel, lime leaves, peppercorns, spices and reserved fat in a pan large enough to hold the legs without layering. Place legs in pan, skin side down. If there is not enough fat to cover the legs, make up the difference with oil, bacon fat or chicken fat. Simmer, but do not boil, over medium-low heat for 2 to 2½ hours, or until meat is tender. Remove from heat, and let cool. Leave cooled duck completely covered with fat, and store in the refrigerator overnight.

Preheat oven to 400°F (200°C). Warm the fat to remove legs from pan, scraping off any residual fat. Heat an ovenproof pan over medium-high heat, and fry legs until skin is crispy. Transfer pan to oven for 10 to 15 minutes, or until meat is hot. Pool sauce on a plate, and top with sliced duck meat. Serve with pickled red cabbage, and offer pickled ginger as a condiment.

Serves 6

TEA-SPICED QUAIL
WITH TOMATO OIL, GREENS
& MUSHROOMS

Sweet roasted quail, marinated in tea, is served with sautéed shiitake mushrooms and mixed greens lightly dressed with vinaigrette. Be sure the greens are washed and ready to be dressed just before serving so that the meat does not overcook.

TOMATO OIL

1	28 oz. (796 mL) can whole tomatoes, undrained	1
1 cup	olive oil	250 mL
2 tsp.	balsamic vinegar	10 mL
¼ tsp.	dried thyme or basil	1 mL
	Pinch coarse salt	
	Pinch freshly ground black pepper	

Blend tomatoes in a food processor. Place in a heavy-bottomed pot, and bring to a low boil. Continue boiling until liquid is reduced by half. Stir in oil, vinegar, thyme or basil, salt and pepper, and cook for 15 minutes. Remove from heat, and let cool, allowing pot to stand until oil rises to the top. Drain off oil, and reserve. Discard the remaining tomato.

Makes 1 cup (250 mL)

GREENS

1 lb.	fresh greens	500 g
3 Tbsp.	vegetable oil	45 mL
1 Tbsp.	toasted sesame oil	15 mL
2 Tbsp.	rice-wine vinegar	25 mL
1 tsp.	lemon juice	5 mL
1 tsp.	toasted sesame seed	5 mL
	Coarse salt & freshly ground black pepper	

Wash, trim and dry greens, and set aside. Combine oils, vinegar, lemon juice and sesame seed in a jar, and shake. Season with salt and pepper to taste. Refrigerate vinaigrette until needed.

QUAIL

¼ cup	dried black tea leaves	50 mL
½ cup	boiling water	125 mL
	Zest & juice of 1 orange	
½ cup	soy sauce	125 mL
¼ cup	brown sugar	50 mL
5 Tbsp.	roasted Szechuan peppercorns	65 mL
8	scallions, cut into 1-inch (2.5 cm) lengths	8
1	2-inch (5 cm) stick cinnamon	1
1	2-inch (5 cm) piece fresh ginger, thinly sliced	1
1 tsp.	coarse salt	5 mL
12-18	quail (2 or 3 per person)	12-18
18	fresh shiitake mushrooms, whole caps (stems removed)	18
2 Tbsp.	vegetable oil	25 mL

Brew tea leaves in boiling water, then cool. In a roasting pan, mix tea together with orange zest, orange juice, soy sauce, sugar, peppercorns, scallions, cinnamon, ginger and salt. Place quail in pan, and allow to marinate in refrigerator for 5 hours or overnight.

Preheat oven to 400°F (200°C). Remove quail from marinade, and strain marinade into a large saucepan. Place quail on a rack in a roasting pan, and roast for 20 to 25 minutes.

In the meantime, boil marinade for 5 minutes, and keep warm.

Lightly sauté mushroom caps in oil. Set aside, and keep warm.

Using just enough vinaigrette to moisten, toss greens immediately before quail is served. Drizzle tomato oil around the rim of each plate. Place dressed greens in the middle. Arrange quail around outside, and top with warm mushrooms. Drizzle with hot marinade.

Serves 6 to 8

Our Daily Bread

With the founding of the Pan Chancho bakery in 1994, Zal and Rose at last satisfied Chez Piggy's voracious appetite for traditional crusty bread. Under the direction of Pandora De Green, the Pan Chancho bakers developed authentic bread-making techniques and recipes, baking the bread in humidity-sensitive ovens.

Bread making is part art and part science. The most fundamental ingredients— hard bread flour, filtered water, sea salt and baker's yeast—and the hands of a sensitive baker combine to create some of the tastiest bread you'll ever find. Readers should remember that our bread is baked in a controlled environment. The home baker has to contend with fluctuating levels of humidity and temperature, and that's going to have an impact on bread-baking success. What doesn't work the first time may very well work the next; in bread making, patience and the willingness to experiment are necessary virtues.

The sweet and savory recipes offered here are, we think, the most accessible to the home baker: Pain Ordinaire, Pita, Rye, Whole Wheat, Sourdough and Multigrain, as well as some of the bakery's favorite treats—our giant Lemon-Currant Rolls and Raspberry & White-Chocolate Scones. Sometimes, you just have to open your own bakery to get what you want.

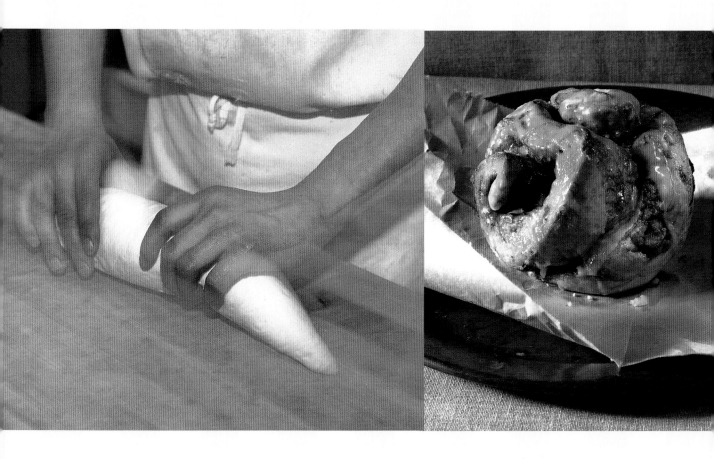

BREAD WINNERS, from left to right: Pan Chancho's breadbasket of assorted fresh loaves greets customers; head baker Paul Muller wields a peel; the touchy-feely art of shaping free-form loaves; the mouth-watering giant Lemon-Currant Roll is Pan Chancho's sweet roll of choice.

WHOLE WHEAT BREAD

We use this moist, tasty bread at the restaurant for sandwiches.

Day 1
STARTER

2 Tbsp.	active dry yeast	25 mL
¾ cup	warm water	175 mL
⅔ cup	buttermilk	150 mL
1¾ cups	unbleached hard white flour	425 mL

In a large bowl, stir yeast into water until dissolved. Add buttermilk, and gradually add flour, mixing until smooth. Cover, and let stand overnight in a cool place.

Day 2
STARTER

2 cups	warm water	500 mL
	Starter from Day 1	
2½ cups	whole wheat flour	625 mL
2¼ cups	unbleached hard white flour	550 mL
⅔ cup	wheat germ	150 mL

Stir water into starter. Gradually add flours, then wheat germ, mixing thoroughly. Cover, and refrigerate overnight.

Day 3
DOUGH

1½ cups	starter	375 mL
1½ cups	warm water	375 mL
1 Tbsp.	active dry yeast	15 mL
2½ cups	whole wheat flour	625 mL
2 cups	unbleached hard white flour	500 mL
1 Tbsp.	sea salt	15 mL
2 Tbsp.	honey	25 mL

Place starter in a large bowl (remaining starter will keep in the refrigerator for a few days). Add remaining ingredients, and mix well with a countertop mixer or your hands. Turn out onto a floured board, and knead until smooth.

Let rise at room temperature until nearly doubled in size. Punch dough down, and divide in two. Shape into free-form loaves, or put into loaf pans. Let rise again until not quite doubled.

Preheat oven to 425°F (220°C). Slash tops of loaves with a razor blade. A few minutes before putting bread in oven, place a pan of boiling water on the bottom rack. After bread has baked for 15 minutes, reduce heat to 375°F (190°C), and remove water. Bake for 25 minutes longer or until loaves are evenly browned.

Makes 2 loaves

RYE BREAD

This aromatic rye loaf gets its extra-sweet flavor from buttermilk. The inside texture of the loaf is smooth, but the crust is crispy. You may need a countertop mixer to blend the dough.

Day 1
MILK SOUR

1½ cups	buttermilk, room temperature	375 mL
¾ cup	whole rye flour	175 mL

In a large bowl, mix buttermilk and flour by hand until there are no lumps. Let stand at room temperature overnight.

Day 2
RYE STARTER

2½ tsp.	active dry yeast	12 mL
1 cup	warm water	250 mL
	Milk sour from Day 1	
2 cups	unbleached hard white flour	500 mL
½ cup	whole rye flour	125 mL

Stir yeast into water, and let stand for 5 minutes, until bubbles start to form on the surface. Add yeast mixture to milk sour. Gradually add flours, and mix well. Cover, and refrigerate overnight. Dough should nearly triple in size.

Day 3
DOUGH

	Rye starter from Day 2	
½ cup	water	125 mL
1 tsp.	honey	5 mL
1 Tbsp.	sea salt	15 mL
3 cups	unbleached hard white flour	750 mL
1	egg white beaten with a little water to make egg wash	1
3 Tbsp.	caraway seed	45 mL

Bring rye starter to room temperature. Place in a large bowl to mix by hand or in the bowl of a stand-up mixer to mix with the paddle attachment. Blend in water, honey and salt, and gradually incorporate flour.

Pour onto a floured surface. Dust hands with flour, and knead. Dough should be sticky, so try not to add more flour. Let rise at room temperature for 1 hour.

Punch dough down, and divide in two. Shape into round or oval loaves. Let rise for 40 minutes.

Preheat oven to 400°F (200°C). Slash tops of loaves with a razor blade, and brush with egg wash. Sprinkle caraway seed on top. Bake for 15 minutes. Reduce heat to 375°F (190°C), and bake for 25 minutes longer.

Makes 2 loaves

PAIN ORDINAIRE

It is important to use hard white flour in this recipe. It is equally important to use sea salt rather than table salt; otherwise, the bread will be overly salty. The rising process is much slower than in most bread recipes because of the salt, which inhibits the action of the yeast. Although you can make this bread in as little as two days, the flavor will improve when the process is extended over three days. If you decide to bake the bread free-form rather than in a loaf pan, it can be baked on a pizza stone dusted with cornmeal. Baking the loaf on a hot stone will brown the bottom.

Day 1
STARTER

1 Tbsp.	active dry yeast	15 mL
2 cups	warm water	500 mL
2 cups	unbleached hard white flour	500 mL

Stir yeast into water until dissolved. Gradually add flour, stirring until well mixed. Cover, and refrigerate overnight.

Day 2
DOUGH

1 Tbsp.	active dry yeast	15 mL
1 cup	warm water	250 mL
	Starter from Day 1	
	Pinch ascorbic acid crystals	
	or ¼ tsp. (1 mL) lemon juice	
4-5 cups	unbleached hard white flour	1-1.25 L
1 Tbsp.	sea salt	15 mL

In a large bowl, stir yeast into water. Add starter and ascorbic acid or lemon juice. Add flour 1 cup (250 mL) at a time, up to 4 cups (1 L). Reserve 1 cup (250 mL) flour for kneading the dough. Blend with a hand mixer on low speed until you have a rough dough. Scrape out onto a well-floured work surface. Sprinkle salt over top, and knead, gradually incorporating the remaining 1 cup (250 mL) flour. The kneaded dough should be silky and satiny but slightly sticky. Resist adding too much flour. Place in a large oiled bowl. Cover, and refrigerate overnight.

Day 3
FINISHED LOAF

Remove dough from refrigerator, and punch down. Divide dough in two. Either shape by hand into free-form loaves, or place in loaf pans. Let rise at room temperature for 1½ to 2 hours.

Preheat oven to 450°F (230°C). Ideally, you want to begin baking the loaves before they have doubled in size; otherwise, they will fall when they come into contact with the heat.

When loaves are about three-quarters risen, slash tops of loaves with a razor blade. Just before you put the bread into the oven, place a pan of boiling water on the bottom rack. Bake loaves for 10 minutes, then reduce heat to 375°F (190°C), and remove pan of water. Continue to bake for 30 to 35 minutes.

Check loaves throughout baking process, and if they get too dark on top, cover loosely with aluminum foil. If you are baking the bread in loaf pans, turn loaves out onto oven rack, bottoms up or on sides, for the last 10 minutes to firm up bottom and sides.

Makes 2 loaves

PUMPKIN-SEED BREAD

You can also make this loaf sans seeds for a very nice "pain de campagne".

SEED MIX

½ cup	sunflower seed	125 mL
½ cup	sesame seed mixed with	125 mL
	2 tsp. (10 mL) tamari sauce	
1 cup	pumpkin seed	250 mL
1 tsp.	cumin seed, ground	5 mL

Day 1
STARTER

1 Tbsp.	active dry yeast	15 mL
2½ cups	warm water	625 mL
1½ cups	whole rye flour	375 mL
1 cup	unbleached hard white flour	250 mL

In a large bowl, dissolve yeast in water, then gradually stir in flours. Cover, and refrigerate overnight.

Day 2
DOUGH

2½-3 cups	unbleached hard white flour	625-750 mL
2 tsp.	sea salt	10 mL
	Starter from Day 1	

Mix seeds together in a small bowl, and set aside. Gradually add flour and salt to starter, and mix into a soft dough. Add seed mix. Turn out onto a floured board, and knead for 4 to 5 minutes. Let rise for 1 hour or until doubled.

Preheat oven to 350°F (180°C). Punch dough down, and divide in two. Shape into oval loaves, and let rise again until not quite doubled. Slash tops of loaves with a razor blade, and bake for 45 minutes.

Makes 2 loaves

MULTIGRAIN BREAD

This textured bread is another of our favorites for sandwiches.

SEED MIX

1 Tbsp.	bran	15 mL
1 Tbsp.	rolled oats	15 mL
1 Tbsp.	bulgur	15 mL
1 Tbsp.	soft wheat berries	15 mL
1 Tbsp.	rye berries	15 mL
1 Tbsp.	cornmeal	15 mL
1 Tbsp.	flax seed	15 mL
¼ cup	amaranth seed	50 mL
¼ cup	kamut kernels	50 mL
¼ cup	sunflower seed	50 mL
¼ cup	sesame seed	50 mL

Mix all ingredients together, and cover with ½ inch (1 cm) water to soak overnight. Drain before using.

Day 1
STARTER

2 Tbsp.	active dry yeast	25 mL
¾ cup	warm water	175 mL
⅔ cup	buttermilk	150 mL
1¾ cups	unbleached hard white flour	425 mL

In a large bowl, stir yeast into water until dissolved. Add buttermilk, and gradually add flour, mixing until smooth. Cover, and let stand overnight in a cool place.

Day 2
STARTER

2 cups	warm water	500 mL
	Starter from Day 1	
2½ cups	whole wheat flour	625 mL
2¼ cups	unbleached hard white flour	550 mL
⅔ cup	wheat germ	150 mL

Stir water into starter. Gradually add flours, then wheat germ, mixing thoroughly. Cover, and refrigerate overnight.

The first home of the little bakery that could. When Pan Chancho outgrew its original space, Rose and Zal moved the bakery to a limestone building they renovated in the heart of downtown Kingston.

Day 3
DOUGH

1½ cups	starter	375 mL
1½ cups	warm water	375 mL
1 Tbsp.	active dry yeast	15 mL
2½ cups	whole wheat flour	625 mL
2 cups	unbleached hard white flour	500 mL
1 Tbsp.	sea salt	15 mL
2 Tbsp.	honey	25 mL

Place starter in a large bowl (remaining starter will keep in the refrigerator for a few days). Add remaining ingredients, and mix well with a countertop mixer or your hands. Mix in 1½ cups (375 mL) seed mix. Turn out onto a floured board, and knead until smooth.

Let rise at room temperature until nearly doubled in size. Punch dough down, and divide in two. Shape into free-form loaves, or place in loaf pans. Let rise again until not quite doubled.

Preheat oven to 425°F (220°C). Slash tops of loaves with a razor blade. A few minutes before putting bread in oven, place a pan of boiling water on the bottom rack. After bread has baked for 15 minutes, reduce heat to 375°F (190°C), remove water, and bake for 25 minutes longer or until evenly browned.

Makes 2 loaves

CHEZ PIGGY SOURDOUGH STARTER

*When making a sourdough starter, you'll need patience and a large mixing container.
If you want to keep the starter active and ready to use, "feed" it every day.*

Days 1 & 2

1 cup	unbleached hard white flour	250 mL
1½ cups	spring water, room temperature	375 mL

Mix flour and water together in a clean container. Cover with a tea towel or
cheesecloth, and let stand for 2 days at room temperature.

Day 3

1 cup	unbleached hard white flour	250 mL
1 cup	spring water, room temperature	250 mL

Feed the starter: Mix flour and water together in a measuring cup. Stir the
starter, then mix in the slurry of flour and water, and blend thoroughly. At the
end of **Day 3**, the mixture should be bubbly and smell a little boozy. If it doesn't,
let stand for another day or two before feeding again.

Day 4

½ cup	unbleached hard white flour	125 mL
½ cup	spring water, room temperature	125 mL

Before you feed the starter, discard all but 1 cup (250 mL). From now until
Day 7, feed the starter its volume in flour and water. On **Day 5**, feed it a slurry
of 1 cup (250 mL) flour and 1 cup (250 mL) water. On **Day 6**, feed it 2 cups
(500 mL) flour and 2 cups (500 mL) water.

Olive & Rosemary
Sourdough

Day 7

The starter is ready to use at room temperature. If you are baking frequently, continue to feed starter once a day. If you bake only once a week, store starter in refrigerator until needed. (To limit the size of the ever-growing starter, remove and discard 1 cup/250 mL starter before each weekly feeding.) To reactivate starter, bring it (or a portion of it) to room temperature and feed for a few days. Starter can also be stored in the freezer in portions once it has become active; it can then be reactivated as needed.

OLIVE & ROSEMARY SOURDOUGH

One of the most flavorful loaves you can eat with soup or a salad—or on its own.

3½ cups	unbleached hard white flour	875 mL
1 tsp.	chopped fresh rosemary	5 mL
⅔ cup	active sourdough starter (*see facing page*), room temperature	150 mL
1 cup	water	250 mL
½ tsp.	sea salt	2 mL
½ cup	chopped kalamata olives	125 mL

Mix flour and rosemary together in a bowl. In a separate large bowl, add starter to water. Gradually add flour mixture to starter mixture, mixing by hand and bringing ingredients together to form a loose ball.

Let dough rest for at least 5 minutes to let flour absorb water and to allow gluten to start developing. Dough should be smooth, soft and fairly sticky.

Add salt, and knead for 5 to 10 minutes, until dough has a silky texture. Mix in olives. (You may need to add a small amount of flour at this point to offset the moisture from the olives.)

Form dough into a ball, and place in a lightly oiled bowl, turning dough to coat with oil. Cover with plastic wrap, and let stand for 1 hour at room temperature. Transfer to refrigerator, and leave overnight to allow flavors to develop.

The next day, remove dough from refrigerator 2 hours before baking. Turn out onto a lightly floured board. Shape dough into a free-form loaf. Place on a rimless floured sheet, and let rise at room temperature until nearly doubled in size.

An hour before baking, preheat oven to 500°F (260°C), and place a baking stone in the bottom third of the oven. Pour 1 cup (250 mL) water into a baking pan, and set on oven floor 15 minutes before baking.

When loaf is ready to bake, cut a circular cap on the dome of the dough using a razor blade or an extremely sharp knife. Slide loaf onto the baking stone, and reduce oven temperature to 450°F (230°C). Bake for 10 minutes, then reduce oven temperature to 400°F (200°C). Bake for 10 minutes more, then remove pan of water. Continue to bake for 20 to 35 minutes. The finished loaf should make a hollow sound when you thump the bottom. Let cool completely on a baking rack before slicing.

Makes 1 loaf

DOUBLE TROUBLE

Loaves that rise a second time should never be allowed to double in size. The key is to put the bread into the oven while it is still on its way "up." If it has already reached its maximum size, the loaf may fall when it comes into contact with the heat.

Vegetarian Focaccette

VEGETARIAN FOCACCETTE

*This is one of our favorites. You can dress focaccette with a variety
of inventive toppings, from grated cheese or grilled vegetables to browned meats.
We recently made one with pan-fried potatoes ringed with fresh spinach
and mustard seed. All-purpose flour will give this loaf a soft, chewy texture.*

TOPPING

¼ cup	olive oil	50 mL
2 tsp.	balsamic vinegar	10 mL
1	clove garlic, coarsely chopped	1
1 Tbsp.	tomato paste	15 mL
	Coarse salt & freshly ground black pepper	
¼	red onion, coarsely chopped	¼
½	zucchini, coarsely chopped	½
¼	eggplant, coarsely chopped	¼
4	button mushrooms, sliced	4

Preheat oven to 350°F (180°C). Mix oil, vinegar, garlic, tomato paste and
salt and pepper to taste. Coat onion, zucchini, eggplant and mushrooms with
dressing, and place in a roasting pan. Roast for 30 to 45 minutes, stirring
occasionally. Set vegetables aside.

DOUGH

½ tsp.	active dry yeast	2 mL
½ cup	warm water	125 mL
2½ cups	unbleached hard white or all-purpose flour	625 mL
½ tsp.	sea salt	2 mL
½ cup	cool spring water	125 mL
1 Tbsp.	extra-virgin olive oil	15 mL
¼ cup	active sourdough starter (*see page 198*), room temperature	50 mL
	Olive oil for brushing loaves	
2 tsp.	chopped fresh rosemary	10 mL
	Sea salt & freshly ground black pepper	

Stir yeast into water in a small bowl. Set aside until yeast has fully dissolved.

Measure flour into a large mixing bowl, and stir in salt, using a wooden spoon. Form a well in center of flour, and pour in yeast mixture, spring water, 1 tablespoon (15 mL) oil and starter. Thoroughly mix all ingredients together, using your hands, if necessary.

Turn dough onto a floured work surface, and knead for about 5 to 10 minutes, or until dough is smooth and elastic. Shape dough into a free-form ball, and place in a clean oiled bowl, turning to coat with oil. Cover with a towel, and let rise until nearly doubled in size, about 1½ hours.

Punch dough down, and turn in bowl. Cover, and let rise again until nearly doubled in size, about 45 minutes.

Turn dough out onto a floured board. Divide in half, and gently press into 2 free-form pizza rounds. Set on a floured rimless baking sheet, and cover with a towel. Let rise until nearly doubled in size, about 50 minutes.

In the meantime, place a pan of water on the floor of the oven, and set a baking stone on the lower oven rack. Preheat oven to 425°F (220°C). When dough is ready, dimple tops with the tips of your fingers, then brush loaves with oil. Garnish with roasted vegetables, and sprinkle with rosemary. Season with salt and pepper to taste.

Slide loaves onto the baking stone, and bake for about 30 minutes, or until they are golden brown, removing pan of water after 10 minutes. Remove bread from oven, and brush with oil. Let cool before serving.

Makes 2 loaves

PITA BREAD

This recipe produces a slightly puffier pita than the traditional unleavened Middle Eastern bread. We like to dress the top with zaatar, a seasoning mixture of ground herbs and spices.

2 scant Tbsp.	active dry yeast	25 mL
¼ tsp.	sugar	1 mL
2 cups	warm water	500 mL
⅓ cup	olive oil	75 mL
4 tsp.	sea salt	20 mL
5½ cups	flour	1.4 L
½ cup	whole wheat flour	125 mL
	Cornmeal	

In a large bowl, dissolve yeast and sugar in ½ cup (125 mL) water, and allow to proof in a warm place until yeast begins to foam. Stir in remaining 1½ cups (375 mL) water, oil and salt, and mix in flour 1 cup (250 mL) at a time. Turn dough onto a floured board, and knead until smooth and elastic, about 10 minutes.

Grease a mixing bowl with butter. Place dough in bowl, and turn to coat all sides. Cover, and let rise in a warm place until doubled in size.

Punch dough down, and let rest on a floured board for 10 minutes. Divide into eight pieces, and shape each piece into a ball. Cover with a clean tea towel, and let rest for 30 minutes. Flatten each ball with a rolling pin into an 8-inch (20 cm) circle.

Preheat oven to 500°F (260°C). Sprinkle a baking sheet or stone with cornmeal, and bake pitas (probably two at a time) by first placing on the lowest oven rack for 5 minutes, then transferring to a higher rack for 3 to 5 minutes, or until pitas have puffed up and are lightly browned.

Makes 8 pitas

Chocolate-Chip (*background*) **and Cranberry Scones**

RASPBERRY & WHITE-CHOCOLATE SCONES

*Raspberry jam and white chocolate make a satisfyingly
sweet combination in this "party" scone.*

2²/₃ cups	flour	650 mL
1 Tbsp.	baking powder	15 mL
¹/₂ tsp.	salt	2 mL
¹/₃ cup	sugar	75 mL
¹/₂ cup less 1 Tbsp.	cold, unsalted butter, cut into pea-size pieces	110 mL
¹/₂ cup	white chocolate chips	125 mL
1 cup less 5 tsp.	buttermilk	225 mL
¹/₃ cup	raspberry jam	75 mL
1	egg beaten with 2 Tbsp. (25 mL) milk	1

When measuring flour, spoon it into the measuring cup. In a large bowl, combine flour, baking powder, salt and sugar. Place a handful of dry mixture on a work surface. Rub in butter pieces, just enough to coat but not blend. Add flour-coated butter to dry mixture, and mix thoroughly. Add chocolate, and mix to coat with flour. Add buttermilk, and mix with a fork or a pastry cutter until mixture just holds together. Do not overmix.

Preheat oven to 425°F (220°C). Place dough on a rolling surface. Using your hands or a rolling pin, gently form dough into a rough-edged square (about 9 by 9 inches/23 by 23 cm). Cut into six triangles. Use a spoon to make a shallow dent in the top of each scone, and fill with jam. Brush with egg-milk wash. Place apart on a baking sheet. Bake for 12-15 minutes, until scones are lightly browned, and let stand for 5 to 10 minutes. (Be careful—the jam is hot.)

Makes 6 scones

SCONE HEADS

Pan Chancho makes a variety of scrumptious scones. You can adapt this scone recipe simply by substituting either semisweet chocolate chips or cranberries for the white chocolate and omitting the raspberry jam.

LEMON-CURRANT ROLLS

These lemon-currant rolls are a daily feature at the bakery. The dough has a tender, elastic texture, and the filling and lemony icing are not too sweet. This recipe is for the oversize variety we like to make—one usually satisfies two people.

DOUGH

2 Tbsp.	active dry yeast	25 mL
½ tsp.	sugar	2 mL
¾ cup	warm water	175 mL
3	eggs	3
1¼ cups	warm milk	300 mL
½ cup	unsalted butter, softened	125 mL
7 cups	flour	1.75 L
½ cup	sugar	125 mL
2 tsp.	sea salt	10 mL
¾ cup	currants	175 mL

FILLING

½ cup	unsalted butter, softened	125 mL
1¼ cups	brown sugar	300 mL
4 tsp.	cinnamon	20 mL

ICING

2 Tbsp.	lemon juice	25 mL
1½ cups	icing sugar	375 mL

In a large bowl, dissolve yeast and ½ teaspoon (2 mL) sugar in water, and leave to proof in a warm place, until yeast begins to foam. Add eggs, milk and butter. In a separate bowl, mix together flour, ½ cup (125 mL) sugar, salt and currants. Fold dry ingredients into liquid ingredients.

Turn out onto a floured board, and knead until smooth. Shape dough into a ball, and place in a bowl greased with butter. Turn dough to coat thoroughly, and cover with a clean tea towel. Let rest in a warm place until dough has doubled in size.

To make filling, cream together butter, brown sugar and cinnamon in a clean bowl. Set aside.

Preheat oven to 350°F (180°C). Turn dough out onto a floured surface, and roll into a rectangle about ¾ inch (2 cm) thick. Spread filling evenly over dough. Roll dough into a cylinder. Cut dough into 18 slices, each 3 inches (8 cm) thick. Place each piece in a greased muffin-tin cup. Bake for 30 minutes. Remove from oven, and allow to cool.

To make icing, in a small saucepan, warm lemon juice and add icing sugar, stirring until sugar dissolves. Drizzle over slightly warm rolls.

Makes 18 rolls

HOT CROSS BUNS

*These hot cross buns are a wonderful homemade version of the sticky-bun classic.
You'll find them easy to prepare and well worth every minute.*

SPICE MIX

4 tsp.	ground nutmeg	20 mL
1 tsp.	ground cloves	5 mL
1 tsp.	allspice	5 mL
1½ tsp.	ground ginger	7 mL
1 tsp.	ground cumin	5 mL
1 tsp.	cinnamon	5 mL

Combine all ingredients together in a small bowl, and set aside.

DOUGH

1 Tbsp.	active dry yeast	15 mL
2 cups	warm water	500 mL
½ cup	butter, softened	125 mL
2	eggs, lightly beaten	2
1 cup	milk powder	250 mL
6 cups	flour	1.5 L
¾ cup	extra-fine white sugar	175 mL
1 Tbsp.	spice mix	15 mL
1 Tbsp.	sea salt	15 mL
1½ cups	currants	375 mL
1½ cups	sultana raisins	375 mL
1 cup	candied citrus peel	250 mL
1	egg beaten with 2 Tbsp. (25 mL) milk	1

ICING

2 Tbsp.	lemon juice	25 mL
1½ cups	icing sugar	375 mL
	Zest of 1 lemon	

In a large bowl, dissolve yeast in water. Stir in butter, 2 lightly beaten eggs
and milk powder. Add flour, sugar, spice mix, salt, currants, raisins and citrus
peel, mix well, and turn out onto a floured board. Knead until silky. Leave to
rise in a warm place for 2 to 3 hours, until dough has doubled in size.

Punch dough down, and shape into 18 buns. Place on a greased baking
sheet, and let rise again until not quite doubled.

Preheat oven to 375°F (190°C). Slash tops of buns with a razor blade. Just
before putting the buns in the oven, brush tops with egg-milk wash. Bake for
20 minutes.

To make icing, warm lemon juice in a small saucepan, stir in sugar until
dissolved, and add lemon zest. Ice slightly cool buns with a cross of icing.

Makes 18 buns

Sweetest Last

In keeping with its reputation for going for the gusto, Chez Piggy has a list of desserts that challenges the hardest heart. We want our desserts to taste like their ingredients rather than whipped-up confectionery extravaganzas. In the first blush of June, summer arrives at your table as a Strawberry Short-cake With Brandied Cream or a Strawberry-Rhubarb Pie. By August, ripe peaches are the centerpiece of Chez Piggy's incomparable Peach Almond Pie. For fans of traditional desserts, we have old-fashioned offerings with a twist—a gingerbread laced with chocolate chips; an apple pie that would do any mother proud. We also cater to appetites driven by a desire for richer fare with our creamy cheesecakes, Chocolate Mousse and Caramel Pecan Tart. For a sweet and satisfying conclusion to any meal, you can't go wrong with Blueberry Crème Brûlée, Lemon Pots de Crème or Flan Español.

JUST DESSERTS, from left to right: Chez Piggy sign at twilight; father-and-son patrons toast their favorite eatery; Susan Newbury, queen of the desserts; restaurant foyer decked out for the holidays.

BLUEBERRY CRÈME BRÛLÉE
WITH A CINNAMON CRUST

*On the baked-custard continuum, this version of crème brûlée is the ultimate dessert,
loaded with blueberries—wild, if possible—and topped with a crispy cinnamon crust.*

4 cups	35% B.F. cream	1 L
¼ cup	granulated sugar	50 mL
9	egg yolks	9
1 tsp.	vanilla extract	5 mL
4 cups	fresh blueberries	1 L
½ cup	flour	125 mL
¼ cup	brown sugar	50 mL
1 tsp.	cinnamon	5 mL
¼ tsp.	ground nutmeg	1 mL
½ cup	unsalted butter, chilled & cut into bits	125 mL

Preheat oven to 350°F (180°C). In a large saucepan, heat cream and ¼ cup
(50 mL) granulated sugar over medium heat until sugar dissolves, but do not
allow cream to boil. Set aside.

Place egg yolks in a large bowl, and temper them by whisking in 1 cup
(250 mL) hot cream. Gradually whisk in remaining cream, and stir in vanilla.
Pour into four individual ovenproof custard cups. Bake in a hot-water bath
for 30 minutes.

Remove custard cups from water, and place on a baking sheet. Top with
blueberries, and set aside. Turn on broiler.

Place flour, brown sugar, cinnamon and nutmeg in a food processor,
and blend. Add butter, and using the pastry blade, process briefly, just to
incorporate. The mixture should be crumbly, and you should be able to
sprinkle it on top of the custard. Heap the cinnamon mixture over the
blueberries. Broil for 3 to 7 minutes, or until butter melts and a crust forms.
Serve warm or cold.

Serves 4

LEMON POTS DE CRÈME

This lemon-flavored custard is best topped with seasonal berries. For a savory variation,
substitute lime juice for the lemon juice and add a few threads of saffron.

1½ cups	35% B.F. cream	375 mL
⅔ cup	sugar	150 mL
1	egg	1
4	egg yolks	4
½ cup	lemon juice	125 mL
1 Tbsp.	lemon zest	15 mL

Preheat oven to 325°F (160°C). Place cream in a saucepan, and gently warm
to body temperature. Pour into a bowl, and stir in sugar until it dissolves. Beat
together egg and egg yolks. Whisk eggs into cream mixture. Stir in lemon juice
and lemon zest. Ladle into four individual ovenproof custard cups, and place in
a hot-water bath. Bake for 45 minutes. Remove from hot water, and let cool.
Serves 4

FLAN ESPAÑOL

Simple to make, Flan Español combines the comforting taste and texture
of custard with a delicious caramelized syrup. This dessert has been one of the
most popular on our menu since the day Chez Piggy opened.

½ cup + 5 Tbsp.	sugar	125 mL + 65 mL
2 Tbsp.	orange juice	25 mL
3¼ cups	whole milk, warmed	800 mL
3	eggs	3
2	egg yolks	2
1 Tbsp.	vanilla extract	15 mL

Combine ½ cup (125 mL) sugar and orange juice in a heavy wide-bottomed
pan, and stir to mix. Place over medium-high heat, and allow sugar to melt
and begin to brown and caramelize. Stir constantly with a wooden spoon until
liquid turns the color of maple syrup, but do not let it burn or smoke. While
the caramel is still hot, divide equally among four to six small ovenproof
custard cups. Set aside to harden.
Preheat oven to 375°F (190°C). Dissolve remaining 5 tablespoons (65 mL)
sugar in milk. In a separate bowl, beat eggs and egg yolks together, then whisk
into milk mixture. Stir in vanilla. Set custard cups in a hot-water bath. Ladle
custard mixture into each. Bake for 45 to 60 minutes, or until custard is fully
cooked. Remove from hot water, and let cool. To serve, run a knife around the
edge of each cup and turn out onto a serving dish.
Serves 4 to 6

CHOCOLATE MOUSSE

There are a million tricks to making a successful chocolate mousse.
Because this recipe does not include cream, as many others do, it is more difficult
to make. Be aware of humidity and temperature. If the chocolate is too cold when
you add the egg whites, for instance, it will produce a custardlike density;
if it is too hot, it will cause the egg whites to separate out of the final preparation.
If you overwhip the egg whites, the finished mousse will be grainy.

6 oz.	semisweet chocolate	175 g
1 Tbsp.	unsalted butter	15 mL
2 Tbsp.	dark rum	25 mL
2 Tbsp.	hot coffee	25 mL
2	large egg yolks	2
6	large egg whites, room temperature	6
1 Tbsp.	lemon juice	15 mL

Place chocolate, butter, rum and coffee in a double boiler over warm water, and stir constantly until chocolate and butter melt. Set aside to cool slightly. When chocolate mixture has cooled to precisely body temperature, whisk in egg yolks. Chocolate should thicken slightly. Scrape chocolate into a large bowl, and set aside.

In a mixing bowl, whip egg whites until peaks begin to form. Add lemon juice, and continue to whip until peaks are stiff but not dry. Gently fold whites into chocolate mixture with a wire whisk, one-third at a time. The whites should be incorporated, but do not overmix. Immediately spoon into individual serving glasses, and chill.

Serves 6

Raspberry Cheesecake With
White-Chocolate Sauce

RASPBERRY CHEESECAKE
WITH WHITE-CHOCOLATE SAUCE

Be sure to use real chocolate for the white-chocolate sauce, which adds the perfect finishing touch to this creamy, rich raspberry cheesecake. The sauce is also delicious on ice cream or drizzled over fresh berries. The basic cheesecake technique is to seal the outside at a high temperature, then bake it for the duration at a low temperature. It is important to watch carefully—many a cheesecake has been ruined because the baker forgot to reduce the heat.

CHEESECAKE

2 Tbsp.	butter, melted	25 mL
¾ cup	graham cracker crumbs	175 mL
1 Tbsp.	icing sugar	15 mL
1 cup + 2 Tbsp.	granulated sugar	250 mL + 25 mL
1 lb.	cream cheese, room temperature	500 g
4	eggs, separated	4
1 tsp.	vanilla extract	5 mL
1 cup	frozen unsweetened raspberries, thawed, with juice	250 mL
1 Tbsp.	flour	15 mL

WHITE-CHOCOLATE SAUCE

1½ cups	35% B.F. cream	375 mL
12 oz.	white chocolate, chopped	375 g

Preheat oven to 450°F (230°C). Line the sides and bottom of a 9-inch (2.5 L) springform pan with parchment or wax paper. Set aside.

Place butter in a large bowl, and add graham cracker crumbs and icing sugar. Using an electric mixer, blend until mixture is consistency of wet sand. Press crumbs into bottom of pan, and set aside.

In a large bowl, cream 1 cup (250 mL) granulated sugar together with cream cheese. Add egg yolks, and beat with an electric mixer until creamy. Beat in vanilla, raspberries and flour until thoroughly mixed. Set aside.

In a clean mixing bowl, whip egg whites until soft peaks form. Slowly add remaining 2 tablespoons (25 mL) granulated sugar, and continue beating until peaks are stiff, being careful to stop before whites become dry. Fold whites into raspberry mixture, one-third at a time.

Pour mixture into prepared pan, being careful not to disturb the crust. Place on middle rack of oven, and bake for 10 minutes. Immediately reduce temperature to 250°F (120°C), and bake for 1¼ hours. Remove from oven, and let cool to room temperature before springing pan.

To make white-chocolate sauce, heat cream to a boil in a large saucepan. Place chocolate in a deep bowl, and add hot cream. Stir until chocolate is completely melted. Drizzle a few tablespoons over individual slices of cheesecake. (Makes 2½ cups/625 mL sauce.)

Serves 10 to 12

LEMON CHEESECAKE
WITH LIME CRÈME FRAÎCHE

This cheesecake, Zal's favorite, is creamy, rich and pleasantly tart
at the same time. It is one of the easiest cheesecakes to prepare.

LIME CRÈME FRAÎCHE

1 1/3 cups	35% B.F. cream	325 mL
1 1/3 cups	sour cream	325 mL
	Juice & zest of 3 limes	
2 Tbsp.	sugar	25 mL

In a small bowl, blend cream and sour cream with a hand blender. Cover with a clean tea towel, and let stand at room temperature overnight.

The next day, line a sieve with a clean tea towel. Set sieve in a large bowl, and pour in crème fraîche mixture. Drain for 12 hours, until mixture is consistency of sour cream. Discard liquid that has drained off. Stir in lime juice, lime zest, and sugar, and refrigerate. It can be stored in the refrigerator for up to 2 weeks.

CHEESECAKE

2 Tbsp.	butter, melted	25 mL
3/4 cup	graham cracker crumbs	175 mL
3/4 tsp.	icing sugar	4 mL
1 1/2 lb.	cream cheese, room temperature	750 g
1 cup	granulated sugar	175 mL + 50 mL
4	eggs, separated	4
	Juice & zest of 2 lemons	

Preheat oven to 450°F (230°C). Line bottom and sides of 9-inch (2.5 L) springform pan with parchment or wax paper.

In a large bowl, combine butter, graham cracker crumbs and icing sugar. Press into bottom of pan.

In a mixing bowl, cream together cream cheese and 3/4 cup (175 mL) granulated sugar until smooth and light. Beat in egg yolks, lemon juice and lemon zest.

In a separate bowl, whip egg whites with remaining 1/4 cup (50 mL) granulated sugar until soft peaks form. Fold egg-white mixture into cream-cheese mixture. Pour into prepared pan.

Bake for 10 minutes, then reduce heat to 250°F (120°C), and bake for 1 hour. Turn off oven, and slightly open oven door. Let cheesecake stand in warm oven for 1 hour. Remove, and let cool completely. Unmold and chill. Serve garnished with a dollop of lime crème fraîche.

Serves 10

PEACHES & CREAM CHEESECAKE

You can use either fresh or canned peaches to make this cheesecake.
With canned, however, be sure the peaches are packed in juice,
rather than syrup, and drain well before making the purée.

CHEESECAKE

¾ cup	graham cracker crumbs	175 mL
2 Tbsp.	butter, melted	25 mL
1 Tbsp.	icing sugar	15 mL
1¾ lb.	cream cheese, room temperature	875 g
¾ cup + 2 Tbsp.	granulated sugar	175 mL + 25 mL
4	eggs, separated	4
3 Tbsp.	peach schnapps (optional)	45 mL
¾ cup	puréed peaches	175 mL

TOPPING

1 cup	sour cream	250 mL
4 tsp.	sugar	20 mL
¾ tsp.	vanilla extract	4 mL

Preheat oven to 450°F (230°C). Line a 9-inch (2.5 L) springform pan with parchment or wax paper. Mix together graham cracker crumbs, butter and icing sugar in a small bowl, and press into the bottom of pan. Set aside.

In a large bowl, cream together cream cheese and ¾ cup (175 mL) granulated sugar. Beat in egg yolks, schnapps, if using, and peaches. Set aside.

In a separate bowl, whip egg whites while gradually adding remaining 2 tablespoons (25 mL) granulated sugar until stiff peaks form. Fold whites into cream-cheese mixture. Pour batter into prepared pan. Bake for 10 minutes, then reduce temperature to 250°F (120°C), and bake for 1 hour.

Meanwhile, prepare topping. Whisk together sour cream, sugar and vanilla. Gently spread sour-cream mixture on top of hot baked cake, and bake at 250°F (120°C) for an additional 10 minutes. When cake is done, turn off oven, and let cake cool in oven with door open.

Serves 10

STRAWBERRY SHORTCAKE
WITH BRANDIED CREAM

When local strawberries ripen, we make this dessert every day.

TEA BISCUITS

3 cups	flour	750 mL
2 Tbsp.	sugar	25 mL
1 Tbsp. + 1½ tsp.	baking powder	15 mL + 7 mL
¾ tsp.	cream of tartar	4 mL
¾ tsp.	salt	4 mL
¾ cup	shortening, chilled	175 mL
1	egg	1
¾ cup	milk	175 mL

FILLING

3 pints	strawberries, cleaned & hulled	1.5 L
¼ cup	sugar	50 mL

BRANDIED CREAM

¾ cup	sour cream	175 mL
¼ cup	sugar	50 mL
1 Tbsp.	lemon juice	15 mL
1 Tbsp.	brandy	15 mL
1 cup	35% B.F. cream, whipped & chilled	250 mL

To make tea biscuits, preheat oven to 400°F (200°C). Mix together flour, sugar, baking powder, cream of tartar and salt in a large bowl. Cut in shortening until mixture forms pea-size pieces. Stir in egg and milk until just mixed. Turn dough out onto floured board, and roll to a 1-inch (2.5 cm) thickness, taking care not to overhandle. Cut out 24 biscuits with a 1½-inch-diameter (4 cm) round cutter. Place ½ inch (1 cm) apart on an ungreased baking sheet. Bake for 15 minutes. Let cool before assembling.

To make filling, slice strawberries and mix with sugar. Let stand until cream is prepared.

To make brandied cream, place sour cream in a medium-size bowl, and stir in sugar, lemon juice and brandy. Fold in whipped cream.

Cut biscuits horizontally, and arrange three pieces each on individual plates. Spoon on strawberries, and generously cover with brandied cream. Top with remaining biscuits.

Serves 8

LEMON CHIFFON CAKE
WITH LEMON CURD FILLING

Light chiffon in texture but rich in lemony tastes, this cake is a perfect summer dessert.

CAKE

2¼ cups	cake flour	550 mL
1¼ cups + 2 Tbsp.	sugar	300 mL + 25 mL
½ tsp.	baking soda	2 mL
½ tsp.	salt	2 mL
½ cup	vegetable oil	125 mL
6	egg yolks	6
⅔ cup	water	150 mL
2 Tbsp.	lemon juice	25 mL
1 Tbsp.	lemon zest	15 mL
1 tsp.	vanilla extract	5 mL
8	egg whites	8
1 tsp.	cream of tartar	5 mL
	Icing sugar for garnish	

LEMON FILLING

½ cup	lemon juice	125 mL
¼ cup	sugar	50 mL
6	egg yolks	6
1	egg	1
⅓ cup	unsalted butter, chilled & chopped	75 mL
1 cup	35% B.F. cream, whipped	250 mL

Preheat oven to 350°F (180°C). Sift together flour, 1¼ cups (300 mL) sugar, baking soda and salt. In a separate bowl, mix together oil, egg yolks, water, lemon juice, lemon zest and vanilla. Beat wet ingredients into dry ingredients to a light, creamy consistency. Set batter aside.

Place egg whites, cream of tartar and remaining 2 tablespoons (25 mL) sugar in a bowl, and beat until stiff peaks form. Fold egg whites into batter. Pour batter into an ungreased 9-inch (3 L) tube pan. Bake for 55 minutes, or until a wooden skewer or a knife tip inserted in center comes out clean.

Let cake cool inverted on a rack. When cooled, remove from pan. When cake is completely cool, cut into three layers horizontally.

To make lemon filling, place lemon juice, sugar, egg yolks and egg in a small bowl, and mix by hand until sugar is dissolved. Place in a double boiler over hot water, stirring constantly until mixture thickens. Remove from heat, and stir in butter until melted. Transfer to a bowl, and let cool. Fold in whipped cream. Refrigerate for 1 hour.

Fill cake layers with lemon filling. Refrigerate for 30 minutes. Dust cake with icing sugar.

Serves 12

PANDORA'S LEMON-MOUSSE CHOCOLATE BROWNIES

One of these mega-rich brownies is plenty to kill two chocoholics.
We serve it in a puddle of chocolate, but don't let that scare you, because the tart lemon
custard adds a much-appreciated contrast in flavors. Melting all the chocolate
required in this recipe will give your double boiler a real workout.

BROWNIE BATTER

13 oz.	semisweet chocolate	400 g
¼ cup	unsalted butter	50 mL
8 oz.	cream cheese, room temperature	250 g
1¾ cups	sugar	425 mL
3	eggs	3
2 tsp.	vanilla extract	10 mL
1½ cups	flour	375 mL
¾ tsp.	baking powder	4 mL
½ tsp.	salt	2 mL

LEMON LAYER

3 oz.	cream cheese, room temperature	75 g
⅓ cup	lemon juice	75 mL
¼ cup	sugar	50 mL
3	eggs	3

CHOCOLATE LAYER

6 oz.	semisweet chocolate	175 g
⅔ cup	35% B.F. cream	150 mL

TOPPING

3 oz.	white chocolate	75 g
¼ cup	35% B.F. cream	50 mL

Preheat oven to 350°F (180°C). To make brownie batter, melt chocolate and butter over warm water in a double boiler. Remove from heat. In a large bowl, cream together cream cheese, sugar and eggs with an electric mixer. Beat in vanilla, flour, baking powder and salt. Add melted-chocolate mixture, and blend until smooth. Pour into a greased, floured 9-by-12-inch (3 L) cake pan.

To make lemon layer, beat together cream cheese, lemon juice and sugar with an electric mixer until smooth. Beat in eggs. Pour over brownie batter.

To make chocolate layer, place chocolate and cream over warm water in a double boiler, and stir until chocolate melts. Remove from heat. Drizzle over lemon layer. Bake for 45 minutes. Let cool, then chill to set.

To make topping, place chocolate and cream over warm water in a double boiler, and stir until chocolate melts. Drizzle over chilled brownies.

Makes 12 to 20 brownies

Pandora's Lemon-Mousse
Chocolate Brownies

LEMON POPPY-SEED POUND CAKE

*Buttery-flavored pound cake is lightened by the tastes of lemon
and poppy seed in this delicious dessert or snacking cake.*

2 cups	flour	500 mL
1½ cups	sugar	375 mL
1 tsp.	baking powder	5 mL
¾ tsp.	salt	4 mL
1 cup + 2 Tbsp.	unsalted butter, room temperature	275 mL
4	eggs, room temperature	4
¼ cup	milk	50 mL
2 tsp.	vanilla extract	10 mL
1 Tbsp.	lemon zest	15 mL
¼ cup	poppy seed	50 mL
⅓ cup	lemon juice	75 mL

Preheat oven to 325°F (160°C). With an electric mixer, beat together
flour, 1 cup (250 mL) sugar, baking powder and salt. Add butter, and mix
until blended.

In a separate bowl, beat eggs, then mix in milk and vanilla. Gradually add
egg mixture to dry ingredients, and beat until smooth. Fold in lemon zest and
poppy seed.

Scrape into a greased, floured Bundt pan. Bake for 1¼ hours, or until tester
comes out clean. Remove from oven, and let cake cool slightly.

Place lemon juice in a saucepan, and stir in remaining ½ cup (125 mL)
sugar over medium heat until dissolved. Drizzle the top and sides of warm
cake with glaze.

Serves 12

Chocolate-Chip
Gingerbread

CHOCOLATE-CHIP GINGERBREAD

Moist gingerbread gets a sweet boost from chocolate chips and a bead of chocolate icing.
At the bakery, we make the gingerbread in mini loaf pans.

GINGERBREAD

	Shortening	
	Breadcrumbs	
1 ¼ cups	flour	300 mL
1 tsp.	baking soda	5 mL
¼ tsp.	salt	1 mL
¾ tsp.	ground ginger	4 mL
¾ tsp.	ground cloves	4 mL
½ tsp.	cinnamon	2 mL
¼ tsp.	dry mustard	1 mL
¼ tsp.	freshly ground black pepper	1 mL
1 Tbsp.	instant coffee	15 mL
½ cup	boiling water	125 mL
½ cup	molasses	125 mL
¼ cup	unsalted butter	50 mL
¼ cup	brown sugar	50 mL
1	egg	1
½ cup	semisweet chocolate chips	125 mL
½ cup	white chocolate chips	125 mL

TOPPING

| 3 oz. | semisweet chocolate | 75 g |
| 1 Tbsp. | unsalted butter | 15 mL |

Preheat oven to 350°F (180°C). Grease a 6-cup (1.5 L) loaf pan or hugelhopf mold with shortening, and dust with breadcrumbs.

In a large bowl, combine flour, baking soda, salt, ginger, cloves, cinnamon, mustard and pepper. In a separate bowl, mix together coffee, water and molasses, and let cool. In another large bowl, cream together butter and brown sugar, and beat in egg. Alternately by thirds, add dry ingredients and molasses mixture to egg mixture. Fold in chocolate chips. Fill prepared pan.

Bake for 45 minutes, or until a wooden skewer inserted in center comes out clean (except if daubed with melted chocolate). Remove from oven, and let cool.

To make topping, melt chocolate and butter over warm water in a double boiler, and drizzle over gingerbread.

Makes 8 slices

LAYERED HAZELNUT MERINGUES

Parchment paper is a necessity when making these giant meringues; wax paper, brown paper and aluminum foil will stick to the finished meringues. Flavor the whipped cream with Frangelico or amaretto, or use flavored chocolate for the decorative curls. Raspberries, strawberries or kiwis (sometimes in combination) make the best fruit filling. Undercooked meringues can be wet, so be sure to leave them in the oven long enough to allow moisture to evaporate fully, but be careful they don't burn.

8	large egg whites	8
1¼ cups	granulated sugar	300 mL
⅓ cup	ground hazelnuts	75 mL
2 Tbsp.	icing sugar	25 mL
1 Tbsp.	cornstarch	15 mL
2 cups	35% B.F. cream, whipped & chilled	500 mL
	Chocolate curls	
	Fresh fruit, sliced	

Draw three 10-inch-diameter (25 cm) circles on parchment paper, and place on a baking sheet. Set aside. Preheat oven to 250°F (120°C).

Place egg whites in a medium bowl, and whip to stiff peaks while slowly adding granulated sugar. Fold in hazelnuts, icing sugar and cornstarch.

Fill icing bag with meringue, and pipe a ½-inch-diameter (1 cm) bead onto parchment-paper circles, starting in the center and spiraling out. With the oven door ajar to allow moisture to escape, bake for 3 hours, or until completely dry.

Remove meringues from paper with a spatula, and let cool to room temperature. Place one meringue on a cake plate, and cover with one-third each of the whipped cream, chocolate curls and fruit. Repeat for remaining two layers.

Serves 12

STREUSEL COFFEE CAKE

You can also make this crumb-topped cake recipe in 12 individual muffin tins. Serve it with fresh raspberries or a raspberry coulis that you make by puréeing fruit with a bit of sugar.

1 cup	whole toasted pecans	250 mL
1 cup	shredded coconut	250 mL
½ cup	brown sugar	125 mL
2 tsp.	cinnamon	10 mL
¼ cup	frozen raspberries, thawed & drained (reserve half the juice)	50 mL
¼ cup	raspberry jam	50 mL
¾ cup	butter	175 mL
1½ cups	sugar	375 mL
3	eggs	3
1½ cups	sour cream	375 mL
2 tsp.	vanilla extract	10 mL
3 cups	flour	750 mL
1½ tsp.	baking soda	7 mL
1½ tsp.	baking powder	7 mL
¼ tsp.	salt	1 mL

Preheat oven to 350°F (180°C). Grease and flour an angel-food cake pan, and set aside.

To make topping, combine ½ cup (125 mL) pecans, ½ cup (125 mL) coconut, brown sugar and cinnamon in a large bowl, and set aside.

In a small bowl, mix together raspberries, reserved juice and jam. Set aside.

In a large bowl, cream butter and sugar together. Gradually beat in eggs, sour cream and vanilla. Sift flour, baking soda, baking powder and salt together, and add to creamed-butter mixture. Fold in remaining ½ cup (125 mL) pecans and remaining ½ cup (125 mL) coconut.

Place half the batter in prepared pan. Spoon raspberry mixture on top, and sprinkle with half the topping. Cover with remaining batter, and sprinkle with remaining topping. Bake for 55 to 60 minutes.

Serves 12

STRAWBERRY HAZELNUT TORTE

*The light hazelnut layers of this torte are filled with strawberries
and creamy orange-flavored butter. As an alternative,
you can substitute kiwis or raspberries in the filling.*

6	eggs, separated	6
1 cup	granulated sugar	175 mL + 50 mL
¾ lb.	toasted hazelnuts, ground	375 g
1 Tbsp.	flour	15 mL
1½ tsp.	orange zest	7 mL
¾ lb.	unsalted butter, room temperature	375 g
¾ cup	icing sugar	175 mL
2 Tbsp.	orange liqueur	25 mL
12-16	strawberries, sliced	12-16

Line sides and bottom of a 9-inch (2.5 L) springform pan with parchment paper. Preheat oven to 350°F (180°C).

In a mixing bowl, beat egg yolks. Add ¾ cup (175 mL) granulated sugar, and beat until light and fluffy. Set aside.

In a large bowl, lightly beat egg whites, and add remaining ¼ cup (50 mL) granulated sugar. Beat until stiff but not dry. Fold egg-yolk mixture into whites. Fold in hazelnuts, flour and 1 teaspoon (5 mL) orange zest.

Pour batter into prepared pan. Bake for 45 minutes. Let cool, then chill. Slice horizontally into three layers. Set aside.

In a large bowl, cream together butter and icing sugar. Whip together with liqueur and remaining ½ teaspoon (2 mL) orange zest at high speed until light and fluffy. Place two-thirds of orange filling in a separate bowl, and gently combine with two-thirds of strawberries.

Place one layer of cake on a plate, and spread with half of the strawberry filling. Add middle layer of cake, and repeat. Put top layer of cake in place, and spread with remaining orange filling. Decorate with remaining strawberries. Refrigerate.

Serves 12

BOURBON PECAN TORTE

*Extremely moist and heavier than a cheesecake (if you can believe it),
this torte is perfect for anyone having a severe chocolate attack.*

TORTE

½ lb.	unsalted butter	250 g
8 oz.	semisweet chocolate	250 g
1½ cups	toasted pecans, chopped	375 mL
1½ cups	sugar	375 mL
1 cup	cocoa	250 mL
6	eggs, room temperature	6
½ cup	bourbon	125 mL
1 cup	toasted pecans, chopped, for garnish	250 mL

GLAZE

8 oz.	semisweet chocolate	250 g
¼ cup	unsalted butter	50 mL

Line sides and bottom of a 9-inch (2.5 L) springform pan with parchment or wax paper. Preheat oven to 350°F (180°C).

Melt butter and chocolate over warm water in a double boiler. Set aside, and let cool slightly.

Place pecans, sugar and cocoa in a bowl, and blend with an electric mixer. Mix in eggs until smooth. Add melted-chocolate mixture and bourbon. Mix until blended, but do not whip. Pour into prepared pan. Bake for 1 hour. Let cool before springing pan. Refrigerate.

To make glaze, melt chocolate and butter over warm water in a double boiler, stirring to mix. Remove from heat, and let cool until chocolate begins to thicken. Spread chocolate on top and sides of cake. Press pecans around the outside. Chill.

Serves 12

CHOCOLATE FRAMBOISE TORTE WITH FRESH RASPBERRY PURÉE

Fudgelike chocolate infused with the taste of raspberries makes the rich filling for this cake. If you are fussy about the consistency of the raspberry purée, strain it through a fine-mesh sieve to remove the seeds.

1 lb.	unsalted butter	500 g
1 generous cup	sugar	250 mL
2 cups	fresh raspberries	500 mL
	(reserve 1 cup/250 mL)	
2 Tbsp.	framboise liqueur	25 mL
1 cup	hot coffee	250 mL
12 oz.	semisweet chocolate, melted	375 g
4 oz.	unsweetened chocolate, melted	125 g
6	eggs, room temperature	6
6	egg yolks, room temperature	6
	Sugar	

In a saucepan, melt butter with sugar. Remove from heat, add 1 cup (250 mL) raspberries, liqueur, coffee and melted chocolate, and stir until mixture has a smooth consistency.

In a separate bowl, beat eggs and egg yolks until frothy. Lightly whisk eggs into chocolate mixture until it thickens.

Preheat oven to 325°F (160°C). Line the sides and bottom of an 8-inch (2 L) springform pan with parchment paper. Pour in batter, and place pan on a heavy baking sheet to catch any leaks. Bake for 1 hour. The torte will be cooked but not set in the center, so let cool for 20 minutes before springing the pan and removing the parchment paper from the sides. Then refrigerate until torte is completely chilled.

Purée the reserved 1 cup (250 mL) raspberries, and sweeten with sugar to taste. Top individual slices with raspberry purée.

Serves 8

WHITE-CHOCOLATE MOUSSE PIE

Unlike a rich cheesecake, this mousse pie is a smooth and deceptively light dessert.
The addition of gelatin takes the pressure off the cook to make a light but firm mousse.

CRUST

2 oz.	semisweet chocolate	50 g
4 oz.	toasted almonds, ground	125 g
3 Tbsp.	apricot jam	45 mL

FILLING

14 oz.	white chocolate	440 g
2¼ tsp.	apricot brandy	11 mL
3 Tbsp.	hot water	45 mL
2¼ tsp.	unflavored gelatin	11 mL
6	egg whites	6
1¾ cups	35% B.F. cream, whipped	425 mL

TOPPING

½ oz.	dark chocolate	15 g
2¼ tsp.	butter	11 mL
1½ tsp.	35% B.F. cream	7 mL

Line sides and bottom of a 10-inch (3 L) springform pan with wax paper, and set aside.

To make crust, gently melt semisweet chocolate over warm water in a double boiler. Remove from heat, and stir in almonds. Press chocolate mixture into bottom of pan with the back of a spoon. Gently heat jam in a small saucepan, and spread in a thin layer over the crust. Set aside.

To make filling, carefully melt white chocolate over warm water in a clean double boiler. Set aside.

Place brandy and water in a mixing bowl, and stir in gelatin until dissolved. In a separate bowl, whip egg whites until stiff but not dry. Fold gelatin mixture into egg whites.

When chocolate has cooled to body temperature, fold into egg-white mixture. Then fold in whipped cream. Pour into crust. Refrigerate for 3 hours before springing pan.

To make topping, place dark chocolate, butter and cream over warm water in a double boiler, and stir until chocolate melts. Drizzle lightly over pie before serving.

Serves 12

EGGNOG

Thick and utterly decadent, this is the richest, booziest eggnog you will ever taste.
It is more dessert than drink and is the great end to a festive feast.
Be sure to serve the eggnog soon after making it, or it will separate.

7	eggs, separated	7
1 cup	sugar	250 mL
2 cups	35% B.F. cream, chilled	500 mL
2 cups	milk, chilled	500 mL
1 cup	bourbon, chilled	250 mL
⅓ cup	amber rum, chilled	75 mL
	Freshly ground nutmeg for garnish	

Using an electric mixer, beat egg whites to soft peaks while slowly adding ½ cup (125 mL) sugar. Set aside.

In a large bowl, beat egg yolks with remaining ½ cup (125 mL) sugar until creamy. Fold egg whites into egg-yolk mixture. Set aside.

Whip cream in a small bowl, and fold into egg mixture. Whisk in milk, bourbon and rum. Ladle into glasses, and garnish with nutmeg.

Serves 6

Eggnog

Peach Almond Pie

SUSAN'S PIE CRUST

We use this basic pie crust for all our dessert pies. The combination of butter and shortening seems to give the crust the right taste and texture, and our bakers generally prebake the bottom crust so that it keeps its texture.

2½ cups	flour, chilled	625 mL
¼ tsp.	salt	1 mL
¼ tsp.	cinnamon	1 mL
⅔ cup	butter, chilled	150 mL
⅓ cup	lard or shortening, chilled	75 mL
1	egg, chilled	1
	Sour cream, chilled	

Make sure all ingredients are thoroughly chilled. In a large bowl, mix together flour, salt and cinnamon. Cut in butter and lard or shortening until mixture forms pea-size lumps. Place egg in a measuring cup, and add enough sour cream to measure ½ cup (125 mL). Beat egg and sour cream, and add to flour mixture, stirring until dough clings together. Wrap dough in plastic, and chill for 2 hours.

Preheat oven to 400°F (200°C). Turn dough out onto floured board, divide in half, and roll into two crusts. Line a 9-inch (23 cm) pie plate with bottom crust. Weight with another pie plate or tin foil and dried beans to prevent puffing, and bake for 12 minutes.

Makes two 9-inch (23 cm) crusts

PEACH ALMOND PIE

*Sour cream added to the peach-almond filling cuts the sweetness of this pie,
which is one of the restaurant's most popular desserts of all time.
We recommend using only sweet, ripe peaches and avoiding those
at the beginning and end of the season, as they tend to be hard or mealy.*

FILLING

¼ cup	flour	50 mL
½ cup	sugar	125 mL
1 tsp.	cinnamon	5 mL
8-12	peaches, blanched, peeled & sliced	8-12
½ cup	sour cream	125 mL
¼ cup	half-and-half	50 mL
1	9-inch (23 cm) prebaked pie crust	1

TOPPING

¼ cup	unsalted butter, cut into small pieces	50 mL
½ cup	brown sugar	125 mL
¼ cup	flour	50 mL
1 tsp.	cinnamon	5 mL
½ cup	sliced almonds	125 mL
	Whipped cream for garnish	

Preheat oven to 350°F (180°C).

To make filling, mix flour, sugar and cinnamon together, and sprinkle over peach slices. Stir in sour cream and half-and-half. Fill cooled crust. Set aside.

To make topping, crumble butter with brown sugar, flour and cinnamon in a mixing bowl. Stir in almonds.

Sprinkle topping over filling, and bake for 55 minutes. Remove from oven, and let cool. Garnish with whipped cream.

Serves 8

MOM'S APPLE PIE

Susan Newbury, the master baker who contributed to this recipe, is a mom, but her own mother also deserves some of the credit for inspiring this big bumpy-top country-fair-style pie.

2	9-inch (23 cm) pie crusts	2
1	egg yolk mixed with 1 Tbsp. (15 mL) water for egg wash	1
8 cups	peeled & sliced apples (Northern Spy or Granny Smith)	2 L
1 tsp.	cinnamon	5 mL
1 tsp.	ground cardamom	5 mL
	Zest of ½ lemon	
1 Tbsp.	lemon juice	15 mL
½ cup	sugar	125 mL
2 Tbsp.	flour	25 mL
	Sliced sharp Cheddar cheese for garnish	

Preheat oven to 425°F (220°C). Roll out bottom crust, and place in a pie plate; brush with egg wash to seal. Chill.

In a large bowl, mix together apples, cinnamon, cardamom, lemon zest, lemon juice, sugar and flour. Spoon into crust. Roll out top crust, and place over filling. Seal edges of pie. Brush top with egg wash. Cut steam vents in top.

Bake on bottom shelf of oven for 10 minutes. Reduce heat to 350°F (180°C), and bake for 40 minutes. Serve with cheese.

Serves 8

STRAWBERRY-RHUBARB PIE

The combination of savory and sweet make this summer pie the best there is at the tail end of the rhubarb season and the beginning of the strawberry season.

2 pints	strawberries, hulled & sliced	1 L
5	stalks rhubarb, cut into ¼-inch (6 mm) chunks	5
½ cup	sugar	125 mL
⅓ cup	flour	75 mL
1 tsp.	cinnamon	5 mL
3 Tbsp.	sour cream	45 mL
1	9-inch (23 cm) prebaked pie crust plus dough for top crust	1
1	egg yolk mixed with 1 Tbsp. (15 mL) milk for egg wash	1

Preheat oven to 350°F (180°C). In a large bowl, mix strawberries and rhubarb with sugar, flour, cinnamon and sour cream, and place in prebaked crust. Roll out top crust to ⅛-inch (3 mm) thickness. Cut into ½-inch (1 cm) strips. Arrange in lattice top on pie, and brush with egg wash. Bake for 35 to 45 minutes.

Serves 8

COCONUT LIME CREAM PIE

This is our version of a truck-stop favorite. The grated coconut gives the filling texture.

1 Tbsp.	unflavored gelatin	15 mL
2 Tbsp.	water	25 mL
1½ cups	unsweetened coconut milk	375 mL
	Salt	
1 cup	sugar	250 mL
6	egg yolks	6
1 cup	grated unsweetened coconut	250 mL
1 tsp.	vanilla extract	5 mL
1 tsp.	lime zest	5 mL
1½ cups	35% B.F. cream	375 mL
3	egg whites, room temperature	3
1	9-inch (23 cm) prebaked pie crust	1
	Whipped cream for garnish	
	Toasted shredded coconut for garnish	

Place gelatin and water in a small bowl, and stir until gelatin is dissolved. Set aside.

Place coconut milk, sugar and a pinch of salt in a large saucepan over medium-high heat, and bring to a boil. Place egg yolks in a large mixing bowl. Pour hot coconut-milk mixture over yolks, whisking constantly. Return mixture to saucepan, and simmer over very low heat, stirring constantly, until it thickens (do not overcook, or mixture will become grainy). Remove from heat once it starts to thicken.

Stir in dissolved gelatin, grated coconut, vanilla and lime zest. Refrigerate, stirring occasionally, until partially set, about 1 hour.

Whip cream, and fold into chilled coconut mixture. Whip egg whites until stiff but moist. Fold into coconut filling. Pour into prebaked pie crust. Refrigerate for 3 hours before serving. Garnish with whipped cream and shredded coconut.

Serves 8

MAPLE PUMPKIN CHIFFON PIE

If you have the time and the patience, serve this fluffy autumn pie garnished with individual marzipan pumpkins, as we do at the restaurant.

CRUST

⅓ cup	butter	75 mL
1¼ cups	graham cracker crumbs	300 mL
2 tsp.	icing sugar	10 mL
¼ tsp.	ground ginger	1 mL

FILLING

¼ cup	hot water	50 mL
1 Tbsp.	unflavored gelatin	15 mL
1 cup	maple syrup	250 mL
3	eggs, separated	3
¼ tsp.	salt	1 mL
¼ tsp.	cinnamon	1 mL
¼ tsp.	ground nutmeg	1 mL
¼ tsp	ground ginger	1 mL
1½ cups	puréed pumpkin	375 mL
½ cup	35% B.F. cream, whipped	125 mL

Whipped cream for garnish
Finely chopped candied ginger for garnish

Melt butter in a saucepan. Stir in graham cracker crumbs, icing sugar and ginger. Press into bottom and sides of an ungreased pie plate. Chill.

To make filling, place water in a mixing bowl. Stir in gelatin to dissolve. Place maple syrup, egg yolks, salt and spices in a double boiler over simmering water. Stir in dissolved gelatin. Cook until thickened, stirring frequently. Remove from heat. Stir in pumpkin, and chill until partially set, about 1 hour.

Fold whipped cream into chilled pumpkin mixture. Beat egg whites until stiff, and fold into pumpkin mixture. Pour into pie shell. Chill until firm. Top with whipped cream mixed with candied ginger.

Serves 8

Caramel Pecan Tart

CARAMEL PECAN TART

This is a surprisingly simple recipe to make, given the wonderful and unique
result of toffee-coated chopped pecans on a shortbread crust.

CRUST

⅓ cup + 2 Tbsp.	unsalted butter	75 mL + 25 mL
1¼ cups	flour	300 mL
5 Tbsp.	sugar	65 mL
2	egg yolks	2

FILLING

⅔ cup	packed brown sugar	150 mL
¼ cup	unsalted butter	50 mL
¼ cup	golden corn syrup	50 mL
2 cups	toasted pecans, coarsely chopped	500 mL
3 Tbsp.	35% B.F. cream	45 mL

Preheat oven to 375°F (190°C). To make crust, line the bottom of a 9-inch
(23 cm) flan pan with parchment paper. Using a pastry cutter or two knives,
cut butter into flour and sugar to form pea-size chunks. Add egg yolks, and
mix until pastry begins to cling together. Press into the bottom and sides of
prepared pan to ¼-inch (6 mm) thickness. Prick crust with a fork, and bake
for 12 minutes. Remove from oven, and let cool.

To make filling, combine brown sugar, butter and corn syrup in a large
saucepan. Bring to a boil. Turn off heat, and stir in pecans and cream. Lightly
press into cooled crust. Bake at 375°F (190°C) for 12 minutes. Let cool, then
cut into thin wedges.

Serves 12

Index

Credits

Illustrations by
Anne Linton

Pan Chancho logo by
Andrew McLachlan

PHOTOGRAPHS
Bernard Clark:
44, 45 (right), 59, 62, 68 (right),
69 (right), 74, 84, 113, 206 (right)

Stephen Homer:
14 (right), 15, 25, 45 (left), 48, 68
(left), 69 (left), 70, 79, 92, 98, 99
(right), 104, 114, 115, 128, 134
(right), 135, 143, 151, 167, 170,
190, 191 (left), 197, 206, 207

Steven Maynard:
160

Garfield Peters:
14 (left), 17, 18, 21, 22, 33, 36, 39,
55, 61, 66, 72, 81, 83, 88, 99, 101,
102, 117, 121, 134, 147, 158, 179,
185, 191 (right), 198, 200, 203,
210, 217, 218, 225, 226, 231

Tracy Read:
12

Bookmakers Press would like
to express a special thanks
to Pamela Cross, Catherine
DeLury, Charlotte DuChene,
Faye Ibbitson, Steven Maynard,
Andrew McLachlan, Jody Morgan,
Connie Morris, Linda Murray,
Mary Patton, Jim and Lorraine
Purvis, Jane Reeves, Lori
Richards and Bill Woods for
their enthusiasm, support and
assistance during this project.